Logging in Java with the JDK 1.4 Logging API and Apache log4j

SAMUDRA GUPTA

```
Logging in Java with the JDK 1.4 Logging API and Apache log4j
Copyright ©2003 by Samudra Gupta
```

All rights reserved. No part of this work may be reproduced or transmitted in any form or by any means, electronic or mechanical, including photocopying, recording, or by any information storage or retrieval system, without the prior written permission of the copyright owner and the publisher.

Printed and bound in the United States of America 12345678910

Trademarked names may appear in this book. Rather than use a trademark symbol with every occurrence of a trademarked name, we use the names only in an editorial fashion and to the benefit of the trademark owner, with no intention of infringement of the trademark.

Library of Congress Cataloging-in-Publication Data

Gupta, Samudra, 1974-

Logging in Java with the JDK 1.4 logging API and Apache log4j / Samudra Gupta.

p. cm.

ISBN 1-59059-099-6 (hardcover : alk. paper)

1. Java (Computer program language) 2. Apache (Computer file : Apache Group) 3. Application logging (Computer science) 4. Application software--Development--Management. 5. Debugging in computer science. I. Title.

QA76.73.J38G86 2003

005.13'3--dc21

2003005480

Technical Reviewer: Jeff Heaton

Editorial Directors: Dan Appleman, Gary Cornell, Simon Hayes, Martin Streicher, Karen Watterson, John Zukowski

Assistant Publisher: Grace Wong

Developmental Editors: Tracy Brown Collins, Ami Knox

Copy Editor: Ami Knox

Production Manager: Kari Brooks

Compositor: Susan Glinert Stevens

Proofreader: Lori Bring

Indexer: Ann Rogers

Artist and Cover Designer: Kurt Krames

Manufacturing Manager: Tom Debolski

Distributed to the book trade in the United States by Springer-Verlag New York, Inc., 175 Fifth Avenue, New York, NY, 10010 and outside the United States by Springer-Verlag GmbH & Co. KG, Tiergartenstr. 17, 69112 Heidelberg, Germany.

In the United States: phone 1-800-SPRINGER, email `orders@springer-ny.com`, or visit `http://www.springer-ny.com`. Outside the United States: fax +49 6221 345229, email `orders@springer.de`, or visit `http://www.springer.de`.

For information on translations, please contact Apress directly at 2560 Ninth Street, Suite 219, Berkeley, CA 94710. Phone 510-549-5930, fax 510-549-5939, email `info@apress.com`, or visit `http://www.apress.com`.

The information in this book is distributed on an "as is" basis, without warranty. Although every precaution has been taken in the preparation of this work, neither the author(s) nor Apress shall have any liability to any person or entity with respect to any loss or damage caused or alleged to be caused directly or indirectly by the information contained in this work.

The source code for this book is available to readers at `http://www.apress.com` in the Downloads section.

To the lotus feet of Bhagavan Sri Ramakrishna

Contents at a Glance

About the Author and Technical Reviewer viii

Acknowledgments ix

Preface x

Chapter 1   Introduction to Application Logging 1

Chapter 2   JDK 1.4 Logging API 11

Chapter 3   Formatting JDK 1.4 Logging Information 59

Chapter 4   Extending the Logging Framework 73

Chapter 5   Understanding Apache log4j 121

Chapter 6   Formatting Logging Information in log4j 177

Chapter 7   Advanced Logging with log4j 199

Chapter 8   Extending log4j to Create Custom
            Logging Components 235

Chapter 9   Using the Apache Log Tag Library 285

Chapter 10 Best Practices 299

Index 315

Contents

About the Author and Technical Reviewer viii

Acknowledgments ix

Preface x

Chapter 1 Introduction to Application Logging 1

What Is Logging? 1
Benefits of Logging 3
Disadvantages of Logging 4
How Logging Works 5
Evaluating a Logging Package 7
Popular Java-Based Logging APIs 7
The Road Ahead 9

Chapter 2 JDK 1.4 Logging API 11

JDK 1.4 Logging API Overview 11
LogManager Object 15
LogRecord Object 17
Logger Object 18
Handler 33
Filter Object 51
File-Based Configuration 55
Formatter Object 58
Conclusion 58

Chapter 3 Formatting JDK 1.4 Logging Information ... 59

Default Formatter Objects 59
Localization of Logging Messages 68
Writing Custom Formatters 69
Conclusion 72

Chapter 4 Extending the Logging Framework 73

Configuring the Logging Framework 73
Writing Custom Handlers 83
Remote Logging 94
Logging in Practice 102
Conclusion 120

Chapter 5 Understanding Apache log4j 121

Installing log4j 121
Overview of the log4j Architecture 122
Configuring log4j 125
Level Object 136
Logger Object 136
LogManager Object 145
Nested Diagnostic Context (NDC) 146
Message Diagnostic Context (MDC) 147
Appender Object 149
Filter Object 166
Layout Object 168
ObjectRenderer 168
A Complete log4j Example 169
Conclusion 175

Chapter 6 Formatting Logging Information in log4j 177

The Layout Hierarchy 177
The Layout Objects in log4j 178
Conclusion 198

Chapter 7 Advanced Logging with log4j 199

A Sample Advanced Logging Application 200
Logging to a Database with JDBCAppender 202
Implementing JMS-Based Logging with JMSAppender 212
Working with SocketAppender 223
Logging to Windows NT Event Log with NTEventLogAppender 228
Distributing Logging Information via SMTPAppender 229
Making Messages Available Through Telnet
    with TelnetAppender 232
Conclusion 232

Chapter 8   Extending log4j to Create Custom Logging Components 235

Creating the Custom WindowAppender 235
Configuring log4j from a Database 243
Custom Logging Framework 258
More on Filtering 270
Error Handling 277
Conclusion 284

Chapter 9   Using the Apache Log Tag Library 285

Installing the Log Tag Library 285
A Simple Example of Using the Log Tag Library 286
Using a Custom Logger with the Log Tag Library 291
Description of Log Tags 292
Creating Custom Tags with the Log Tag Library
    to Use a Custom Level 294
Conclusion 298

Chapter 10 Best Practices 299

Obtaining a Logger 299
Using Logger Hierarchy 301
Logging Messages Efficiently 302
Issues with Localization 304
Using Location Information 304
Formatting Logging Information 305
Using Renderer Objects 305
Using Asynchronous Logging 306
Using Filter Objects 306
Using Nested Diagnostic Context 307
Configuration Issues 308
Comparing log4j and JDK 1.4 Logging API 309
Conclusion 313

Index 315

About the Author and Technical Reviewer

About the Author

Samudra Gupta holds a postgraduate degree in information technology and management from All India Management Association, India, and has around six years of experience in designing and developing Web-based applications ranging from research-based projects to e-commerce applications. He started his career as a research engineer at the Indian Institute of Technology, Kanpur, India, and he is presently working as an independent Java consultant in the United Kingdom, architecting and developing several e-commerce–based applications, content management system software, and retail-based software. Samudra also writes articles for *JavaWorld* and *Java Developer's Journal*, and is a monthly contributor to Java Boutique (http://javaboutique.internet.com). When not programming, he plays a lot of contract bridge.

About the Technical Reviewer

Jeff Heaton is an author, college instructor, and consultant. Jeff lives in Chesterfield, Missouri. The author of three books and over a dozen journal and magazine articles, Jeff specializes in Internet, socket-level/spidering, and artificial intelligence programming. A Sun-certified Java programmer and a member of the IEEE, Jeff has a masters degree in information management from Washington University in St. Louis.

Acknowledgments

ALTHOUGH THERE APPEARS only one name on the cover of this book, the credit for this accomplishment goes to many. I would first of all like to thank everybody in the Apress family for making a dream come true for me by publishing this book. Special thanks go to John Zukowski, Editorial Director, Apress, for signing me to write this book and suggesting many ideas during the course of putting the manuscript together to make this book a better one. Grace Wong, Assistant Publisher, deserves all the credit for her guidance from the manuscript stage to the production stage of this book. Tracy Brown Collins and Ami Knox both have done a splendid job with development and copyediting of this book, contributing so many valuable ideas and making this book coherent and consistent throughout. Without their great efforts, many mistakes might have made their way into this book. I also thank the production team at Apress—Kari Brooks, Production Manager, as well as Susan Glinert Stevens, Lori Bring, and Ann Rogers—for their commendable job in the final production of this book.

I am greatly thankful to Jeff Heaton, Technical Reviewer, who suggested numerous improvements to make this book more accurate and useful. I feel honored to have his name associated with this book. My heartfelt thanks must also go to Paul Burden and Ashish Patel, two of the great programmers I have had the privilege to work with, for contributing their most valuable ideas from the initial stages of this book.

I take this opportunity to express my deepest gratitude and convey my most humble regards to Doctor T. V. Prabhakar, Department of Computer Science and Engineering, Indian Institute of Technology, Kanpur, India, who initiated me into the world of computer science. Without his most valuable and affectionate guidance, it just could not have been the same. My special thanks go to Mr. N. V. Brahmaji Rao, Doctor Amit Neogi, and Doctor Chaitali Roy for encouraging me throughout my efforts in writing this book. Without their encouragement, I might not have ventured to do so.

Lastly, my parents and my elder brother (whom I call Dadabhai) have been a source of constant inspiration and encouragement throughout. I offer them my sincerest regards, and words cannot express my gratitude to them. In the end, I say a big "thank you" to all my friends, too many to name individually, and you know who you are.

Preface

THIS BOOK DEALS WITH the concept of building a flexible and robust application logging framework for Java-based applications. After an introduction to application logging, this book covers the two most popular Java-based logging APIs: the JDK 1.4 logging API and Apache log4j version 1.2.6. The text provides a comprehensive study of these two APIs, and in the final chapter you will find a comparative study of the two logging APIs and a few best practices for using them.

This book is aimed at providing an in-depth guide to the use of the JDK 1.4 logging API and Apache log4j with an emphasis on

- Understanding the internals of these APIs and how they work

- Working with the extremely useful, robust logging features available in these APIs

- Extending the existing logging framework for certain specialized, application-specific needs

The book provides numerous examples, ranging from simple programs to complex ones, written in the Java language. The simple examples explain how the logging APIs work and what they are capable of producing in terms of logging output. The complex examples resemble real-life application scenarios and demonstrate how useful logging can be to maintaining large-scale distributed application components. Finally, the comparison between the JDK 1.4 logging API and Apache log4j will act as a guideline for deciding which of the two discussed APIs to use in your project.

Target Audience

This book, which discusses logging APIs based in the Java language, targets beginning-to-advanced Java language application developers. It provides many simple and straightforward examples that demand only minimal familiarity with the Java language. Thus this book can also be helpful to non–Java language application developers, who can still benefit from the ideas presented in this book.

Chapter Synopsis

This book is mainly divided into two sections: one for the JDK 1.4 logging API, and the other for Apache log4j version 1.2.6. Readers interested in only one particular API can skip the chapters discussing the other. In general, the book comprises the following chapters:

Chapter 1: Introduction to Application Logging

This chapter discusses application logging. It describes the advantages and disadvantages related to the various concepts of application logging. This chapter also discusses a few criteria for a good logging framework.

Chapter 2: JDK 1.4 Logging API

This chapter introduces the JDK 1.4 logging API and provides an in-depth discussion about the internals and use of this API.

Chapter 3: Formatting JDK 1.4 Logging Information

This chapter explores the issues related to the formatting of logging output. It discusses the available formatting options within the JDK 1.4 logging API and also shows how to write custom formatters to do customized formatting.

Chapter 4: Extending the Logging Framework

This chapter is dedicated to explaining and demonstrating how to extend the existing JDK 1.4 logging framework to write custom, application-specific logging components. It provides some real-life examples to illustrate how custom logging components can be developed and used.

Chapter 5: Understanding Apache log4j

This chapter provides an in-depth discussion of Apache log4j based on version 1.2.6. It explains the core objects involved in the log4j framework, and how they work and interact with each other to finally produce logging output.

Chapter 6: Formatting Logging Information in log4j

This chapter discusses different formatting options available within log4j to structure the final logging output. It also shows how to use configurable patterns to format logging information.

Chapter 7: Advanced Logging with log4j

This chapter is dedicated to the advanced logging features of log4j. It details the process of distributing logging information via a database, a Java Message Service (JMS), the Simple Mail Transfer Protocol (SMTP), and various other options available within log4j.

Chapter 8: Extending log4j to Create Custom Logging Components

This chapter focuses on the techniques to extend the existing log4j framework in order to write custom, application-specific logging components. It provides some real-life examples to demonstrate how effective custom logging components can be in certain application scenarios.

Chapter 9: Using the Apache Log Tag Library

This chapter discusses the Apache Log tag library, which can be used along with Java Server Pages (JSPs) to achieve log4j-based logging activity. It describes the installation and use of the Log tag library and also shows how to incorporate custom tags within this tag library.

Chapter 10: Best Practices

This chapter provides a guideline to the best practices involved in using the JDK 1.4 logging API and Apache log4j. It also provides a comparative study of these two logging APIs.

CHAPTER 1
Introduction to Application Logging

IMAGINE IT IS late at night and you are still busy debugging your application. Worse—you are debugging another person's code! You have no clue what is wrong with the system. You are not sure where the problem lies. You cannot find any error trace. You do not know what to do, but you do know what is next—the raging managers, the anxious clients, and still it will take time to debug a piece of code without a trace of what is going on.

What is the problem? It is a well-known fact that no software is bug free. Therefore, we need to assume that application modules may malfunction from time to time, and we need some mechanism to trace what is going wrong. This is precisely the role of application logging. Any commercial application will need logging capability. Debugging an application without any logging trace is time consuming and costly. Indirectly, a hard-to-debug application loses its market value. Indeed, the impact of well-controlled application logging is multilevel. It improves the quality of the code produced, it increases the maintainability of the application, and all this means more market for the product.

In this chapter, we will see what application logging is and its benefits, and also explore a few available Java language–based logging APIs. We will begin with a more detailed definition of logging and its value.

What Is Logging?

Logging in any application generally means some way to indicate the state of the system at runtime. However, we all use logging during development to debug and test our modules. The logging activity carried out during the development phase generally holds no value in the deployment stage, and normally we take out those logging traces after we have successfully tested our modules. The logging activity that should be a part of the application in the deployment phase demands much more thought and care. We almost always want to produce logging that is informative and effective but involves least effort.

Keeping all these points in mind, let's define application logging in the following manner:

> *Logging is a systematic and controlled way of representing the state of an application in a human-readable fashion.*

One important point about logging to note is that it is not synonymous to debugging traces in an application. Logging information can potentially offer more than mere debugging information. However, its usefulness totally depends on how we apply logging within an application. Logging information may be of immense value in analyzing the performance of an application. Moreover, we can bundle internal states of the application in logging information and store that information in a structured manner to reuse in the future.

This definition of logging highlights the following important points:

- It is systematic.

- It is controlled.

- It represents an application's state.

In the following sections, we will examine each of these features one by one.

Logging Is Systematic

Logging should be a systematic approach rather than an arbitrary way of producing information. More often than not, we will need to define a strategy for our logging activity. We need to decide beforehand what information to log, yet these decisions are not always easy. We should look at this problem from more than one angle. Typically, we need to produce logs for debugging and day-to-day maintenance of an application. We may also need to produce detailed logs for system administrators monitoring the performance of the system. Again, we may need to distribute logging information to various remote places to facilitate remote management of the application. The issues are endless. Hence, we need a logging strategy before we embark on writing an application.

Logging Is Controlled

There is one and only one way to log the information we require: We have to write some logging code within our applications. The logging code needs to go through the same controls as the main application code. Like every piece of application code, the logging code can be well written or badly written. Keep in mind that logging is there to support and improve the quality of the application being written. Therefore, the logging code should be written in such a way that it has least impact on the overall performance of the system.

Also, we need to exercise some control over where the logging information is stored and the format of the logging information. The logging information needs to be structured so that is easily readable and can be processed at a future date with the least effort. One example is to prefer logs in XML format rather than in simple text format. Although text format for logging may be desirable in the development stage, XML format is much more reusable and portable when the application is deployed. In other situations, we may need to store logging information in a database to maintain a history of the logs produced.

Logging Information Represents the Application State

The logging information produced may be quite useless if sufficient care is not taken about what to log. To make logging activity most effective, we should aim to represent the internal state of the system wherever required and also to present a clear idea of what stage of control the application is at and what it is doing. If you can visualize your system as a collection of distinct components performing several related and sequential tasks, you may well need to log the state of the system before and after each task is performed.

Benefits of Logging

Almost all projects in software development run on strict schedules. In this context, incorporating logging code in an application demands extra time and effort. Again, all software projects are aimed at success and producing a good end product. To meet such criteria, any application must implement some sort of logging methodology. The benefits offered by incorporating robust logging within an application makes it a worthwhile effort to plan ahead for this capability.

In short, logging within an application can offer the following benefits:

- *Problem diagnosis:* No matter how well written our code is, there may be some problems hidden in it. As soon as the triggering conditions occur, the hidden problems come to the surface. If our applications have well-written code for logging the internal state of the system, we will be able to detect the problems precisely and quickly.

- *Quick debugging:* Once it is easy to diagnose the problem, we know exactly how to solve the problem. The logging trace should be aimed at precisely showing the location of the problem, which means we will be able to debug the application in less time. The overall cost of debugging the application is reduced greatly by well-planned and well-written logging code.

- *Easy maintenance:* Applications with a good logging feature are easy to debug and therefore easily maintainable compared to any application without a similar logging feature. The logging information typically contains more information than the debugging trace.

- *History:* A good logging feature in an application results in logging information being preserved in a structured way at a desired location. The location may be a file, database, or remote machine. All this enables system administrators to retrieve the logging information at a future date by going through the logging history.

- *Cost and time effective:* As explained, well-written logging code offers quick debugging, easy maintenance, and structured storage of an application's runtime information. This makes the process of installation, day-to-day maintenance, and debugging much more cost and time effective.

Disadvantages of Logging

In the previous section, we discussed the benefits of logging. In reality, these benefits do not come without a cost. Some of the disadvantages are inherent in the logging activity itself, and some may arise from improper use of logging. Whatever is the case, in general the following disadvantages can occur with any logging process:

- Logging adds runtime overhead due to the generation of logging information and the device I/O related to publishing logging information.

- Logging adds programming overhead due to the extra code required for producing logging information. The logging process increases the size of the code.

- Badly produced logging information can cause confusion.

- Badly written logging code can seriously affect the performance of the application.

- Last not but not the least, logging requires planning ahead, as adding logging code at a later stage of development is difficult.

However, considering the benefits incurred and the disadvantages involved, logging is considered to be one of the essential elements of producing quality applications. Carefully planned and well-written logging code will often remove some of the demerits that can otherwise be prominent in poorly programmed logging code.

How Logging Works

In the previous sections we discussed the process, benefits, and some of the disadvantages associated with logging. We all want to write an application with a well-designed logging feature. But the question is how to achieve an effective logging mechanism.

You are probably acquainted with the most familiar Java syntax, System.out.println(), and similarly you might know in languages like C the famous printf(). These produce a piece of information that is printed to a console, and they represent the most primitive type of logging that can be embedded within an application. Such items will produce what we want in a nice and simple fashion. But they defeat the purpose of controlled logging in that there is no way we can turn off any of these statements.

You might be wondering why you need to turn off logging statements when you plan and put so much effort into including them. A complex application may have complicated logging activities. One goal of logging may be to produce enough information about the internal state and functioning of the system. Another goal may be to produce enough detail so that in case of malfunction the problem can be detected and debugged quickly. On a good day, when an application is running without any problems, any debugging-related logging information appearing in the logging trace may prevent the logging information from being clean and easily understandable. So we need some mechanism to turn off the debug-related logging trace. On a not-so-good day, we may wish to turn on the debug-related logging to see exactly what is going wrong.

The normal System.out.println() style of logging methodology is not capable of offering such flexibility, because it does not provide a way to modify the behavior of the static logging code. Even if we accept that we always want to see what we produce, the other problem is that it is very difficult to segregate logging messages into different levels of priority. Surely, messages related to a database operation problem are more crucial than messages related to the method entries and exits.

In essence, a robust logging framework means that the messages should be categorized in terms of their severity. Also, we should be able to switch over to any severity level to see messages with that level of severity only. But this sort of flexibility should not mean changes to the source code. We need to achieve this flexibility via some configuration parameters. Thus, a good logging system needs to be highly configurable.

It is also very important that we should be able to redirect logging information to a chosen destination such as a database, file, etc., so that we can reuse that information. Console-based logging activity is pretty much limited, as it is volatile. A robust logging framework should offer flexibility in terms of the logging destination and formatting of the messages.

While it is true that a good logging API will provide a flexible, robust, and feature-rich logging environment, it also demands appropriate and efficient use of all these logging features. In this book, after we examine basic logging techniques with the JDK 1.4 logging API and Apache log4j, we will focus on the best practices involved in using these logging APIs in Chapter 10.

From the architectural point of view, software application modules and logging components reside in two separate layers. The application makes a call to the logging components in the logging layer and delegates the logging responsibility to those components. The logging components receive the logging request and publish the logging information at preferred destinations. Figure 1-1 represents the collaboration of a software module and its logging components.

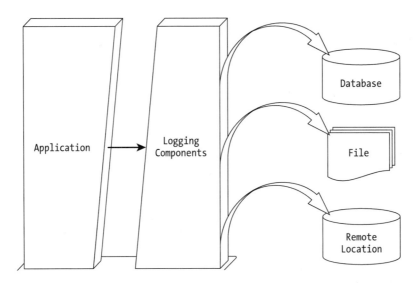

Figure 1-1. The application logging process

As shown in the diagram, the logging components have the freedom to publish logging information to any destination of choice such as a file, console, database, or remote location. The logging components can in turn make use of any other available technologies to achieve localized and distributed logging.

Evaluating a Logging Package

In a large-scale development process, it is crucial that we implement a proper logging mechanism. Whether we develop the logging component in-house or use any third-party logging component, there are certain criteria against which the logging component should be evaluated. In a nutshell, we can summarize the following criteria as features of a good logging package:

- *Configuration:* Logging components may support programmatic and file-based configuration. The latter is better, as it allows us to avoid changing our source code to switch to a different type of logging behavior. Also, the logging package should support dynamic configuration as opposed to static configuration. Dynamic configuration enables us to change logging behavior without taking an application down.

- *Flexibility:* A logging package should provide flexibility in terms of what to log and where to log. Also, we should be able to prioritize logging information based on its level of importance. We require a logging package that supports multiple loggers and multiple levels of messages, and is also capable of publishing logging messages to various destinations.

- *Output:* The way that logging information can be output to a preferred destination is important for the success of any logging package. We must carefully consider how flexible the logging package is in terms of output formats and destinations.

- *Ease of use:* However good the design of a logging package may be, if it is not easy to use, chances are that anyone working on or using the application will not use it. So we need to evaluate any logging package in terms of its ease of use.

Popular Java-Based Logging APIs

Experience has taught people how important application logging is and how to write well-designed logging code. Once logging concepts had been proven successful, they were put into use as generic logging APIs. There are a few Java-based logging APIs available in the market. Some of them are proprietary, and some are open source. Out of all the available APIs, the following are most popular in the Java community.

JDK 1.4 Logging API

Version 1.4 of JDK has its own logging API in its `java.util.logging` package. This API originated from the JSR 47. The JDK 1.4 logging API in essence is a scaled-down version of log4j (discussed in the next section). The logging concepts captured in this API involve logging levels and different logging destinations and formats. The JDK 1.4 logging API is well suited for simple applications with simple logging requirements. Despite a few limitations, this API provides all the basic features that you need to produce effective logging information. Chapters 2 to 4 cover the JDK 1.4 logging API.

Apache log4j

Apache log4j is an open-source logging API from Apache. This API, which evolved from the E.U. SEMPER project, is a popular logging package in Java. It allows great control over the granularity of logging statements. One main benefit of this API is that it is highly configurable through external configuration files at runtime. It views the logging process in terms of different levels of priorities and offers mechanisms to direct logging information to a great variety of destinations such as a database, file, console, Windows NT Event log, UNIX Syslog, Java Message Service (JMS), and so on. It also allows application developers to choose from various formatting styles such as XML, HTML, etc.

Overall, log4j is a feature-rich, well-designed extendible logging framework, and provides more capabilities than the JDK 1.4 logging API. For example, the configuration of log4j is much more flexible than that of the JDK 1.4 logging API. The JDK1.4 logging API can only be configured through a properties-style configuration file, but log4j supports both properties- and XML-style configuration.

In this book, Chapters 5 to 9 are devoted to a discussion of log4j.

Commons Logging API

The Commons logging API is another logging effort from Apache. The goal of this API is to provide a seamless transition from one logging API to another. Depending upon the presence of a logging framework in the classpath, the Commons logging API will try to use the available API to carry out application logging. The Commons logging API runs its own discovery process to find out which logging API is available in the classpath. It tends to provide the lowest common denominator of any two logging APIs. For example, between log4j and the JDK1.4 logging API, it will provide seamless transition for the features common in both—so we would miss any extra features used in log4j.

In terms of operation, the Commons logging API creates a wrapper for all the objects in the logging API. Automatic discovery and the wrapper generation are heavyweight processes and tend to slow down the overall performance. This is a more complex logging framework, as this API tries to combine the efforts of more than one logging API. In reality, it offers the flexibility to switch between different logging APIs without changing the source code. But before using it, determine whether you need such flexibility in exchange for added complexity and performance degradation due to the heavyweight nature of the Commons logging API.

The Commons logging API is a great effort to offer a common interface to logging in that it enables an application to switch to different logging APIs without changes to the application code. Once you understand and appreciate the methodologies adopted by the JDK 1.4 logging API and Apache log4j, it will be fairly easy to understand the philosophy behind the Commons logging API. For this reason, we will not be discussing the Commons logging API further in this book.

The Road Ahead

With this introduction in mind, we will now see how two of the logging APIs mentioned in the previous section, the JDK1.4 logging API and Apache log4j, implement a robust logging framework for Java-based applications. This book will deal with these two different logging APIs separately. Apache log4j was evolving quicker than the chapters in this book were being written, so we will focus on the 1.2.6 version of log4j. The later versions will have the same foundation and thus this book can be a good starting point for using them. After you finish this book, you will be able to compare and decide for yourself which logging API you want to use in your next project.

CHAPTER 2
JDK 1.4 Logging API

THE LOGGING API included in the `java.util.logging` package of the 1.4 version of JDK offers a comprehensive way of managing logging information from within an application. This API provides us with different levels and styles of logging that are vitally important for debugging and auditing any application. The JDK 1.4 logging mechanism concept is centered around different logging levels, configurable logging parameters, flexibility in producing logging information for various destinations, and adaptability of logging messages to different formatting styles.

The highly configurable architecture of the JDK 1.4 logging API offers some great benefits such as the capability to turn logging activity off and on depending on various stages of the project. This enables post-release software to be easily configured to produce detailed logging messages, which makes debugging applications faster and cheaper. In addition, the flexibility of this logging API can be utilized to vary the detail level of logging messages as needed.

In this chapter, we will first look at an overview of the architecture of the JDK 1.4 logging API and examine in detail how the different objects within the API interact with each other to accomplish logging activity.

JDK 1.4 Logging API Overview

The JDK 1.4 logging API (also referred to henceforth as the logging API) consists of several objects that capture logging information and process and publish the intended logging information to any preferred destination. The logging framework essentially consists of the following core objects:

- LogManager: The `java.util.logging.LogManager` object is a singleton that is responsible for managing the logger namespace hierarchy. This class reads a system-wide configuration file to set the initial properties for the logging framework.

 NOTE A *singleton* is a class that is available only once per Java Virtual Machine (JVM) instance of an application.

- `Logger`: The `java.util.logging.Logger` object is responsible for carrying out the logging activity. This object provides a number of logging methods to publish logging information.

- `LogRecord`: The `java.util.logging.LogRecord` object encapsulates all the logging information. Typically, it contains the date and timestamp of the logging message, the origin of the logging activity, and the granularity and priority level of the logging message.

- `Handler`: The `java.util.logging.Handler` object is responsible for publishing logging information to various destinations—a file, console, memory buffers, etc.

- `Filter`: The `java.util.logging.Filter` object is used by `Logger` objects to decide whether logging information should be passed to a `Handler` to deal with it or be ignored. `Handler` objects can also use `Filter` objects to perform more checks on a logging request before publishing it to the final destination.

- `Formatter`: The `java.util.logging.Formatter` object is responsible for providing required structure to the logging information being published. Formatters also perform the localization of logging information, if configured to do so.

The logging API obtains various configuration parameters from a system-wide configuration file. JDK 1.4 supplies a default configuration file, located in the "/jre/lib/logging.properties" file. It can also use any other user-specified configuration file for greater control and, above all, to support programmatic control of the behavior of the logging framework.

The basic architecture of the logging API defines several levels of logging information. The levels describe the priority of a log request, and the logging framework can be tuned to display logging information related to a certain level(s). The levels defined can be categorized in the descending order of priority as follows:

- *SEVERE (highest):* This level is used to log messages about problems that are very critical to the application and need immediate attention to rectify.

- *WARNING:* This level is used to log messages that indicate potential problems with the application.

- *INFO:* This level is the default level used by the logging API. Log messages published with this level are generally normal debug statements helpful in the development phase and day-to-day maintenance of the application.

- *CONFIG:* This level specifies log messages related to the configuration stage of the application. For example, at startup of an application, we could use this level to print configuration-related information.

- *FINE/FINER/FINEST (lowest):* These levels denote the detail of the log messages from less detailed to highly detailed. Use of these logging levels will result in a vast amount of logging information being published in the logging destination.

- *ALL:* This level indicates that all messages should be logged.

All the aforementioned levels are defined in the `java.util.logging.Level` class as `static final int` primitive types with a unique integer value associated with each defined level. If we want to define our own level, then we can do that by extending the `java.util.logging.Level` class and declaring a level with a unique integer value attached to it.

The most essential component of the logging framework is the `Logger` object. The `Logger` object is used to log messages specific to an application or application component. It captures the specified logging messages and creates a `LogRecord` object, which encapsulates all the information related to a logging request. The logging API provides a root logger, which exists as the default logger, without a namespace attached to it. The root logger is capable of printing logging information to the application's console. The default level associated with a `Logger` object is INFO. The amount of information that a logger can publish depends on the level associated with the logger.

Each `Logger` object can also have one or more `Handler` objects associated with it, which are responsible for publishing logging information to different destinations such as consoles, files, streams, sockets, etc. A `Handler` object in turn may have a `Formatter` object associated with it. A `Formatter` object is responsible for structuring logging information in various formats and also localizing logging information whenever needed. The `Handler` object formats logging messages with the associated `Formatter` object(s) before publishing them. It is also interesting to note that `Logger` and `Handler` objects can have one or more `Filter` objects associated with them to help decide whether any particular logging request is logged or ignored. The filtering decision can be made based on any predefined criteria such as levels associated with the log messages or any other application-specific filtering criteria.

The overall control flow of the framework is shown in the UML sequence diagram in Figure 2-1.

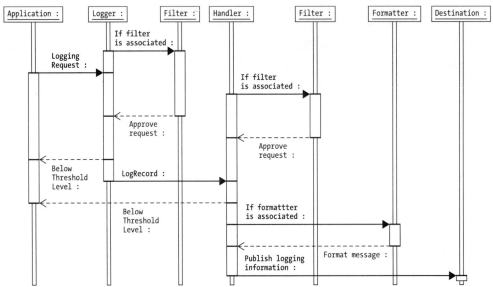

Figure 2-1. *The JDK 1.4 logging API sequence diagram*

The overall framework works like this:

1. The application component makes a call to one of the logging methods available in the Logger object and passes the logging information to it.

2. The Logger object checks the level associated with the message against its own assigned level. If the level of the incoming logging message is the same or above its level, then the Logger object internally creates a LogRecord object and uses any Filter object associated with it to determine whether to process the request or ignore it. The Logger will reject any logging request based on the filtering criteria defined through the associated Filter object or if the message's level falls below the level associated with the Logger.

3. If it decides to process the message, the Logger then passes the internally created LogRecord object to the associated Handler object. The Handler object in turn checks the level of the LogRecord object with its own assigned level.

4. If the level condition is satisfied, the record is passed to any Filter object(s) associated with the Handler object. If the associated Filter object approves the record, then the message is passed to the appropriate Formatter object attached to that particular Handler.

5. The Formatter object then localizes (if required) and returns the formatted logging information back to the Handler. Finally, the Handler prints the logging information to the preferred destination associated with it.

Note that the `Filter` and `Formatter` objects as shown in Figure 2-1 are optional to the framework. Often, if these objects are not specified, the framework uses the default `Filter` and `Formatter` objects. The default configuration of the JDK 1.4 logging API specifies the `SimpleFormatter` object as the default `Formatter` to use, and no `Filter` object is used with the root logger. The only default filtering activity of the logging API is the level-based filtering.

In the next few sections, we will explore the different objects involved in the logging API starting with the `LogManager`. In Chapter 3, we will take an in-depth look at `Formatter` objects, because how the logging information is structured greatly influences the reusability of the logging information.

LogManager Object

Imagine a big system where several loggers are acting together to log messages in various destinations such as sockets, memory, files, consoles, custom logging windows, etc. Each logger may have separate filters, handlers, formatters, and levels associated with them. Managing all these configuration and execution issues with so many loggers can be quite complex. The logging API provides a centralized way of managing all these configuration issues with the `java.util.logging.LogManager` class.

The `LogManager` class operates as a singleton object and has only one instance operating per Java VM instance. We obtain a reference to `LogManager` with the `LogManager.getLogManager()` static method. The `LogManager` object is created by reading a system-wide configuration file at class initialization, and thus cannot be changed afterward.

By default, the `LogManager` class has the following responsibilities:

- It manages a pool of loggers in a hierarchical namespace in a key-value format within a `java.util.logging.Hashtable` object. Whenever a logger reference is requested, if it already exists, the `LogManager` returns the existing instance or else creates a new instance, returns it to the caller application, and stores the newly created instance in the pool.

- It also manages a pool of global `Handler` objects.

The `LogManager` class provides methods for adding, removing, and obtaining `Logger` objects and also for reading configuration properties and removing any default settings acquired from any configuration parameter source. The following static method returns the singleton reference to the `LogManager` object:

```
public static LogManager getLogManager()
```

This next method adds a named logger to the logger namespace hierarchy maintained by the `LogManager` class:

```
public boolean addLogger(Logger logger)
```

If the named logger already exists, it returns `false`. The application using the named logger is responsible for keeping its own local reference of the `Logger` object to avoid any interference with the garbage collection of the `LogManager` class.

The following method obtains the named logger reference:

```
public Logger getLogger(String name)
```

Notice that this method is not static and can't be called directly. The `Logger` class uses this method internally to obtain the reference of an existing named `Logger` instance.

This next method checks if the current application context has the required permission to modify any of the `LogManager` properties:

```
public void checkAccess()
```

Currently, only one logging permission level, named "control", is defined with the default security manager. So any application trying to modify any of the `LogManager` properties is required to have `LoggingPermission("control")`. If the application trying to modify the `LogManager` properties does not have the required permission, a `java.lang.SecurityException` is thrown.

The following method obtains the value of the named property:

```
public String getProperty(String name)
```

It returns null if the named property is not found.

This next method reads and initializes the configuration parameters by reading the configuration file specified at startup:

```
public void readConfiguration()
```

This method fires a `java.beans.PropertyChangeEvent` once this method is invoked, which is handled with a `PropertyChangeListener` defined internally to update the configuration information. If there is a problem reading the configuration file, a `java.io.IOException` is thrown. If the caller application does not have the required permission to instruct the logging framework to read any configuration file, a `java.lang.SecurityException` is thrown.

The following method reads the configuration information from a `java.io.InputStream` source:

```
public void readConfiguration(InputStream inStream)
```

If there is a problem in reading the input stream, a `java.io.IOException` is thrown, and if there is a permission problem, a `java.lang.SecurityException` is thrown. A `java.beans.PropertyChangeEvent` is fired once the properties are read from the given input stream.

The following method removes and eventually closes all the `Handler` objects associated with all the named loggers:

```
public void reset()
```

The `reset()` method is protected by the default `SecurityManager` of the logging API and throws a `java.lang.SecurityException` in case the caller invoking the method does not have the required permission to do so. It sets the level associated with any named logger to null and sets the level of the root logger to Level.INFO. We can then create our own `Loggers` and notify the `LogManager` to manage the created loggers. This is often useful when an application needs to redefine new logging components and get rid of the old ones.

The `LogManager` class is located at startup by looking into the `java.util.logging.manager` system property. The initial configuration file for the `LogManager` class is defined in the "/jre/lib/logging.properties" file in the "JAVA_HOME" directory. It is possible to change the behavior of the logging framework by changing the configuration file. We will take a detailed look at the configuration issues with `LogManager` in Chapter 4.

LogRecord Object

The `Logger` object encapsulates the message string passed to it and any other related information such as the level, etc., within a `LogRecord` object. The `LogRecord` object is the information pool for the logging framework. Once the `LogRecord` object has been created, any modification to it might lead to unexpected logging behavior. The `LogRecord` object is *serializable*, which means it can be transferred to a remote component over the Remote Method Invocation (RMI). This feature of the `LogRecord` object makes the logging framework distributed. We will explore serialization of the `LogRecord` class with RMI in Chapter 4.

The `LogRecord` class consists of the following elements:

- The logging message string

- A logger name

- The logger level

- The timestamp of the logging activity

- The source class name and the source method name

- A unique sequence number

- The ID of the thread that generated the `LogRecord` object

- Optional argument objects (these objects can be used by the `Filter` object to make further decisions about the logging process)

- Optional `java.util.ResourceBundle` object used for localization

- Optional `java.lang.Throwable` object instance to indicate any erroneous conditions in the application

When no explicit source class name and source method name is attached to the `LogRecord` object, the `Logger` object tries to determine this information by analyzing the stack trace. However, this is not a reliable technique and might not produce correct results in cases where the compiler uses any optimization techniques that might completely remove any stack trace.

Logger Object

`Logger` objects are fundamental to the logging framework. To log a message, we always need to obtain a `Logger` object implicitly or explicitly. The `Logger` object provides several logging methods that publish logging information in different ways. In addition, `Logger` objects can have a `java.util.ResourceBundle` attached to them for the localization of logging information.

To use the logging API to log messages, first we need to obtain a reference to a `Logger` object. The logging framework does not allow us to instantiate a `Logger` object on our own. Instead, we use a factory method called `getLogger()` to obtain a reference to the `Logger` object. The `getLogger()` method either creates a new `Logger` object or returns an existing instance by obtaining it from the `LogManager`. The `getLogger(String name)` factory method creates a hierarchical namespace for the different loggers in the system with the specified name. Normally, the name of the `Logger` object is the package name or the class name, but in theory can be any arbitrary string. Obtaining a reference to a `Logger` object is pretty straightforward.

```
Logger logger = Logger.getLogger("my.package");
```

This piece of code will obtain a reference to a `Logger` object with the namespace "my.package".

We can obtain another Logger instance with the namespace "my.package.io". This gives us the freedom to separately manage logging from two packages. However, it is also possible to create an anonymous logger without any namespace attached to it.

```
Logger anoLogger = Logger.getAnonymousLogger();
```

This code will obtain an anonymous logger.

Anonymous logger objects are not stored in the logger namespace. They can operate without being affected by any logging hierarchy. They become particularly useful when we want to share the same logger across different classes within the same application. We can create an anonymous logger, store it in a central location, and then refer to the same logger from each class. This is suitable for small applications where the logging requirement is not hugely complicated. But for large-scale applications, often we will need to maintain different sets of loggers logging different information to different destinations. In such cases, we need to work with several named loggers to identify and segregate the logging information. As a rule, namespaced Logger objects are organized within the framework in a namespace hierarchy, which almost resembles the package hierarchy of the Java language. Figure 2-2 depicts the hierarchical architecture of named Logger objects.

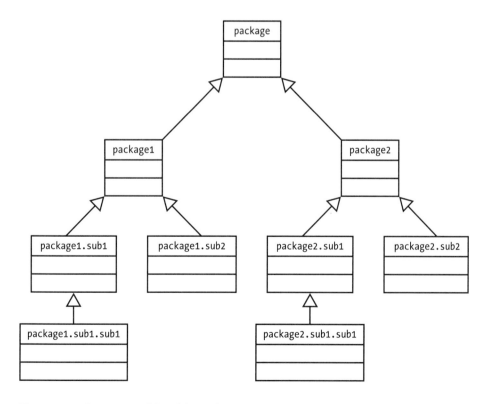

Figure 2-2. The Logger object hierarchy

The parent-child hierarchy shown in Figure 2-2 signifies the dependency and separation of different loggers acting within the same application. It is interesting to note that the top-level root logger object has no namespace associated with it. The hierarchical relationship of the loggers also means that the child loggers inherit several properties from the parent logger. Typically, a child logger inherits the following properties from its parent logger:

- `level`: When the child logger has no level specified explicitly or the level is null, it inherits the level of its immediate parent logger or recursively up the tree until it finds an appropriate level to use.

- `handler`: Each logger can have a `Handler` object explicitly specified to it. If one is not specified for a particular logger, then it obtains a suitable `Handler` from its immediate parent or recursively up the tree.

- `ResourceBundle`: If a logger does not have any `ResourceBundle` explicitly attached to it, it uses the `ResourceBundle` associated with its parents recursively up the tree. `ResourceBundle` is used for the localization of logging messages, which we will discuss in Chapter 3.

NOTE Because of this hierarchical relationship, it is important to note that a child logger can be affected by changing any of the preceding properties of a parent logger when the child logger implicitly uses the properties of its parent loggers.

A Basic JDK 1.4 Logging Example

In reality, writing logging code with the JDK 1.4 logging API is fairly simple. Let's take the following example. Listing 2-1, `BasicLogging.java`, demonstrates the very basic use of the logging feature with the JDK 1.4 logging API.

Listing 2-1. BasicLogging.java

```
package sam.logging;

import java.util.logging.*;
import java.io.*;
public class BasicLogging
{
```

```java
    private static Logger logger = Logger.getLogger("MyLogger");
    private ConsoleHandler console = null;
    private FileHandler file = null;
    public BasicLogging()
    {
        //create a new handler to write to the console
        console = new ConsoleHandler();
        //create a new handler to write to a named file
        try
        {
            file = new FileHandler("basicLogging.out");
        }catch(IOException ioe)
        {
            logger.warning("Could not create a file...");
        }

        //add the handlers to the logger
        logger.addHandler(console);
        logger.addHandler(file);

    }

    public void logMessage()
    {
        //log a message
        logger.info("I am logging test message..");
    }

 public static void main(String args[])
 {
     BasicLogging demo = new BasicLogging();
     demo.logMessage();
 }

}
```

As mentioned in the previous sections, the central point of logging activity is the Logger object. In the beginning of the program, we obtain a named Logger object instance—MyLogger. There is one important consideration to keep in mind while obtaining the Logger instance: Try to obtain it once and only once in the program, and reuse the Logger instance throughout the scope of the program. No matter how many times you try to obtain an instance of a particular named logger, the JDK logging framework will return the single instance of that named logger.

However, attempting to obtain the same named logger several times will make your program inefficient, as it will need to use the JDK logging framework each time to determine the existing instance of the named logger and return it.

Within the constructor, we create instances of `ConsoleHandler` and `FileHandler` objects. We add these `Handler` objects to the named logger. The named logger has two separate `Handler` objects attached to it. One will log the information to the console and the other to a file named "basicLogging.out".

The `doLogging()` method simply calls the `info()` method on the `Logger` object. The `info()` method is designed to publish messages with a level of INFO. We will discuss different logging methods in detail in the relevant sections. Once we execute the program, we will see the following messages printed to the console:

```
18-Dec-2002 20:39:18 sam.logging.BasicLogging logMessage
INFO: I am logging test message..
18-Dec-2002 20:39:18 sam.logging.BasicLogging logMessage
INFO: I am logging test message..
```

Also, a file named "basicLogging.out" will be created in the directory from which we execute the program. The file, shown in the following code snippet, will be in XML format and will contain the same logging information as printed in the console.

```xml
<?xml version="1.0" encoding="windows-1252" standalone="no"?>
<!DOCTYPE log SYSTEM "logger.dtd">
<log>
<record>
  <date>2002-12-18T20:39:18</date>
  <millis>1040243958817</millis>
  <sequence>0</sequence>
  <logger>MyLogger</logger>
  <level>INFO</level>
  <class>sam.logging.BasicLogging</class>
  <method>logMessage</method>
  <thread>10</thread>
  <message>I am logging test message..</message>
</record>
</log>
```

At this point, we have examined how to use the `Logger` and `Handler` objects to publish information to different destinations of our choice. In the following sections, we will look at the internals of how the framework works and provide more examples related to the use of different objects available within the JDK 1.4 logging API.

Logger Relationship Example

In the previous sections, we have seen that Logger objects exist in a namespace hierarchy for a given application instance. At this point, we will see how to develop a sample program that will illustrate the parent-child relationship of Logger objects. Listing 2-2, ParentLogger.java, shows a program that has a package named sam.logging and contains a method named aMethod() that prints logging information to a console.

Listing 2-2. ParentLogger.java

```
package sam.logging;
import java.util.logging.*;

public class ParentLogger
{
  private Logger logger = Logger.getLogger("sam.logging");
  private Level level = null;
  public ParentLogger()
  {
    level = Level.SEVERE;
    //setting the level as SEVERE
    logger.setLevel(level);
  }

  public void aMethod()
  {
    logger.log(level, "Severe message from Parent Logger");
  }
}
```

This program obtains a reference to the Logger object with the namespace "sam.logging". It also assigns SEVERE as the level of logging, which means that this logger will only log messages with the priority SEVERE. All other logging requests will be discarded, as SEVERE is the highest level. When we instantiate the ParentLogger class and invoke the method aMethod(), it will print the logging information to the console.

```
22-Aug-2002 23:08:28 sam.logging.ParentLogger aMethod
SEVERE:  Severe message from Parent Logger
```

As is evident, the logging information contains the date and timestamp of the logging activity, and the names of the class and method from which the logging was invoked. The next line contains information about the level of logging and the logging message itself. We will further explore the formatting of logging information in Chapter 3.

In the sample code shown in Listing 2-3, we will see how to develop a program called `ChildLogger.java`. This program is packaged in `sam.logging.child`. The program is similar to `ParentLogger.java` except the `Logger` object obtained in the `ParentLogger` class will now be the parent logger of the `Logger` object obtained in the `ChildLogger` class. This is due to the fact that the namespace "sam.logging.child" resides below the namespace "sam.logging".

Listing 2-3. ChildLogger.java

```
package sam.logging.child;

import java.util.logging.*;
import sam.logging.ParentLogger;
public class ChildLogger
{
    private Logger logger = Logger.getLogger("sam.logging.child");

    private Level level = null;
    public ChildLogger()
    {
        //level = Level.INFO;
        //setting the level of this child logger, if not specified, it
        // will use the level of the parent logger
        logger.setLevel(level);
    }

    public void aMethod()
    {
        logger.log(Level.INFO, "Info message from Child Logger");
        logger.log(Level.SEVERE, "Severe message from Child Logger");
    }
}
```

In the constructor, we specify the level associated with the `Logger` object obtained as INFO. Within the `aMethod()`, we print two logging messages, one with the level INFO and the other with the level SEVERE. Listing 2-4, `LoggingMonitor.java`, uses both `ParentLogger` and `ChildLogger`.

Listing 2-4. LoggingMonitor.java

```
package sam.logging;
import java.util.logging.*;
import sam.logging.child.ChildLogger;

public class LoggingMonitor
{
    public static void main(String[] args)
    {
        ParentLogger pLogger = new ParentLogger();
        ChildLogger cLogger = new ChildLogger();
        cLogger.aMethod();
    }
}
```

Executing the previous program will print both messages to the console.

```
26-Aug-2002 19:05:42 sam.logging.child.ChildLogger aMethod
INFO: Info message from Child Logger
26-Aug-2002 19:05:42 sam.logging.child.ChildLogger aMethod
SEVERE:  Severe message from Child Logger
```

Interestingly, if we comment out the setting of level in the ChildLogger class constructor, according to the package structure the logger in the ChildLogger class will try to use the Logger and its associated level defined in the ParentLogger class in the parent package sam.logging. In this case, the level associated with the parent logger is SEVERE.

Executing the program in Listing 2-4 with no level attached to the Logger object in the ChildLogger class will result in only the message with level SEVERE printing.

```
26-Aug-2002 19:08:22 sam.logging.child.ChildLogger aMethod
SEVERE:  Severe message from Child Logger
```

This example highlights how the parent-child relationship between Logger objects can affect the logging from within an application. Often, for your own purposes you will discover that this relationship is undesirable, and you will use the setUseParentHandlers() method in the Logger class to set the use of the parent logger and the associated Handlers to false. However, in some cases this parent-child relationship can be judicially employed to log the same message in two different destinations. For example, imagine a situation where the logger sam.logging is designed to write log messages to a file. The program ChildLogger is required to write the information to both console and file. In this situation, the child logger sam.logging.child can use a ConsoleHandler to write to the console, whereas the logging requests will automatically be delegated to the parent logger sam.logging. The parent logger will log the same information to a file.

This example also highlights the fact that the change of configuration in the parent logger can affect the behavior of the child logger. Thus, the use of this parent-child relationship is case specific, and we need to consider this aspect before using it.

Logging Information with Logger Objects

Each Logger provides a number of different logging methods. The design of different logging methods is governed by the fact that a LogRecord can contain a simple text message and a few other logging parameters. These additional parameters can be used by the Filter and Formatter objects for any logging decision or localization information; or, if the logging is intended to highlight some error condition, the logging information might carry the information about the exception. The Object argument to the log() methods is typically used by Filter objects to achieve fine-grained control over the information. The Filter objects then can analyze the Object argument and decide whether it should be logged or not, depending on any criteria set by the application and defined within the Filter objects. The Object argument can be any Java type, which will by default always extend the java.lang.Object.

The methods provided in the Logger class can be divided into the categories discussed in the following sections.

Basic Logging Methods

The following methods allow us to specify a logging level, the message string, the optional log record parameters, and an instance of java.lang.Throwable, which contains any error and exception details. The last method in this category accepts a LogRecord object and processes any information attached to the LogRecord object.

```
public void log(Level level, String message);
public void log(Level level, String message, Object param1);
public void log(Level level, String message, Object[]params);
public void log(Level level, String message, Throwable thrown);
public void log(LogRecord record);
```

As previously pointed out, the optional Object parameter to the logging methods can be used by Filter objects. For example, if we want to record the information for orders more than $100, we can pass an Order object to the logging methods as an optional parameter. Any `Filter` object associated with the `Handler` or `Logger` objects can then check for the order value and accordingly accept or reject the logging request.

Precise Logging Methods

The following methods are the same as the basic logging methods, except they explicitly specify the source class name and the source method name. On the surface this seems a simple aspect of logging information, but it can be a very important issue in logging. The JDK 1.4 logging API by default attempts to determine the location information for any particular logging request by analyzing the stack trace. This is a CPU-intensive operation and the outcome often cannot be trusted. Therefore, wherever you want the source class and source method names to be part of the logging information, you should use the precise logging methods.

```
public void logp(Level level, String sourceClass, String sourceMethod,
Stringmessage);
public void logp(Level level, String sourceClass,
String sourceMethod, String message, Object param1);
public void logp(Level level, String sourceClass,
String sourceMethod, String message, Object[] params);
public void logp(Level level, String sourceClass,
String sourceMethod, String message, Throwable thrown);
```

Logging with ResourceBundle

The following methods are the same as the precise logging methods, except they take a `ResourceBundle` name that will be used for localization purposes by the `Formatter` objects.

    The `java.util.ResourceBundle` is a technique to make our program language independent. With this technique, at the simplest level we use certain keys within our program. These keys map to certain messages (values) and are defined within a properties file. The `ResourceBundle` properties files are locale specific. For example, we can define messages in English and German in two separate properties files named "MyResources_en.properties" and "MyResources_de.properties". In the program we can use the `ResourceBundle` object with the name `MyResource.properties`. In a situation where the locale requires German, our program will automatically pick up the resource named `MyResources_de.properties`.

    In the `ResourceBundle`-based logging methods of the `Logger` class, the message parameter is used as the key for the resource bundle to locate the localized message value.

```
public void logrb(Level level, String sourceClass,
String sourceMethod, String bundleName, String message);
public void logrb(Level level, String sourceClass,
String sourceMethod, String bundleName, String message,
Object param1);
public void logrb(Level level, String sourceClass,
String sourceMethod, String bundleName,
String message, Object[] params);
public void logrb(Level level, String sourceClass,
String sourceMethod, String bundleName, String message,
Throwable thrown);
```

Level-Based Logging

The `Logger` class provides logging methods that use a particular logging level. The methods that fall into this category are discussed in this section.

The following method prints the message parameter with the Level.INFO logging level:

```
public void info(String message);
```

The following set of methods print messages with Level.FINE, Level.FINER, and Level.FINEST logging levels. The only difference among these methods is in the granularity of the logging message.

```
public void fine(String message);
public void finer(String message);
public void finest(String message);
```

The following method prints messages with the Level.CONFIG logging level and is generally used to print the configuration-related information:

```
public void config(String message);
```

The following method prints messages with the Level.WARNING logging level. Such messages usually contain any information about potential risks to the system that should be attended to immediately.

```
public void warning(String message);
```

The following method prints messages with the Level.SEVERE logging level. These messages often contain information that is extremely critical to the system about problems that may be causing the system to malfunction.

```
public void severe(String message);
```

However, it purely depends on the application developers to decide which level to use for logging a certain piece of information. It is often a good practice to decide the levels that should be used to publish certain categories of information. For example, messages indicating problems related to database access operation are crucial to the system. These sorts of messages can be published with the level SEVERE. On the other hand, the debug traces from within an application can be published with the level INFO.

The appropriate separation of levels for messages becomes beneficial at the deployment stage of the application. You can configure loggers to publish messages that are crucial to the system only with SEVERE or WARNING levels. However, you will likely configure to a lower level the loggers that provide detailed information for debugging the application.

Method-Related Logging

The following are convenience methods for tracking method-level activities such as the entry and exit to any method.

```
public void entering(String sourceClass, String sourceMethod);
public void entering(String sourceClass, String sourceMethod, Object param1);
public void entering(String sourceClass, String sourceMethod, Object params[]);
public void exiting(String sourceClass, String sourceMethod);
public void exiting(String sourceClass, String sourceMethod, Object param);
public void exiting(String sourceClass, String sourceMethod, Object[] params);
```

These methods internally use the Level.FINER logging level to log messages, and as a result should only be used to create debug traces.

Logger Example

As discussed in the previous sections, the Logger class provides various convenience methods for logging. Application developers can choose to use any of the methods depending on various other conditions within the application. Listing 2-5, LogMethods.java, will demonstrate the use of different logging methods within the Logger class.

Listing 2-5. LogMethods.java

```java
package sam.logging;

import java.util.logging.*;
import java.io.IOException;
public class LogMethods
{
    private static Logger logger = Logger.getLogger("sam.logging");
    public LogMethods()
    {
        //first obtain the logmanager instance
        LogManager manager = LogManager.getLogManager();
        //remove all the associated handlers with this manager
        manager.reset();
        //create a new handler for the logger to write messages
        // to the console
        ConsoleHandler ch = new ConsoleHandler();
        ch.setLevel(Level.FINEST);

        //setting the logger level and handler
        logger.setLevel(Level.FINEST);
        logger.addHandler(ch);

    }

    /**
     * This method demonstrates the basic logging methods
     */
    public void printBasicMethods()
    {
        logger.log(Level.INFO, "THIS IS INFO LEVEL MESSAGE");

        //creating a log record on our own
        LogRecord record = new LogRecord(Level.SEVERE, "OUR OWN LOGRECORD OBJECT");

        //logging the log record object
        logger.log(record);

    }

    /**
     * This method demonstrates the precise logging methods
     */
```

```java
    public void printPreciseMethods()
    {
        logger.logp(Level.INFO, "LogMethods", "printPreciseMethods",
"PRECISE METHODS..");
    }

    /**
     * This method demonstrates the level based logging methods
     */
    public void printLevelMethods()
    {

        logger.fine("THIS IS A FINE LEVEL MESSAGE");
        logger.finer("THIS IS A FINER LEVEL MESSAGE");
        logger.finest("THIS IS A FINEST LEVEL MESSAGE");
        logger.config("THIS IS CONFIG LEVEL MESSAGE");
    }

    /**
     *This method demonstrates the method level logging methods
     */
    public void printMethod()
    {

        logger.entering("LogMethods", "printMethod");
        logger.exiting("LogMethods", "printMethod");
    }

    public static void main(String[] args)
    {
        LogMethods lm = new LogMethods();
        lm.printBasicMethods();
        lm.printPreciseMethods();
        lm.printLevelMethods();
        lm.printMethod();
    }
}
```

This program demonstrates some important concepts about how the logging framework works in real life. By default, the logging framework sets up a default root logger, which is always present. The root logger has a `ConsoleHandler` object associated with it as the default handler, capable of printing information to `System.err`. The application can obtain any other named or anonymous `Logger` instance, and can then potentially attach any other Handler object to the Logger. If no Handler object is explicitly attached to the Logger instance, and the use of parent handlers is enabled, the Logger then will use the Handler objects associated with its parent loggers.

The default level associated with the ConsoleHandler is Level.INFO, which means that this handler will ignore any message with a lower level. In this scenario, logging methods such as log.fine(), log.finer(), etc., will not print any message. To avoid this problem, we can programmatically remove any handler associated with the LogManager of the current Java VM instance, and assign our own Handler object to the logger with the appropriate logging level associated with it.

In Listing 2-5, we first obtain a named Logger instance, sam.logging. In the constructor, we remove all the preset Handler and Formatter objects associated with the LogManager instance by calling the reset() method of the LogManager class. We create an instance of the ConsoleHandler, which by default prints the logging information to System.err. We set the level of the Handler and the Logger objects to the lowest level, Level.FINEST.

NOTE The use of the reset() method is shown in the example to illustrate what it does. You have to remember it has the global effect of resetting the whole logging framework. To disable the use of the root logger or any parent logger associated with a particular logger, the best practice is to use the setUseParentHandlers(false) method. The same effect is apparently achieved by the reset() method of the LogManager class at a global level. Using this method will also affect any other logger in the application willing to use the parent logger.

With this little arrangement, we will be able to see all the messages being printed to the console. Note that the basic level logging methods automatically determine the source class name and source method name. The precise logging methods print the source class name and the source method name as supplied to the logging methods. Although the basic level logging methods are capable of determining the source class name and the source method name, this is not reliable. It is worth mentioning again that several optimization techniques used with compilers can completely remove stack traces, in which case the logger will not be able to identify the source class and methods or may do it completely wrong. Hence, it is advised to explicitly specify the source class and source method names wherever needed.

After executing the example program in Listing 2-5, the following output will be printed to the console:

```
07-Oct-2002 19:06:04 sam.logging.LogMethods printBasicMethods
INFO: THIS IS INFO LEVEL MESSAGE
07-Oct-2002 19:06:04 sam.logging.LogMethods printBasicMethods
SEVERE: OUR OWN LOGRECORD OBJECT
07-Oct-2002 19:06:04 LogMethods printPreciseMethods
INFO: PRECISE METHODS..
07-Oct-2002 19:06:04 sam.logging.LogMethods printLevelMethods
FINE: THIS IS A FINE LEVEL MESSAGE
07-Oct-2002 19:06:04 sam.logging.LogMethods printLevelMethods
FINER: THIS IS A FINER LEVEL MESSAGE
07-Oct-2002 19:06:04 sam.logging.LogMethods printLevelMethods
FINEST: THIS IS A FINEST LEVEL MESSAGE
07-Oct-2002 19:06:04 sam.logging.LogMethods printLevelMethods
CONFIG: THIS IS CONFIG LEVEL MESSAGE
07-Oct-2002 19:06:04 LogMethods printMethod
FINER: ENTRY
07-Oct-2002 19:06:04 LogMethods printMethod
FINER: RETURN
```

It might seem that a Logger object itself is capable of publishing the logging information with its convenience methods; but in reality, it does so through its associated Handler objects, which we will look at in the next section.

The Logger object can be associated with any number of preferred Handler through the addHandler() method. If no Handler is specified, it uses its default Handler, which is a ConsoleHandler according to the default parameters specified in the JDK configuration file. It is important to note that a Logger uses its own Handler as well as any Handler registered with its parent logger and passes on the LogRecord to the parent. The use of the parent logger can be controlled through the logger's setUseParentHandlers() method.

NOTE In the previous example, we did not disable the use of the parent logger. But by using the reset() method on the LogManager, we have removed all the associated default Handler objects from the parent logger (the root logger, in this case). Hence, the logging information is not duplicated in the console. Refer back to the section "Logger Relationship Example" for more details on the parent-child logger relationship.

Handler

The `Handler` object is mainly responsible for publishing logging information to various destinations. It receives a `LogRecord` object from the `Logger` and sends it to the appropriate destination. The destination can be a file, console, stream, etc., depending on the type of handler being used. Each `Handler` object has its own default setting for its level of logging, as well as `Filter` and `Formatter` objects. The default values of the logging `Level`, `Filter`, and `Formatter` objects are determined by using the `LogManager` properties that the `LogManager` acquires by reading the configuration file. Each `Handler` may have different default settings depending on its type.

In the logging API, depending on the intended destination of the logging information, the following five categories of `Handler` objects are defined:

- `java.util.logging.FileHandler`: This writes the logging information to a file.

- `java.util.logging.ConsoleHandler`: This prints the logging information to the console or the command line shell.

- `java.util.logging.StreamHandler`: This writes the logging information to any particular stream.

- `java.util.logging.MemoryHandler`: This writes the logging information to a memory buffer.

- `java.util.logging.SocketHandler`: This writes the logging information to a server component listening to a particular port using TCP/IP.

All the preceding types of `Handler` objects basically subclass an `abstract` class called `Handler`. This class defines `abstract` methods for publishing the logging information encapsulated within a `LogRecord` object and closing and flushing any stream being used by the `Handler` to publish the logging messages. Any `Logger` object internally calls the overridden `publish(LogRecord record)` method of its registered `Handler` to publish the logging information. It is important to know that the `publish()` method in all `Handlers` is synchronized. This makes the logging activity thread-safe. It is also possible to write our own customized `Handler` object; to do so we have to extend our `Handler` object from the abstract `Handler` class and override the preceding methods. We will discuss how to develop a custom `Handler` in Chapter 4.

The relationship of different `Handler` objects within the logging API is shown in the UML class diagram in Figure 2-3.

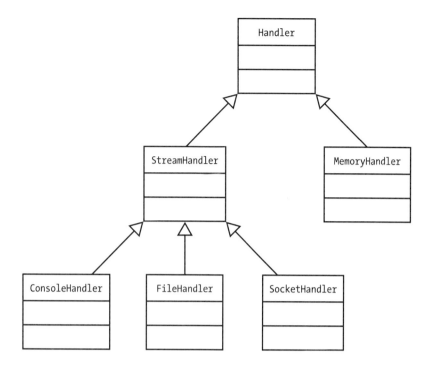

Figure 2-3. The Handler class hierarchy

StreamHandler

The StreamHandler class acts as a base class for any stream-based handler. It is possible to specify a java.io.OutputStream object to StreamHandler so that StreamHandler will print the logging information to the specified OutputStream. The default configuration properties for StreamHandler are initialized using the LogManager configuration properties.

With the default JDK 1.4 setting, a StreamHandler acquires the following initialization properties:

- level: This reads the java.util.logging.StreamHandler.level property and defaults to Level.INFO.

- filter: This reads the java.util.logging.StreamHandler.filter property and defaults to no filter.

- formatter: This reads the java.util.logging.StreamHandler.formatter property and defaults to java.util.logging.SimpleFormatter.

- encoding: This reads the java.util.logging.StreamHandler.encoding property and defaults to platform-specific encoding style.

The `StreamHandler` object can write to any kind of `OutputStream` object including `System.out`. In `StreamHandlerDemo.java`, shown in Listing 2-6, we will publish logging information to `System.out` with the help of a `StreamHandler`.

Listing 2-6. StreamHandlerDemo.java

```java
package sam.logging;
import java.util.logging.*;
import java.io.*;

public class StreamHandlerDemo
{
    private StreamHandler handler = null;
    private OutputStream outStream = null;
    private static Logger logger = Logger.getLogger("sam.logging");
    public StreamHandlerDemo()
    {
        //creating an outputstream as System.out
        outStream = System.out;

        //creating a stream handler
        handler = new StreamHandler(outStream, new SimpleFormatter());
        //setting the handler to the logger
        logger.addHandler(handler);
        //setting the user of parent logger to false
        logger.setUseParentHandlers(false);

    }

    /**
     *This method demonstrates the stream handler logging capability
     */
    public void logMessage()
    {
        //publishing the logging information
        logger.info("StreamHandler is working…");
    }

    public static void main(String[] args)
    {
        StreamHandlerDemo demo = new StreamHandlerDemo();
        demo.logMessage();

    }
}
```

In this example, first we obtain a named `Logger` instance, `sam.logging`. In the constructor, we create a `StreamHandler` object by passing a reference to `System.out`. This acts as the output stream to which to write the logging information and also pass a `SimpleFormatter` object instance to format the logging message. We assign the `StreamHandler` object as a handler to the logger. Noticeably, we set the use of parent loggers to `false`. This will stop the logging request being forwarded to the parent loggers. On the other hand, if the use of parent loggers is enabled, the logging message will appear several times in the output depending on the number of parent loggers associated with a particular logger.

In the `logMessage()` method, we invoke the `info()` method of the `Logger` class with the logging message. It is important to note that the level of the `StreamHandler` object should be equal to or greater than the level used with the `Logger` object. By default, the `StreamHandler` has a level of INFO. If the level falls below the threshold level of the `StreamHandler`, the logging message will be ignored. In the end, we publish the logging message using the `info()` method of the `Logger` class.

Executing the program in Listing 2-6 will produce the following output to the console:

```
07-Aug-2002 18:42:30 sam.logging.StreamHandlerDemo logMessage
INFO: StreamHandler is working...
```

However, the `StreamHandler` object is rarely used in isolation. `FileHandler`, `ConsoleHandler`, and `SocketHandler` are subclasses of `StreamHandler` that provide richer functionality for stream-based logging.

ConsoleHandler

`ConsoleHandler` is a built-in handler in the JDK 1.4 logging API. It is used to print logging information to `System.err`, as opposed to `System.out`, and therefore extends the `StreamHandler` class. `ConsoleHandler` is one of the default handlers used by the `Logger` object when no handler is explicitly defined for the that object.

By default, the `ConsoleHandler` object is initialized by reading the configuration properties of the `LogManager` object. It acquires the following default properties when properties are not explicitly set:

- `level`: This reads the `java.util.logging.ConsoleHandler.level` property and defaults to Level.INFO.

- `filter`: This reads the `java.util.logging.ConsoleHandler.filter` property and defaults to no filter.

- `formatter`: This reads the `java.util.logging.ConsoleHandler.formatter` property and defaults to `java.util.logging.SimpleFormatter`.

- `encoding`: This reads the `java.util.logging.ConsoleHandler.encoding` property and defaults to platform-specific encoding style.

It is interesting to note that the overridden method `close()` of the `ConsoleHandler` only flushes any buffer to the `System.err` stream but leaves `System.err` open.

FileHandler

`FileHandler` is a very useful `Handler` object provided within the JDK 1.4 logging API. It writes logging information into a file. It extends the `StreamHandler` object and overrides the necessary method to implement file-based logging. `FileHandler` has a couple of useful features for managing the file to which logging information is logged and to locate the file within a file system in an OS-independent manner. As a feature-rich file-based handler, it has the following characteristics:

- It can write the logging information to a single file, or it can write to a rotating set of files. When a particular file reaches the maximum size limit, the logging information is continued in a different file. The history of the logging file is maintained with a sequential numbering scheme such as "0, 1, 2 . . ." added to the base filename.

- It is possible to specify log files by using a pattern instead of specifying an absolute path. The pattern is a string that can contain the expressions shown in Table 2-1.

Table 2-1. The Patterns in FileHandler

Expression	Meaning
/	The path separator of the local OS
%t	A directory suitable for storing temporary logging files, such as the temp directory of the OS
%h	A directory such as the "user.home" location, which is suitable to store user-specific data in the system
%g	A log generation number to rotate log files
%u	A number to make a log file unique to avoid any conflicts
%%	A literal percent sign

FileHandler will use the pattern string to resolve the log file's name and location in the following way:

- If the pattern expression contains / or %t, then the location of the log file is either the current working directory or the temporary file directory specific to the OS. For example, if the pattern is %t/logging/info.out, then in Solaris OS, it will be read as "/var/tmp/logging/info.out" and in Windows it will be read as "c:/temp/logging/info.out".

- If the pattern contains the expression %t/logging/info%g.out, then the logging information will be written to "/var/tmp/logging/info0.out" and rotated to "/var/tmp/logging/info1.out", etc.

- %u is a unique identification number to resolve any conflict with the logging file. If FileHandler tries to open a file and finds that it is already in use by another process, then it tends to use %u to generate some unique number and adds that number to the end of the base filename after a dot. For example, the pattern %t/logging/info%u.%g.out, with a count 2, may produce log filenames such as "/var/tmp/logging/info0.0.out", "/var/tmp/logging/info0.1.out", and "/var/tmp/logging/info0.2.out". If "info0.2.out" generates a conflict, the logging information will be rotated to "info1.2.out".

In line with other Handler objects, the FileHandler object is also initialized with the LogManager properties. By default, FileHandler acquires the following properties:

- level: This reads the java.util.logging.FileHandler.level property and defaults to Level.ALL.

- filter: This reads the java.util.logging.FileHandler.filter property and defaults to no filter.

- formatter: This reads the java.util.logging.FileHandler.formatter property and defaults to java.util.logging.XMLFormatter formatting style.

- encoding: This reads the java.util.logging.FileHandler.encoding property and defaults to the platform-specific encoding style.

- limit: This reads the java.util.logging.FileHandler.limit property. The limit property specifies an approximate amount of data in bytes to be written to the file. If this is set to zero, then there is no limit to the data size. This property defaults to no limit. It is important to note that the limit is specified in bytes, *not* in kilobytes or megabytes or any other units. If the data exceeds the file size limit property, then the file is rotated.

- count: This reads the `java.util.logging.FileHandler.count` property and denotes the number of output files to cycle through. It defaults to 1.

- pattern: This reads the `java.util.logging.FileHandler.pattern` property. It defaults to %h/java%u.log.

- append: This reads the `java.util.logging.FileHandler.append` property. It defaults to `false`. If it is set to `true`, then log messages are appended to the log file until the limit is reached. Otherwise, the logging information is overwritten to the file.

The `FileHandler` class provides the following constructors to create the object:

- `public FileHandler()`: This is the default constructor, and is initialized entirely with `LogManager` properties.

- `public FileHandler(String pattern)`: Constructor with the pattern to use. The file size limit is set to none and the file count is set to 1. Only one file will ever be created to write the log messages. The `append` property is set to `false`.

- `public FileHandler(String pattern, Boolean append)`: Constructor with the pattern to append to the log file if the `append` property is set to `true`.

- `public FileHandler(String pattern, int limit, int count)`: Constructor specifying the pattern, the size limit of each log file, and the number of files to be created for rotation. Once the number of files required to write the complete amount of log information exceeds the specified count, the log messages are rotated back to the first file. The count value must be at least 1.

- `public FileHandler(String pattern, int limit, int count, Boolean append)`: Same as the preceding constructor, except it includes a specific appending instruction.

Listing 2-7, `FileHandlerDemo.java`, demonstrates the use of a pattern with the `FileHandler` class.

Listing 2-7. FileHandlerDemo.java

```
package sam.logging;

import java.util.logging.*;
import java.io.IOException;
```

```java
public class FileHandlerDemo
{
    private FileHandler handler = null;
    private static Logger logger = Logger.getLogger("sam.logging");

    public FileHandlerDemo(String pattern)
    {
        try
        {
            //creating a file handler object with 1000 bytes limit for
            //each file and with count 2
            handler = new FileHandler(pattern,1000, 2);
            //adding the handler to the logger
            logger.addHandler(handler);
        }catch(IOException ioe) {
            ioe.printStackTrace();
        }
    }

    /**
     * This method logs the message with the FileHandler
     */
    public void logMessage()
    {
        LogRecord record = new LogRecord(Level.INFO, "Logged in a file..22.");
        logger.log(record);
        handler.flush();
        handler.close();
    }

    public static void main(String[] args)
    {
        FileHandlerDemo demo = new FileHandlerDemo("%h/log%g.out");
        demo.logMessage();
    }
}
```

In this example, we use the constructor with a pattern, size of each logging file, and count of files. We specify the pattern to be %h/log%g.out. According to Table 2-1, %h denotes the user.home system property. Once we go to the same location, we will find the log files are created. If we have exceeded the limit of each file (one way of doing so is to run the program in Listing 2-7 a couple of times in a loop), then the log file will be rotated; in that case, we will get files "log0.out" and "log1.out", as the count is specified as 2.

FileHandler by default uses the XMLFormatter object to write logging information. We will look at the XMLFormatter object in detail in Chapter 3. But in short, the logging information will be XML formatted and the XML data will be logged into the logging files. For the preceding application, the log file will contain the following logging information:

```
<?xml version="1.0" encoding="windows-1252" standalone="no"?>
<!DOCTYPE log SYSTEM "logger.dtd">
<log>
<record>
  <date>2002-08-30T22:19:02</date>
  <millis>1030742342998</millis>
  <sequence>0</sequence>
  <level>INFO</level>
  <thread>10</thread>
  <message>Logged in a file...</message>
</record>
</log>
```

The XML logging information is structured data and therefore can be a very useful way of maintaining logging information for further processing. For example, any other customized error manager can parse the XML data and produce user-friendly, meaningful error messages to the user of the application. It is also possible to specify any other formatting style to be associated with the FileHandler object by using the setFormatter() method. We can specify any existing Formatter objects in the JDK 1.4 logging API, or we can create our own formatter and attach it to FileHandler.

FileHandler can prove useful in various situations. With the concept of patterns, it is possible to specify a location without indicating the absolute path, which helps in implementing a file-based logging system in an OS-independent way. Arguably, this bit of information can be made configurable, but that means we need to change the configuration file every time the logging platform changes. Thus, the way FileHandler reads the system properties and determines the location of the logging files can be very helpful.

MemoryHandler

Imagine a situation in which you want to log messages only when a certain triggering condition is achieved and discard any logging information that doesn't meet the triggering condition. `MemoryHandler` is the answer for these types of logging activity. A `MemoryHandler` object writes data to a circular buffer in the memory. By condition, a `MemoryHandler` is not itself capable of publishing information to any destination and will have another `Handler` object associated with it as a target `Handler`. When the triggering condition is reached, the logging information is passed to the target `Handler` object for further processing.

By default, the `MemoryHandler` acquires the following default properties by using the `LogManager` properties:

- `level`: This reads the `java.util.logging.MemoryHandler.level` property and defaults to Level.ALL.

- `filter`: This reads the `java.util.logging.MemoryHandler.filter` property and defaults to no filter.

- `size`: This reads the `java.util.logging.MemoryHandler.size` property, which defines the size of the memory buffer. It defaults to 1000 bytes.

- `pushLevel`: This reads the `java.util.logging.MemoryHandler.pushLevel` property. This defines the triggering condition with respect to the logging level for the `MemoryHandler` to release its buffer to the specified target `Handler` object.

- `target`: This reads the `java.util.logging.MemoryHandler.target` property and defines the target `Handler` to be used for publishing the logging information.

It is interesting to note that the `MemoryHandler` has no `Formatter` object associated with it. Instead, it uses the `Formatter` object associated with its target `Handler` object. The `MemoryHandler` object has the following constructor other than the default constructor:

```
public MemoryHandler(Handler target, int size, Level pushLevel)
```

This constructor creates a `MemoryHandler` with the specified target `Handler`, the number of `LogRecords` to buffer, and also the push level. Note that the size argument has no relation to the length of the memory buffer. These values will override any default values specified in the logging configuration file. Also, the `MemoryHandler` object provides us with various convenience methods to control the memory buffer and the associated target `Handler` object.

The following method pushes any buffered output to the associated target `Handler`:

```
public void push()
```

This next method flushes any output buffer used by the associated Handler:

```
public void flush()
```

It is important to note that MemoryHandler itself has no output stream to write to and uses the associated target Handler to open any stream and write the logging information.

The following method closes any output stream used by the associated target Handler object:

```
public void close()
```

It eventually closes the associated Handler and all its resources.

There are three possible situations in which MemoryHandler will try to release its buffered content to the associated target Handler object:

- When the incoming LogRecord object has a level greater than the push level of the MemoryHandler object. Here level matching is the triggering condition.

- When any external class calls the push() method of the MemoryHandler object.

- When any subclass of the MemoryHandler object overrides the method publish(LogRecord record), checks certain conditions, and decides to release the buffered content.

Listing 2-8, MemoryHandlerDemo.java, illustrates the use of MemoryHandler.

Listing 2-8. MemoryHandlerDemo.java

```java
package sam.logging;
import java.util.logging.*;

public class MemoryHandlerDemo
{
    private ConsoleHandler handler = null;
    private MemoryHandler mHandler = null;
    private static Logger logger = Logger.getLogger("sam.logging");

    public MemoryHandlerDemo(int size, Level pushLevel) {
        handler = new ConsoleHandler();
        //instantiating the MemoryHandler object with the specified
        //size, pushLevel and a ConsoleHandler as target Handler
        mHandler = new MemoryHandler(handler, size, pushLevel);
```

```java
        //adding the memory handler to the logger
        logger.addHandler(mHandler);
        //set the use of parent logger to false
        logger.setUseParentHandlers(false);

    }
    /**
     *This method publishes the log messages
     */
    public void logMessage() {
        LogRecord record1 = new LogRecord(Level.SEVERE, "This is
SEVERE level message");
        LogRecord record2 = new LogRecord(Level.WARNING, "This is
WARNING level message");

        logger.log(record1);
        logger.log(record2);

        //this block of code is commented out initially. Will explain the use
of this block in the discussion below.
        /*
        //sequence that will force both the records
        logger.log(record2);
        logger.log(record1);

        //sequence that will discard one record according to the size
        logger.log(record2);
        logger.log(record2);
        logger.log(record1);
        */
    }

    public static void main(String args[]) {
        //creating a MemoryHandler object with size limit 1000 bytes
        // and pushLevel as Level.SEVERE
        MemoryHandlerDemo demo = new MemoryHandlerDemo(2, Level.SEVERE);
        demo.logMessage();
    }
}
```

This program looks very simple. In essence, we create a `MemoryHandler` object with 2 as the specified number of `LogRecord` objects to be logged and the push level as Level.SEVERE. Within the constructor we assign a `ConsoleHandler` object as the target `Handler` object. Within the `logMessage()` method, we create two `LogRecord` objects, record1 and record2, with two different logging levels, Level.SEVERE and Level.WARNING. We then attempt to publish the record objects.

The `MemoryHandler` object will internally check the level of each record with the specified push level. If the level of the record is greater or equal to the push level, then the record is passed to the associated target `Handler` object (in this example, the `ConsoleHandler` object). Upon execution of the preceding program, we will only see the record with level SEVERE being printed to the console.

```
31-Aug-2002 17:48:50 null
SEVERE: This is SEVERE level message
```

It all looks so simple, but there is an order to the messaging that is important. If we try reversing the order of the record object, then we will get the following output:

```
31-Aug-2002 17:53:11 null
WARNING: This is WARNING level message
31-Aug-2002 17:53:11 null
SEVERE: This is SEVERE level message
```

This is no nasty surprise. What is important is the order of messaging. When we reverse the order of publishing the record as

```
//publishing the logging information
logger.log(record2);
logger.log(record1);
```

record 2 has a level of Level.WARNING and record1 has a level of Level.SEVERE. When `MemoryHandler` processes the publishing request with record2, it finds the level is lower than the push level (Level.SEVERE) and therefore decides not to pass it to the target `Handler` object. But when it processes the publish request with the record1 object, it finds the level is equal to the push level and hence decides to pass it to the target `Handler` object. At this point of time, it loops through an internal storage of all the `LogRecord` objects that have issued a publish request and passes all the `LogRecord` objects to the target `Handler`. The target `Handler` object then prints all the records to the destination. This is the reason why with the reversing of logging sequence both messages with level WARNING and SEVERE appear in the console.

One last thing to discuss is the role of the size parameter in the constructor of the `MemoryHandler` object. The size parameter as discussed restricts the number of `LogRecords` to be logged in memory. In our previous example, we specify the number of log records to be buffered as 2. When the triggering condition is reached, such as the level of a log record being greater or equal to the push level of the MemoryHandler, then the MemoryHandler tries to release all the previous log records within the range of the specified size parameter. If we try to print the log record in the following sequence:

```
//sequence that will discard one record according to the size
logger.log(record2);
logger.log(record2);
logger.log(record1);
```

we will see the following output:

```
31-Aug-2002 18:27:13 null
WARNING: This is WARNING level message
31-Aug-2002 18:27:13 null
SEVERE: This is SEVERE level message
```

Only one of the record2 objects is printed along with the record3 object, as the size argument is specified as 2. If we change the size parameter now to 3, we will see all the messages being printed.

SocketHandler

Often it is the case that in a distributed computing scenario we have several components of an application running in different places over a network. Although the components are distributed, we tend to manage the components centrally. In this scenario, logging information from each individual component needs to be wired to a central location. SocketHandler is designed to send messages across the network using TCP/IP to a server component that is listening to a particular port for such messages. SocketHandler is a very simple network-based Handler that extends the StreamHandler class. It has the following constructor:

```
public SocketHandler(String host, int port)
```

If the host or the port is unreachable, it throws a java.io.IOException. If the host or port number specified is invalid, then a java.lang.IllegalArgumentException is thrown. By default, SocketHandler is initialized with the LogManager properties, and it acquires the following properties:

- level: This reads the java.util.logging.SocketHandler.level property and defaults to Level.ALL.

- `filter`: This reads the `java.util.logging.SocketHandler.filter` property and defaults to no filter.

- `formatter`: This reads the `java.util.logging.SocketHandler.formatter` property and defaults to the `java.util.logging.XMLFormatter`.

- `encoding`: This reads the `java.util.logging.SocketHandler.encoding` property and defaults to the platform-specific encoding.

- `host`: This reads the `java.util.logging.SocketHandler.host` property. It specifies the host to which to connect in order to pass the logging information.

- `port`: This reads the `java.util.logging.SocketHandler.port` property. It specifies the port number to a particular host to connect to.

The I/O operation performed by `SocketHandler` is buffered, but the buffer is flushed after each `LogRecord` object is written. Listing 2-9, `SocketHandlerDemo.java`, and Listing 2-10, `LoggingServer.java` (shown a little later in this section), illustrate the use of the `SocketHandler` object.

Listing 2-9. SocketHandlerDemo.java

```java
package sam.logging;
import java.util.logging.*;
import java.io.IOException;

public class SocketHandlerDemo
{
    private SocketHandler handler = null;
    private static Logger logger = Logger.getLogger("sam.logging");

    public SocketHandlerDemo(String host, int port)
    {
        try {
            //instantiating a SocketHandler with the given host & port
            handler = new SocketHandler(host, port);
            //adding the handler to the logger
            logger.addHandler(handler);
        }catch(IOException ioe) {
            ioe.printStackTrace();
        }
    }
}
```

```
    /**
     * This method logs the logging information
     */
    public void logMessage()
    {
        logger.warning("SocketHandler is working...");
    }

    public static void main(String args[]) {
        //creating a SocketHandlerDemo with localhost and 2020 port
        SocketHandlerDemo demo = new SocketHandlerDemo("localhost", 2020);
        demo.logMessage();
    }
}
```

This program in essence obtains a named `Logger` instance, `sam.logging`, creates an instance of the `SocketHandler` object, and assigns it as the `Handler` of the `Logger` instance. In the `logMessage()` method, it sends the logging message to the server. Notice that we do not disable the use of the parent logger property for the newly obtained `Logger` instance. This is just to make sure we see the logging information at the client side as well. To avoid printing the logging message in the client side, we can disable the use of the parent logger by including `setUseParentHandlers(false)`.

Listing 2-10, `LogginServer.java`, shows the server-side program for accepting this logging request.

Listing 2-10. LoggingServer.java

```
package sam.logging;

import java.net.*;
import java.util.logging.*;
import java.io.*;

public class LoggingServer
{
  private ServerSocket serverSocket = null;
  private Socket socket = null;
```

```java
    public LoggingServer(int port)
    {
      try
      {
        serverSocket = new ServerSocket(port);
        socket = serverSocket.accept();
      }catch(IOException ioe)
      {
        ioe.printStackTrace();
      }
    }

    /**
     *This method starts receiving the messages
     */
    public void acceptMessage()
    {
      try
      {
        //get the inputStream of the received socket
        InputStream inStream = socket.getInputStream();
        BufferedReader reader =new BufferedReader(new InputStreamReader(inStream));
        String str = null;
        while( (str = reader.readLine()) !=null)      {
          System.out.println(str);
        }
      }catch(IOException ioe)
      {
        ioe.printStackTrace();
      }
    }

    public static void main(String args[])
    {
      LoggingServer server = new LoggingServer(2020);
      server.acceptMessage();
    }
}
```

In this program we start a server that listens to port 2020. The accept() method on the java.net.ServerSocket object provides us with the InputStream of the opened socket connection. We then construct a java.io.BufferedReader object with the InputStream obtained to read the content.

The client program, SocketHandlerDemo, creates a java.util.logging.SocketHandler with the same port number to the host named "localhost" (which is the current machine by default). It then creates a LogRecord object and publishes it over the network.

The server program running listens to the request and receives the LogRecord object passed to it. Upon receiving the input, it prints out the information to the console. As SocketHandler uses the XMLFormatter object by default, we get the following message printed to the console:

```
<?xml version="1.0" encoding="windows-1252" standalone="no"?>
<!DOCTYPE log SYSTEM "logger.dtd">
<log>
<record>
  <date>2002-08-31T20:48:47</date>
  <millis>1030823327564</millis>
  <sequence>0</sequence>
  <level>WARNING</level>
  <thread>10</thread>
  <message>Socket handler is working</message>
</record>
</log>
```

We will discuss the java.util.logging.XMLFormatter formatting style in detail in Chapter 3. The fact that SocketHandler writes the logging information in XML format makes it particularly reusable in the server side. It is easier to read the input stream from the socket and parse the incoming XML data, which can then be organized into different Java objects for use across the application for various purposes. It is important to note that after the log record has been passed to the listening server, the SocketHandler object needs to be closed. If there is a problem connecting to the specified host and port number, a java.io.IOException is thrown.

Filter Object

java.util.logging.Filter objects are useful when we want more fine-grained control over the logging. We have already seen that logging information is filtered with its associated logging level. But in situations where we need to analyze the log record before making a final decision whether it should be logged, we need to implement separate Filter objects. A Filter can be attached to both Logger objects and Handler objects. Each can apply separate Filter objects to one particular LogRecord before logging it. It is possible to set Filter objects programmatically through the setFilter() methods, or they can be specified in the configuration file.

Filter objects by rule have to implement the `java.util.logging.Filter` interface, which defines a single method, `isLoggable(LogRecord record)`, returning a Boolean value. Before a `Logger` passes a `LogRecord` object to its associated `Handler`, it calls the `isLoggable()` method on any attached `Filter` and passes the `LogRecord` to the `Handler` only if the `Filter` approves it. Similarly, the `Handler` object invokes the `isLoggable()` method on its associated `Filter` before sending it to the final destination. Listing 2-11, `Person.java`, defines a `Person` object, and Listing 2-12, `AgeFilter.java`, creates a `Filter` that is capable of making some logging decisions based on a person's age.

Listing 2-11. Person.java

```java
package sam.logging;

public class Person
{
 private String name = null;
 private int age;

 public Person(String name, int age)
 {
  this.name = name;
  this.age = age;
 }

 public void setName(String name)
 {
  this.name = name;
 }

 public String getName()
 {
  return name;
 }

 public void setAge(int age)
 {
  this.age = age;
 }

 public int getAge()
 {
  return age;
 }
}
```

Listing 2-12, `AgeFilter.java`, implements the `java.util.logging.Filter` interface and provides an implementation for the method `public boolean is Loggable(LogRecord record)`. For simplicity, let's assume that the `LogRecord` object passed to it will have only one `Person` object associated with it. We then obtain and check the age from the `Person` object and return `true` if the age is greater than 30; otherwise, we return `false`. If the return value is `true`, then the `LogRecord` object is passed to the next processor in the line, or else the `LogRecord` object is discarded.

Listing 2-12. AgeFilter.java

```java
package sam.logging;

import java.util.logging.*;

public class AgeFilter implements Filter {
    public AgeFilter() {
    }
    /**
     * This is the overridden method from the Filter interface.
     * It checks the Person object associated with the LogRecord
     * checks the age>30, and returns true
     *@param record the LogRecord object
     *@return boolean true/false
     */
    public boolean isLoggable(LogRecord record) {
        boolean result = false;
        //obtaining the Person object from the record
        Object[] objs = record.getParameters();
        Person person = (Person)objs[0];

        //check if person is not null
        if(person !=null) {
            //obtain the age
            int age = person.getAge();
            if(age>30)
                result =  true;
            else
                result =  false;
        }
        return result;
    }
}
```

Once we have the infrastructure ready, we next create the program in Listing 2-13, FilterDemo.java, that will use the AgeFilter. In the constructor, we obtain a Logger object with the sam.logging package structure. We then instantiate a AgeFilter object, and assign the Filter to the Logger. Now we will create two Person objects with age 32 and 29 and try to log some messages with the logger.log() method by passing the reference to the respective created Person objects.

Listing 2-13. FilterDemo.java

```java
package sam.logging;

import java.util.logging.*;

public class FilterDemo
{
   private Logger logger = null;
   private AgeFilter filter = null;

   public FilterDemo()
   {
     //obtaining a logger object
     logger = Logger.getLogger("sam.logging");
     //creating a AgeFilter object
     filter = new AgeFilter();
     //attaching the filter to the logger
     logger.setFilter(filter);
   }

   /**
    * This method logs the message
    */
   public void logMessage(Person person)
   {
     //logging the message with Person object as parameter
     logger.log(Level.INFO, "Person has age "+person.getAge(), person);

   }
```

```
  public static void main(String args[])
  {
    FilterDemo demo = new FilterDemo();
    //creating  Person objects
    Person person1 = new Person("Paul", 32);
    Person person2 = new Person("sam", 29);
    //logging with each Person object
    demo.logMessage(person1);
    demo.logMessage(person2);
  }
}
```

The `Logger` object in Listing 2-13 has the `AgeFilter` attached to it, which only allows a `Person` object with age greater than 30 to be logged. Therefore, executing this program will print the following logging information to the console:

```
01-Sep-2002 13:01:06 sam.logging.FilterDemo logMessage
INFO: Person has age 32
```

The preceding listing is a very simplistic example of the usage of `Filter` objects in the logging framework. You can easily figure out how useful `Filter` objects might become to greatly reduce the number of log messages being published and also how they can help to log only the information that is needed. `Filter` objects become really beneficial when you need to print only selected logging information at the time of debugging.

File-Based Configuration

In the examples provided in previous sections, we have seen how to configure the JDK 1.4 logging API programmatically by using the methods available in different objects. However, programmatic configuration is not flexible. Anytime you decide to change the configuration such as the level for a particular logger, you will need to go back to the source code and make necessary changes.

The JDK 1.4 logging API supports configuration via a configuration file. The configuration file supports the configuration parameters to be defined in a key-value format. For example, recall the example in Listing 2-9, `SocketHandlerDemo.java`. We can rewrite the program without providing any configuration for the `Logger` within the program by defining the required configuration in a configuration file.

Listing 2-14, `ConfigDemo.java`, rewrites `SocketHandlerDemo` without the code for the configuration.

Listing 2-14. ConfigDemo.java

```java
package sam.logging;

import java.util.logging.Logger;
import java.util.logging.SocketHandler;

public class ConfigDemo
{
    private static Logger logger = Logger.getLogger("sam.logging");

    public ConfigDemo()
    {
        try
        {
          logger.addHandler(new SocketHandler());
        }catch(Exception e)
        {
            e.printStackTrace();

        }
    }
    /**
     * This method logs the logging information
     */
    public void logMessage()
    {
        logger.warning("SocketHandler is working...");
    }

    public static void main(String args[]) {
        //creating a SocketHandlerDemo with localhost and 2020 port
        ConfigDemo demo = new ConfigDemo();
        demo.logMessage();
    }
}
```

We can now create a configuration file to use with `ConfigDemo`. Listing 2-15, "config.properties", is the sample configuration file.

Listing 2-15. config.properties

```
#define the logger level
sam.logging.level=INFO

#define the properties for the SocketHandler
java.util.logging.SocketHandler.level=INFO
java.util.logging.SocketHandler.host=localhost
java.util.logging.SocketHandler.port=2020
```

Notice that we have defined the host, port, and level configurations for the SocketHandler in the configuration file rather than the application. This gives us the power to change any configuration without changing the source code.

Execute the program in Listing 2-14 with the following command:

```
java -Djava.util.logging.config.file=config.properties sam.logging.ConfigDemo
```

With the server program running as explained in the example in Listing 2-10, we will see the following output printed to the console of the server in XML format:

```
<?xml version="1.0" encoding="windows-1252" standalone="no"?>
<!DOCTYPE log SYSTEM "logger.dtd">
<log>
<record>
  <date>2002-12-22T15:47:22</date>
  <millis>1040572042929</millis>
  <sequence>0</sequence>
  <logger>sam.logging</logger>
  <level>WARNING</level>
  <class>sam.logging.ConfigDemo</class>
  <method>logMessage</method>
  <thread>10</thread>
  <message>SocketHandler is working...</message>
</record>
</log>
```

For a giggle, let's change the configuration file to use SimpleFormatter with SocketHandler by adding the following line:

```
java.util.logging.SocketHandler.formatter=java.util.logging.SimpleFormatter
```

We will see the following output:

```
22-Dec-2002 15:59:49 sam.logging.ConfigDemo logMessage
WARNING: SocketHandler is working...
```

This is the advantage of specifying the configuration via a configuration file. We will discuss configuration in more detail in Chapter 4.

Formatter Object

Handler objects are capable of filtering logging requests and printing them to different destinations. Before finally printing logging information, Handler objects use Formatter objects to convert logging information to different human-readable representations. Formatter objects help structure data in any formatting style that is useful for the application. It is also vitally important to render logging information in a well-structured and meaningful manner so that it can be used for future analysis. We will discuss Formatter objects in detail in Chapter 3.

Conclusion

In this chapter, we have examined various objects in the JDK 1.4 logging API. We have discussed how the different objects in the framework interact with each other. We have also seen sample usage of each object. By now, you should have a proper understanding of the working of the logging API. In the next chapter, we will explore the different formatting styles used by the Formatter objects available within the API and develop our own custom Formatter object.

CHAPTER 3
Formatting JDK 1.4 Logging Information

THE GOAL OF the JDK 1.4 logging API is to provide a way to encapsulate logging information at the appropriate level of detail. In the previous chapter, we explored various objects that are utilized to capture logging information, how to tell the logging API the detail level of the logging activity that should be performed, and also how to change and pass different configuration parameters to the API at runtime to control logging information. However, another important aspect of any logging mechanism is the way the logs are produced and maintained. It is vitally important for an application to structure and produce logging information that can be analyzed and processed later. In order to achieve this aspect of logging, it is essential that logging information can be produced in different formats. The JDK 1.4 logging API provides two basic mechanisms for producing logging information that is human readable and appropriate for any future processing. The objects that accomplish the task of producing log information in different formats are called Formatter objects. In this chapter, we will examine the default Formatter objects provided within the API and explore how to write new Formatter objects.

Default Formatter Objects

It is important you have an understanding of the architecture of the JDK 1.4 logging API before we discuss Formatter objects in detail, so let's briefly review it. We have seen in the previous chapter that the central point of the framework is the Logger object. The Logger object internally creates a LogRecord object. The LogRecord object encapsulates the logging information. The Logger object has an associated Handler object, which manages the distribution of log messages. Each Handler object will have a Formatter object associated with it that is responsible for formatting the log messages with appropriate formatting styles. If a Formatter is not explicitly specified with the Handler object, it uses the default Formatter object associated with the respective Handler objects or any other Formatter object associated with the parent Handler object.

Figure 3-1 depicts the collaboration of different objects within the logging framework.

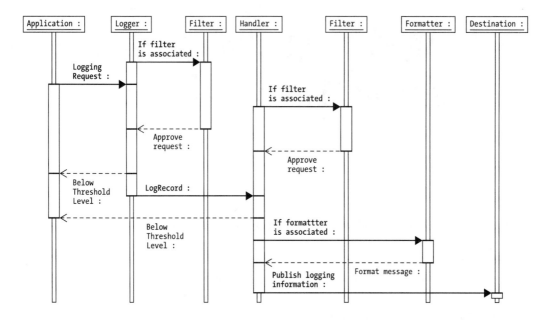

Figure 3-1. The sequence diagram of the JDK 1.4 logging objects

Apart from producing log messages in different structures, the Formatter objects are also responsible for localization of data. The localization of logging information is performed by attaching a java.util.ResourceBundle object to the LogRecord object. Formatter objects use the ResourceBundle associated with each LogRecord object, and the bulk of the formatting and localization work is done within the formatMessage() method of the Formatter object. Most of the logger methods use a message string as a parameter. This message parameter can also represent the localization key. If the LogRecord object has a ResourceBundle associated with it, and the ResourceBundle has a mapping for the message string, the message string is replaced by the localized values. If no mapping is found in the ResourceBundle, then the message string itself is used as the output message.

Formatter objects typically use the java.text.MessageFormat style of formatting. A Formatter object first tries to locate the specified ResourceBundle objects with the active thread's ContextClassLoader. If the ContextClassLoader is null, then it tries to locate the ResourceBundle with the SystemClassLoader. We will see how to develop a localization example later in this chapter.

There are two types of Formatter objects defined in the JDK 1.4 logging API:

- java.util.logging.SimpleFormatter: This produces a brief, human-readable summary of the logging information.

- java.util.logging.XMLFormatter: This produces logging information in a structured XML format.

Figure 3-2 shows the class hierarchy of the two default Formatter objects in the JDK 1.4 logging API.

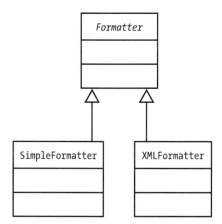

Figure 3-2. The class hierachy of the Formatter objects in the JDK 1.4 logging API

We will discuss these in more detail in the following sections.

SimpleFormatter Object

The SimpleFormatter class represents the simplest way of presenting logging information in a human-readable format. It produces the output in one or two lines of information. Listing 3-1, BasicLogging.java, is a simple program intended to produce very basic logging information.

Listing 3-1. BasicLogging.java

```
package sam.logging;
import java.util.logging.*;

public class BasicLogging
{

  public static void main(String args[])
  {
     Logger logger = Logger.getLogger("current.package");
     logger.info("Simple formatted message..");

  }
}
```

Executing this program will produce the following output in the console—an example of a log message following the `SimpleFormatter` pattern:

```
12-Aug-2002 21:16:23 sam.logging.BasicLogging main
INFO: Simple formatted message..
```

The first line shows the date and timestamp of the logging activity, and the fully qualified name of the class and name of the method from which the logging was posted. The second line shows the logging level and the logging message. The structure of the information is divided into the segments displayed in Table 3-1.

Table 3-1. Message Structure with SimpleFormatter

Timestamp	Class Name	Method Name	Level and Message
12-Aug-2002 22:51:50	sam.logging.BasicLogging	main	INFO: Simple formatted message

The `SimpleFormatter` class extends the `abstract Formatter` class and provides an implementation for the `abstract String format(LogRecord record)` method. It formats the given `LogRecord` object and returns the formatted string. The implementation of the `format()` method in the `SimpleFormatter` class is synchronized. The `format()` method internally uses a `StringBuffer` object to construct and format log messages. The construction of the `StringBuffer` is kept thread-safe by declaring this method as `synchronized`. The `SimpleFormatter` obtains the runtime information about the source class and the source method from which the logging is invoked by calling the `getSourceClassName()` and `getSourceMethodName()` methods respectively on the `LogRecord` object and includes these in the logging information to be produced. This object uses the `java.text.MessageFormat` style to output the logging messages.

The formatting style of the `SimpleFormatter` object is particularly useful for outputting logging messages to a console or a separate logging application such as a logger window, in which we might want to show some very basic logging information. If an application is particularly interested in tracing the control of the program flow by logging different method entries and exits, then `SimpleFormatter` is the most suitable formatter. We are most likely to use a `SimpleFormatter` object with any `Handler` object intended to produce logging output to a console. The `ConsoleHandler` provided within the JDK 1.4 logging API uses the `SimpleFormatter` object to output logging information to consoles. It is possible to change the formatting style associated with a `SimpleFormatter` object by extending the class and overriding the `format()` method of the class.

XMLFormatter Object

The XMLFormatter object produces logging information in a standard XML format. The formatted XML-encoded logging information can be stored in an external file or output to any other device such as a console. While formatting the log message, the XMLFormatter object uses the default document type definition (DTD) as specified in the Java logging specification. The specified DTD can be located in the URL http://java.sun.com/j2se/1.4.1/docs/guide/util/logging/overview.html. The top-level element of the XML data is the <log> element. The immediate child element to the <log> element is the <record> element, which contains the bulk of the logging information.

The <record> element consists of several child elements, of which <date>, <millis>, <sequence>, <level>, <thread>, and <message> are compulsory and will always be present in logging information formatted through the XMLFormatter object. The other optional elements are constructed depending on certain situations, which we will discuss later. The recommended character encoding with the XMLFormatter object is UTF-8, but in theory any character-encoding scheme can be used.

In the sample program shown in Listing 3-2, XMLLogging.java, we will see how we can send the XML-formatted output to a file and also how we can use the ConsoleHandler object along with the XMLFormatter object to produce the output on a console. Here we are using ConsoleHandler to produce messages related to any exception that may occur because the ConsoleHandler class by default writes the output to the System.err stream.

Listing 3-2. XMLLogging.java

```
package sam.logging;
import java.util.logging.*;
import java.io.*;

public class XMLLogging
{
    private     ConsoleHandler ch ;
    private     XMLFormatter formatter ;
    private     FileHandler handler = null;

    /**
     * constructor
     */
    public XMLLogging() {
        ch = new ConsoleHandler();
        formatter  = new XMLFormatter();
    }
```

```java
/**
 * This method demonstrates the logging using XMLFormatter
 * and should there be an exception, the exception
 * is logged into the console with ConsoleHandler and formatted
 * withXMLFormatter.
 */

public void logMessage()
{
    //creating a LogRecord object with level and message
    LogRecord record = new LogRecord(Level.INFO, "XML message..");

    try
    {
        //creating a StreamHandler object to file output the xml message
        handler = new FileHandler("newxml.xml");
        handler.setFormatter(formatter);

        //publishing the log message to the file and flushing the buffer
        handler.publish(record);
        handler.flush();
    }catch(Exception e) {
        //creating a log record object with the WARNING level
        //and exception message
        LogRecord rec = new LogRecord(Level.WARNING,e.toString());

        //setting the formatter for the consolehandler as
        //XMLFormatter and publishing the message
        ch.setFormatter(formatter);
        ch.publish(rec);
    }
}
public static void main(String args[]) {
    XMLLogging logging = new XMLLogging();
    logging.logMessage();
}
}
```

CAUTION Although the previous program uses the Handler object and its publish() method to print logging information, this is not the recommended way of logging information. The application should use the Logger object to print the logging information. The reason for adopting a nonstandard way in this example is to demonstrate the difference in the logging output, as will be explained in the following sections.

The bulk of the work in this program is done in the logMessage() method of the XMLLogging class. It starts with creating a LogRecord object with the level of the logging and the message to be published, and then instantiates a FileHandler object with "newxml.xml" as the output filename. It then sets the XMLFormatter object instance as the associated Formatter object to the FileHandler. Finally, it invokes the publish() method of the FileHandler class to log the message.

Similarly, in the exception block, we create a new LogRecord object with the log message containing the exception message. We set the XMLFormatter object instance as the Formatter associated with the ConsoleHandler object. If any exception is thrown, the ConsoleHandler will publish the exception information to the console.

If we want the class and method names to be a part of the LogRecord object, then we have to explicitly specify them with the setter methods defined in the LogRecord class. If no source class name or source method name is set, then that information will be omitted from the log messages.

Perhaps you noticed in the earlier example of the SimpleFormatter object (in Listing 3-1) that we use a Logger object and its info() method to produce simple formatted logging information. This displays the source class name and the method name, even though we never explicitly specified them, because the logging framework finds out the calling class and the method by analyzing the stack trace of the application. However, this is unreliable due to its being subject to the level of optimization performed by the Java Virtual Machine in question, which in some cases might completely remove the stack trace and can make it impossible for the logging framework to determine the source class and method from which the logging was invoked. In order to reliably contain this information as a part of the log message, we have to pass the source class and method names explicitly to the LogRecord object.

Next, we create a StreamHandler object that will be responsible for writing the XML-formatted data to a java.io.OutputStream object. Within the constructor, we define and pass a java.io.FileOutputStream object that points to the "logmessage.xml" file as the destination, and pass a default XMLFormatter object to it. Each Handler object inherits from an abstract superclass called Handler, which has an abstract method named publish(LogRecord). The StreamHandler class provides a stream-based implementation of the same and writes the LogRecord object to the destination. At the end, we need to call the flush() method, which flushes any buffered messages. The "logmessage.xml" file will contain the following XML data:

```
<?xml version="1.0" encoding="windows-1252" standalone="no"?>
<!DOCTYPE log SYSTEM "logger.dtd">
<log>
<record>
  <date>2002-08-15T20:40:38</date>
  <millis>1029440438292</millis>
  <sequence>0</sequence>
```

```
    <level>INFO</level>
    <thread>10</thread>
    <message>XML message..</message>
  </record>
</log>
```

We also define a `ConsoleHandler` object to demonstrate how the XML-formatted logs can be sent to a console. As the `ConsoleHandler` object by default writes logging information to the `System.err` stream, we utilize it to log any exception generated in the program. If we just specify the filename used to construct the `FileOutputStream` object as "" or null, then we will simulate a faulty situation, and an exception will be thrown. The `ConsoleHandler` will use the passed `XMLFormatter` object to format the log message before printing it to the console, as shown here:

```
<?xml version="1.0" encoding="windows-1252" standalone="no"?>
<!DOCTYPE log SYSTEM "logger.dtd">
<log>
<record>
   <date>2002-08-15T21:19:09</date>
   <millis>1029442749165</millis>
   <sequence>1</sequence>
   <level>WARNING</level>
   <thread>10</thread>
   <message>java.io.FileNotFoundException:   (The system cannot find the path specified)</message>
  </record>
</log>
```

The preceding sample program demonstrates a deliberate use of `XMLFormatter` with different `Handler` objects. The API provides another convenient handler called `FileHandler`, which by default uses the `XMLFormatter` object to format the log messages associated with it. The program in Listing 3-3, `AlternateXML.java`, demonstrates the use and output of the `FileHandler`.

Listing 3-3. AlternateXML.java

```
package sam.logging;

import java.util.logging.*;

public class AlternateXML
{

 public static void main(String args[])
 {
```

```
    try
    {
      FileHandler handler = new FileHandler("alterxml.xml");
      Logger logger = Logger.getLogger("sam.logging");
      logger.addHandler(handler);
      logger.log(Level.INFO, "alternative xml");
    }catch(Exception e)
    {
      e.printStackTrace();
    }
  }
}
```

The use of `FileHandler` is simple. However, it would be interesting to look at the difference in the final XML output of the first program and the second. The `AlternateXMLLogging` class writes the XML output in the "alterxml.xml" file as shown here:

```
<?xml version="1.0" encoding="windows-1252" standalone="no"?>
<!DOCTYPE log SYSTEM "logger.dtd">
<log>
<record>
  <date>2002-08-16T20:23:20</date>
  <millis>1029525800176</millis>
  <sequence>0</sequence>
  <logger>current.package</logger>
  <level>INFO</level>
  <class>AlternateXML</class>
  <method>main</method>
  <thread>10</thread>
  <message>alternative xml</message>
</record>
</log>
</record>
```

There is a subtle but very important difference in the output produced by `XMLLogging.java` and by `AlternateXML.java`. The `AlternateXML.java` example (Listing 3-3), which includes the `FileHandler` object along with a `Logger` object to produce log messages, contains the source class name and the source method name of the logging activity. The XML produced by the `XMLLogging.java` program (Listing 3-2) omits the information about the source class and source method name. This is due to the way the logging framework tries to determine the source class and source method name when they are not explicitly specified.

The `LogRecord` class only determines the caller class and method names if it finds a `java.util.logging.Logger` class instance in the stack trace. In the example in Listing 3-2, we avoid using the `Logger` class by including the `StreamHandler` and `XMLFormatter` classes, and hence the logging framework does not encounter the `java.util.logging.Logger` class in the stack trace and does not attempt to determine the caller source class and method. In the example in Listing 3-3, we include the `Logger` class, and hence the framework attempts to determine the caller source class and method.

Localization of Logging Messages

Localization is a technique used in Java to cater to different languages without having to change the source code. The localization of logging messages is accomplished by using the Java `ResourceBundle` technique. We define log messages in an appropriate properties file in a key-value format, and pass the properties file to the Java runtime. Most logger methods in the logging API take a message argument. If a `ResourceBundle` name is specified, the `Logger` objects will try to find a mapped text against the passed message string as the key. The logger will first look in the thread's `ContextClassLoader` for the specified `ResourceBundle`. If this is null, then it looks in the `SystemClassLoader` for the `ResourceBundle`. Once a `ResourceBundle` is located and it contains a mapping for the message string, then the message string is replaced by the localized value; otherwise, the message string is printed. Listing 3-4, `LocalizeLogging.java`, demonstrates the localization technique with the JDK 1.4 logging API.

Listing 3-4. LocalizeLogging.java

```java
package sam.logging;
import java.util.logging.*;
import java.io.*;
import java.util.ResourceBundle;

public class LocalizeLogging
{
    private static Logger logger = Logger.getLogger("sam.logging");
    private String rbName = null;

    public LocalizeLogging(String rbName)
    {
        this.rbName = rbName;

    }

    public void logMessage()
```

```
    {
        logger.logrb(Level.INFO, "LocalizeLogging", "logMessage", rbName,
"success");

    }

    public static void main(String args[]) {
        //collect the name of the resource bundle
        String rbName = args[0];
        LocalizeLogging lLogging = new LocalizeLogging(rbName);
        lLogging.logMessage();
    }
}
```

We create two `ResourceBundle` properties files named "localizeText.properties" and "localizeText_fr.properties" for English and French messages, respectively, as shown here:

localizeText.properties	localizeText_fr.properties
progress = "Progressing"	progress = "Tres Bein"
success = "Done"	success = "Fini"

The application in Listing 3-4 accepts the name of the `ResourceBundle` as a command line parameter or any other configuration source. The application obtains a `Logger` instance with the name `sam.logging` and then sets the `ResourceBundle` name. It then invokes the `logrb()` method of the `Logger` class with the logging message and the `ResourceBundle` name. The logging message string will be considered the localization key and the corresponding value from the `ResourceBundle` file will be displayed as the logging message.

Executing the preceding application with the French text version will produce the following output message to the console:

```
>> java  sam.logging.LocalizeLogging localizeText_fr
16-Aug-2002 22:33:12 LocalizeLogging logMessage
INFO: "Fini"
```

Writing Custom Formatters

While it is useful to apply the default `Formatter` objects available within the JDK 1.4 logging API, different applications might need to produce logging messages in a more application-specific manner. For these situations, it is possible to define custom Formatter objects. To write a custom Formatter object, we just need to extend the java.util.logging.Formatter class and override the format() method in it. For example, let's imagine an application that needs to store different method entries and logging messages used in those method calls in a Java properties-style format. To achieve this, we will design a very simple custom Formatter object that will format the message and return it to the appropriate Handler object being used by the application. Listing 3-5, CustomFormatter.java, shows how to develop a custom Formatter object for this scenario.

Listing 3-5. CustomFormatter.java

```
package sam.logging;
import java.util.logging.*;
public class CustomFormatter extends Formatter
{

  public CustomFormatter()
  {
  }

/**
 This method formats the given log record, in a java properties file style
 */
  public synchronized String format(LogRecord record)
  {
    String methodName = record.getSourceMethodName();
    String message = record.getMessage();
    StringBuffer buffer = new StringBuffer(50);
    buffer.append(methodName);
    buffer.append("=");
    buffer.append(message);

    return buffer.toString();
  }
}
```

The CustomFormatter object defined in Listing 3-5 overrides the abstract format(LogRecord record) method of the parent class Formatter. It simply constructs a string in key-value format and returns to the parent handler. We can see from the code that it totally depends on the LogRecord object to obtain the name of the method from which the logging was invoked, and this object does not attempt to determine the source method from the stack trace. Thus, it is the sole responsibility of the user of this custom Formatter object to supply the source method name as a part of the LogRecord object. Of course, we can write a more complex formatter that can potentially do much more complicated formatting activity.

The client program in Listing 3-6, CustomFormatterTest.java, uses the CustomFormatter object. It attempts to write the information in a properties file so that a Java program can pick up the information at a later date in a java.util.Properties object. The client application first obtains an instance of the named logger, sam.logging. It then creates a FileHandler object to write to a given file and assigns a new instance of the CustomFormatter object as the Formatter object associated to the FileHandler instance. Finally, the Logger invokes the info() method to log any logging message.

Listing 3-6. CustomFormatterTest.java

```
package sam.logging;
import java.util.logging.*;
import java.io.*;

public class CustomFormatterTest
{
    private static Logger logger = Logger.getLogger("sam.logging");
    private String fileName = null;

    public CustomFormatterTest(String fileName)
    {
        this.fileName = fileName;
        try
        {
            FileHandler fh = new FileHandler(fileName);
            CustomFormatter formatter = new CustomFormatter();
            fh.setFormatter(formatter);

            logger.addHandler(fh);
        }catch(IOException ioe)
        {
            ioe.printStackTrace();
        }
    }

    /**
     * This method performs the logging activity
     */
```

```
    public void logMessage()
    {
        logger.info("log this message");

    }

    public static void main(String args[]) {
        CustomFormatterTest test = new CustomFormatterTest(args[0]);
        test.logMessage();

    }
}
```

Executing this client application will output the logging information to a file specified on the command line.

```
>>java sam.logging.CustomFormatterTest custom.properties
```

The final properties file obtained, "custom.properties", contains the method name and the message in a key-value pair format.

```
CustomFormatterTest.logMessage=log this message
```

Conclusion

In this chapter, we have seen how different Formatter objects work, their internals, and how to write custom Formatter objects and use them. We have also explored the localization aspect of log messages. Now it is time to start using this logging framework in real-life applications. Often we will find that we require a custom-logging framework tailored to an application's needs. In the next chapter, we will examine how to extend the existing logging API framework to meet more application-specific needs.

CHAPTER 4

Extending the Logging Framework

IN THE PREVIOUS CHAPTERS, we dealt in great detail with the different objects available in the JDK 1.4 logging API and how they operate. We also analyzed different formatting techniques that can be applied along with the logging framework, and developed our own Formatter object. The API already provides a great number of logging features sufficient for small-scale applications. Using the logging framework in an effective way, it is possible to enhance the maintainability of any application.

However, in other more complicated cases, the default capabilities of the JDK 1.4 logging API might fall a little short. This is the time when we need to extend the framework to suit our needs—after all, a good object-oriented API means a framework that is always extendible.

In this chapter, we will first discuss configuration issues involving the JDK 1.4 logging API and develop custom Handler objects. Later, we will explore remote logging with the JDK 1.4 logging API and see a real-life example to demonstrate a practical application of the logging framework.

Configuring the Logging Framework

In Chapter 2, we saw how to configure the JDK 1.4 logging API programmatically. Using different methods exposed by different objects in the logging API, we can configure individual Logger and Handler objects. The main drawback of programmatic configuration is that it makes it impossible to change the configuration without changing the source code. To avoid such bottlenecks, the JDK 1.4 logging API also supports configuration via configuration files. In general, the configuration of the JDK 1.4 logging API can be achieved in the following ways:

- By using different methods available within the API

- By defining the configuration parameters in a configuration file

- By writing a separate configuration class that has the responsibility of configuring the logging components

By now, you are familiar with the first option—that is, how to configure logging components programmatically. In the coming sections, we will explore the other two options for configuring the JDK 1.4 logging API.

File-Based Configuration

The `java.util.logging.LogManager` class in the logging framework is the core class responsible for reading the configuration file and initializing different objects with defined configuration parameters. The logging API relies on the configuration information being passed to it from a standard configuration file. The `LogManager` class uses the `java.util.logging.config.file` system property to read the initial configuration information from a configuration file.

If this property is not passed to the logging framework at startup, by default, `LogManager` reads a configuration file located in the "JAVA_HOME/jre/lib/logging.properties" file. This configuration file defines the default configuration parameters for the logging framework to work. It is possible to override the default location and specify our own configuration file by passing a command line option to the Java runtime as:

```
java -Djava.util.logging.config.file=configuration file name
```

The logging configuration in a configuration file is divided into two sections. One section holds the global configuration information, and the other includes the `Handler` object-specific configuration information. The global configuration properties are loaded at Java VM startup, and the `Handler`-specific configuration properties are loaded when respective `Handler` objects are initialized. Each property defined is preceded by the fully qualified name of the `Handler` class (e.g., `java.util.logging.FileHandler.formatter`).

We will take a closer look at these two parts of the logging configuration in the next sections.

Global Configuration

The global configuration has only two parameters to define: the global `Handler` objects to be loaded and the global level of the logging. These parameters are defined as follows:

```
handlers= java.util.logging.ConsoleHandler
.level= INFO
```

Extending the Logging Framework

The handlers property defines the global Handler object to be loaded. Although the default configuration defines the java.util.logging.ConsoleHandler object as the only Handler to initialize, we can define several Handler objects for initialization as a comma-separated list. For example, the following line can load the java.util.logging.ConsoleHandler and the java.util.logging.FileHandler objects as the default global Handlers:

handlers= java.util.logging.FileHandler, java.util.logging.ConsoleHandler

This means that the root logger will now use two separate Handler objects to write the logging information to two separate destinations, such as a console and a file.

NOTE The defined global Handler object class needs to be in the system classpath. At JVM startup, the class file is located in the classpath and loaded into the VM, and a new instance of the class is created with any configuration parameter defined specific to the global Handler object.

The level property defines the global level of logging to be used. This level acts as a threshold level to the global Handler objects defined and blocks any message with a lower level.

The global configuration of level is inherited by all the Logger objects within the same instance of the application. However, it is possible to configure each individual Logger object used within an application. For example, the following line defines the level for a Logger named com.abc.myapp:

com.abc.myapp.level=INFO

It is important to note that any subpackage of com.abc.myapp will inherit this level if not configured individually.

Configuration Order

The configuration order of different Logger objects within the same configuration file must be sequential. In other words, the parent logger must be configured before the child logger. In the JDK 1.4 logging API, the parent configuration always overrides the child configuration. This becomes crucial for the Logger objects having a parent-child relationship.

For example, the following configuration does NOT configure the `Logger` objects as we expect:

```
com.abc.myapp.net.level=INFO
com.abc.myapp.level=SEVERE
```

This configuration order does not set the level for the logger `com.abc.myapp.net` to INFO. This is because the parent logger `com.abc.myapp` is later assigned a level SEVERE. The logger `com.abc.myapp.net` will also have a level SEVERE.

Handler-Specific Configuration

The different `Handler` objects provided within the JDK 1.4 logging API have the following common properties present in all of them:

- `level`

- `filter`

Apart from the preceding properties, which are common to all the `Handlers`, specific `Handlers` such as `java.util.logging.FileHandler` can use some other properties such as `pattern`, `limit`, etc., to publish logging information.

Here is a sample configuration file for the logger `com.abc.io`. Assume that the logger uses a `SocketHandler`. The configuration file first defines the level for the logger. Next, the configuration parameters for the `SocketHandler` are defined:

```
#setting the level of the logger
com.abc.io.level=INFO

#setting the handler properties
java.util.logging.SocketHandler.level=INFO
java.util.logging.SocketHandler.formatter=java.util.logging.SimpleFormatter
java.util.logging.SocketHandler.filter=com.apress.logging.AgeCheckFilter
java.util.logging.SocketHandler.host=localhost
java.util.logging.SocketHandler.port=2020
```

The preceding configuration for the `SocketHandler` defines the basic properties such as `level`, `formatter`, and `filter`. In addition, it defines its own parameters for connection information such as `host` and `port`.

Once the parameters are defined for a `Handler`, the `LogManager` class stores the configuration key and configuration value in a `java.util.Properties` object. When each `Handler` is initialized by an application, the appropriate configuration information is extracted from the `LogManager` class and used within the specific

Handler class. If any of the configuration parameters are missing, then properties of the parent handler are used.

> **NOTE** We need to make sure that all the values specified are valid, or else they will be ignored and parent properties will be used.

We will now explore the configuration options available for each of the Handler objects in the next few sections.

ConsoleHandler Parameters

java.util.logging.ConsoleHandler has the configurable properties defined in Table 4-1.

Table 4-1. ConsoleHandler Configuration Parameters

Property	Meaning	Default
encoding	Character encoding to use	Default platform-specific encoding
filter	Filter to attach	No filter
formatter	Formatting for the logging information	java.util.logging.SimpleFormatter
level	The level of logging	Level.INFO

A sample configuration for ConsoleHandler might look like the following:

```
#configuration for the ConsoleHandler
java.util.logging.ConsoleHandler.level = INFO
java.util.logging.ConsoleHandler.formatter =java.util.logging.SimpleFormatter
```

This configuration sets the threshold level of the ConsoleHandler to Level.INFO and the formatter associated with the ConsoleHandler is a SimpleFormatter object. Any message with a level equal to or above Level.INFO will be published to System.err (the default destination for the ConsoleHandler) in a SimpleFormatter formatting style.

FileHandler Parameters

The `java.util.logging.FileHandler` has the configurable properties defined in Table 4-2.

Table 4-2. FileHandler Configuration Parameters

Property	Meaning	Default
append	Item to append to the existing file	false
count	The number of files to rotate through	Defaults to 1
encoding	Character encoding to use	Default platform-specific encoding
filter	Any filter to attach	No filter
formatter	Formatting for the logging information	java.util.logging.XMLFormatter
level	The level of logging	Level.ALL
limit	The approximate maximum number of bytes to write to a file	No limit (If set to zero, it means no limit.)
pattern	Pattern for generating the output filename	%h/java%u.log

Here is a sample configuration file for the `FileHandler`:

```
#configuration for the FileHandler
java.util.logging.FileHandler.pattern = %h/java%u.log
java.util.logging.FileHandler.limit = 5000
java.util.logging.FileHandler.count = 1
java.util.logging.FileHandler.formatter = java.util.logging.SimpleFormatter
```

We have already discussed the patterns related to the `FileHandler` in Chapter 2. The default configuration parameters just shown for the `FileHandler` object define the location of the logging output file to be the "/user-home" directory, and each logging file will be named with a unique number added to its base name such as "java0.log", "java1.log", etc. The `limit` property defines the size limit for each file and is set to 5000 bytes. Exceeding the limit will force the creation of a new logging file with the pattern defined in the `pattern` configuration property. The `count` property defines the number of `LogRecord` objects to be logged, and the `formatter` property defines `SimpleFormatter` to be the default `Formatter` object for the `FileHandler`.

SocketHandler Parameters

`java.util.logging.SocketHandler` has the configurable properties defined in Table 4-3.

Table 4-3. SocketHandler Configuration Parameters

Property	Meaning	Default
encoding	Character encoding to use	Default platform-specific encoding
filter	Filter to attach	No filter
formatter	Formatting for the logging information	java.util.logging.XMLFormatter
host	The host to connect to	No default
level	The level of logging	Level.ALL
port	The port to connect to	No default

Here is a sample configuration file for the `SocketHandler`:

```
#configuration for SocketHandler
java.util.logging.SocketHandler.level=INFO
java.util.logging.SocketHandler.formatter=java.util.logging.SimpleFormatter
java.util.logging.SocketHandler.filter=com.apress.logging.AgeCheckFilter
java.util.logging.SocketHandler.host=localhost
java.util.logging.SocketHandler.port=2020
```

This configuration sets a `Filter` named `AgeCheckFilter` as part of the `SocketHandler` configuration. This means that this `SocketHandler` instance will verify with the `Filter` that it can proceed to log the information. The destination host and port are also defined in the configuration file. A server program running in the defined host and listening to the defined port will receive logging information from this `Handler` instance.

MemoryHandler Parameters

`java.util.logging.MemoryHandler` has the configurable properties defined in Table 4-4.

Table 4-4. MemoryHandler Configuration Parameters

Property	Meaning	Default
filter	Filter to attach	No filter
level	The level of logging	Level.ALL
push	The push level to release the buffer	Level.SEVERE
size	The buffer size	1000 records
target	The target Handler to use	No default

Here is a sample configuration file for the `MemoryHandler`:

```
#configuration for MemoryHandler
java.util.logging.MemoryHandler.level=INFO
java.util.logging.MemoryHandler.size=2000
java.util.logging.MemoryHandler.push=WARN
java.util.logging.MemoryHandler.target=java.util.logging.ConsoleHandler
```

We have already discussed `MemoryHandler` in great detail in Chapter 2. Knowing what we do about `MemoryHandler`, this configuration has an interesting aspect. The `level` and `push` properties both define the level for the `MemoryHandler` to work. However, the subtle distinction is that the `level` property is the level for the `MemoryHandler` itself, and any logging message with a lower level will always be ignored. On the other hand, the `push` property defines the level criteria for messages to be pushed to the associated `Handler` objects for publishing.

Besides the default `Handler` objects, if we develop some new custom `Handler` objects and want to define the initialization parameters for the `Handlers`, we can do so in the default "logging.properties" file or in any custom configuration file we specify at startup, in the same fashion as other `Handlers` are defined. We will see an example of this later in this chapter.

Class-Based Configuration

In the JDK 1.4 logging API, the `LogManager` class is capable of reading a configuration file located on the same machine. But with this logging API, it is also possible to load the configuration information located on a remote machine from any data source such as a file or database. In order to do that, we need a custom configuration class that is responsible for reading configuration information from the relevant data source and populating the configuration parameters required by the logging framework. It is important to note that the configuration class specified is only loaded and instantiated by the LogManager without attempting to invoke any other method in the configuration class. Hence, all the initialization work needs to be completed within the scope of class instantiation only.

If we want to defer the initialization to any other method of the configuration class, we have to override the LogManager functionality to invoke the method after the instantiation of the configuration class. Note that this is quite unnecessary and possibly overkill, as we tend to perform the initialization operation within the constructor of the configuration class only. To use a custom configuration class, we can pass the name of the configuration class as a system property in the command line as follows:

```
java -Djava.util.logging.config.class=MyClass
```

where myClass is the class responsible for reading the configuration information from the relevant data source. For example, let's assume that the configuration file is situated in a remote location—http://www.XYZ.com/config.properties.

Listing 4-1, RemoteConfigReader.java, is a sample program that will read configuration information from the remote location over HTTP and populate the initialization parameters of the LogManager class.

Listing 4-1. RemoteConfigReader.java

```java
package sam.logging.config;

import java.util.logging.LogManager;
import java.net.URL;
import java.net.URLConnection;
import java.net.MalformedURLException;
import java.io.InputStream;
import java.io.IOException;

public class RemoteConfigReader
{
 private String urlString = "http://www.xyz.com/config.properties";
 private URL url = null;
 private URLConnection urlConn = null;
 private InputStream inStream = null;
 private LogManager manager = null;
```

```java
/**
 * The constructor obtains a connection to the URL specified in the
 * urlString object, obtains an InputStream on the URL and
 * calls the readConfiguration(InputStream) of the LogManager class
 * to perform the initialization
 */
public RemoteConfigReader()
{
 try
 {
  url = new URL(urlString);
  urlConn = url.openConnection();
  inStream = urlConn.getInputStream();
  manager = LogManager.getLogManager();
  manager.readConfiguration(inStream);
 }catch(MalformedURLException mue)
 {
  System.out.println("could not open url: "+urlString);
 }catch(IOException ioe)
 {
  System.out.println("IOException occured in reading: "+urlString);
 }catch(SecurityException se)
 {
  System.out.println("Security exception occured in class RemoteConfigLoader");
  }
 }
}
```

This class is a simple one that constructs a `URL` object out of the `urlString` specifying the location of the remote configuration file. It opens a `java.net.URLConnection` object to the remote location and obtains a `java.io.InputStream` object from the `URLConnection` object. It then passes the `InputStream` object to the `readConfiguration(InputStream)` method of the `LogManager` class to perform the initialization.

The "config.properties" file located in the remote location `http://www.XYZ.com/config.properties` defines the level of the `ConsoleHandler` class as Level.WARNING. Assume that the configuration file has a line like this:

```
java.util.logging.ConsoleHandler.level = WARNING
```

The `LogManager` will be initialized with the preceding property. Now start up an application with the system property `java.util.logging.config.class` set as `sam.logging.config.RemoteConfigReader` and print the `level` property of the `java.util.logging.ConsoleHandler` class as follows:

```
public class RemoteLoaderTest
{
   public static void main(String args[])
   {
      LogManager manager = LogManager.getLogManager();
      String level =
      manager.getProperty("java.util.logging.ConsoleHandler.level");
      System.out.println("The ConsoleHandler level: "+level);
   }
}
```

If we run the previous program with the following command:

```
java -Djava.util.logging.config.class=sam.logging.config.RemoteConfigReader
 RemoteLoaderTest
```

we will see the level being printed as WARNING. This shows that the initialization parameters are obtained from the remote HTTP location instead of the default JDK location

Writing Custom Handlers

The default `Handler` objects provided by the JDK 1.4 logging API are capable of printing information in a console, to a file, to any stream, and to a socket. In most applications, logging activity is directed to one of these destinations. But in complex applications, sometimes logging activity demands more than the capabilities of the default `Handler` objects provided with the API.

Imagine a situation where you are doing some distributed computing, and logging information is required to be sent to a remote location to be logged. In such situations, you may want to pass logging information to the remote location using Java RMI. But this mandates that the object that encapsulates the logging information must be `serializable` in order to be transferred over RMI. Within the JDK 1.4 logging API, the only object that is `serializable` is the `LogRecord` object. Thus, one solution is to use the `LogRecord` object and serialize it to some Java RMI component every time you are interested in logging some information. This can easily become a big pain in the process of application development and can shift the focus to writing code for logging activity rather than concentrating on application coding.

In such scenarios, often it is advised to develop a custom `Handler` object to cater to such needs. We can then just associate the custom `Handler` object to the obtained `Logger` objects and continue performing the normal logging activity without being worried about the underlying RMI implementation of the logging. In complex application scenarios, developing a custom `Handler` object can be worth the time spent and often is a good design practice.

Writing a custom `Handler` object can be a fairly simple task depending on what we want the `Handler` to do with the given `LogRecord` object. In essence, we just need to inherit the abstract `Handler` class and override the abstract methods defined in the `Handler` base class.

In JDK 1.4 logging API, the methods discussed next are declared abstract in the `Handler` base class.

The following method does the bulk of the work of publishing the logging information encapsulated within the `LogRecord` object to the destination defined within the `Handler` object:

```
public abstract void publish(LogRecord record)
```

This next method closes the `Handler` and frees all the acquired resources:

```
public abstract void close()
```

The following method flushes any buffered output in any associated stream with the `Handler` object:

```
public abstract void flush()
```

The custom `Handler` class can inherit all other methods from the base `Handler` class.

NOTE It is important to emphasize that several methods in the base `Handler` class are implemented as `synchronized` to make the `Handler` thread-safe. The overridden `publish()` method has to be specially synchronized in order to avoid multiple threads acting on the method at the same time, which might lead to a disordered sequence of messages being published.

Custom Window Handler

Imagine you want to create an application that can print all its logging messages to a small window. In order to achieve this, we will see how to develop a custom Handler object in this section. Listing 4-2, LogWindow.java, is a sample program that creates a small Java window to display logging information. It uses a javax.swing.JFrame object, and displays the messages to an attached javax.swing.JTextArea object.

Listing 4-2. LogWindow.java

```java
package sam.logging.handler;

import javax.swing.JFrame;
import javax.swing.JTextArea;
import javax.swing.JScrollPane;

public class LogWindow extends JFrame
{
 private int width;
 private int height;
 private JTextArea textArea = null;
 private JScrollPane pane = null;

 public LogWindow(String title, int width, int height)
 {
  super(title);
  setSize(width,height);
  textArea = new JTextArea();
  pane = new JScrollPane(textArea);
  getContentPane().add(pane);
  setVisible(true);

 }
 /**
  * This method appends the data to the text area.
  *@param data the Logging information data
  */
 public void showInfo(String data)
 {
  textArea.append(data);
  this.getContentPane().validate();
 }
}
```

The LogWindow is a simple component extending the javax.swing.JFrame class. It defines the title and the dimension of the frame through the constructor. It also defines a javax.swing.JScrollPane instance that contains a javax.swing.JTextArea object. The logging information will be contained in the defined JTextArea. The showInfo() method takes the logging information as a String parameter and appends it to the existing data within the JTextArea. The content pane of the frame is validated after each piece of data is written.

With this simple output device in place, we will now see how to develop a WindowHandler class that will print the logging information to the LogWindow. Listing 4-3, WindowHandler.java, is a custom Handler object that uses the logging window and prints logging information to that window.

Listing 4-3. WindowHandler.java

```java
package sam.logging.handler;

import java.util.logging.*;

public class WindowHandler extends Handler
{
 //the window to which the logging is done
 private LogWindow window = null;
 private Formatter formatter = null;
 private Level level = null;
 //the singleton instance
 private static WindowHandler handler = null;

 /**
  * private constructor, preventing initialization
  */
 private WindowHandler()
 {
  configure();
  if(window == null)
   window = new LogWindow("Logging window",500,200);
 }
 /**
  * The getInstance method returns the singleton instance of the
  *      * WindowHandler object
  * It is synchronized to prevent two threads trying to create an
  *      * instance simultaneously.
  * @return WindowHandler object
  */
```

```java
    public static synchronized WindowHandler getInstance()
    {
      if(handler == null)
      {
       handler = new WindowHandler();
      }
      return handler;
    }
    /**
     * This method loads the configuration properties from the
            *JDK level configuration
     * file with the help of the LogManager class. It then
            * sets its level, filter and formatter
     * properties.
     */
    private void configure()
    {
      LogManager manager = LogManager.getLogManager();
      String className = this.getClass().getName();
      String level = manager.getProperty(className+".level");
      String filter = manager.getProperty(className+".filter");
      String formatter =
manager.getProperty(className+".formatter");

      //accessing super class methods to set the parameters
      setLevel(level !=null ? Level.parse(level):Level.INFO);
      setFilter(makeFilter(filter));
      setFormatter(makeFormatter(formatter));

    }
    /**
     * private method constructing a Filter object with the filter name.
     *@param filterName the name of the filter
     *@return the Filter object
     */
    private Filter makeFilter(String filterName)
    {
     Class c = null;
     Filter f = null;
```

```
  try
  {
   c = Class.forName(filterName);
   f = (Filter)c.newInstance();
  }catch(Exception e)
  {
   System.out.println("There was a problem to load the
filter class: "+filterName);
  }
  return f;
 }
 /**
  *private method creating a Formatter object with the
       * formatter name. If no name is
  *specified, it returns a SimpleFormatter object
  *@param formatterName the name of the formatter
  *@return Formatter object
  */
 private Formatter makeFormatter(String formatterName)
 {
  Class c = null;
  Formatter f = null;

  try
  {
   c = Class.forName(formatterName);
   f = (Formatter)c.newInstance();
  }catch(Exception e)
  {
   f = new SimpleFormatter();
  }
  return f;
 }

 /**
  *This is the overridden publish method of the abstract
       * super class Handler.
  * This method writes the logging information to the
       * associated Java window.
  *This method is synchronized to make it thread-safe. In case
         * there is a problem,
  * it reports the problem with the ErrorManager, only once and
       * silently ignores the others.
```

```
 *@record the LogRecord object
 *
 */
public synchronized void publish(LogRecord record)
{
 String message = null;
 //check if the record is loggable
 if( !isLoggable(record))
  return;
 try
 {
  message = getFormatter().format(record);
 }catch(Exception e)
 {
  reportError(null, e, ErrorManager.FORMAT_FAILURE);
 }

 try
 {
  window.showInfo(message);
 }catch(Exception ex)
 {
  reportError(null, ex, ErrorManager.WRITE_FAILURE);
 }

}

public void close()
{
}

public void flush()
{
}
}
```

Following the steps to write a custom Handler object, as described previously, the WindowHandler class extends the java.util.logging.Handler class and overrides the abstract methods. Notably, it has defined the publish() method as synchronized to make the logging thread-safe. The design and implementation of the WindowHandler object is guided by the following factors:

- It uses the LogWindow object instance to publish the message.

- We need one and only one instance of the LogWindow to be active in the application context. Hence, before creating an instance of the LogWindow, the WindowHandler object checks if the LogWindow instance is null.

- The instantiation of the LogWindow class is performed in the constructor of the WindowHandler. So with every instance creation, there is a chance that a separate instance of the LogWindow is created; this could result in the problem of having several LogWindow instances being alive within the application lifetime, which will end up showing multiple logging windows.

- To avoid this problem, we make the WindowHandler object a singleton. Thus, in one application context, one and only instance of the WindowHandler object is available.

- Since the publish() method is synchronized, we safely avoid the risk of wrongly sequenced messages being published.

- The alternative could be to make the LogWindow instance a singleton. This might prove inadequate in cases where we decide to create two LogWindow instances to display messages from two different Handlers, which require the same functionality of displaying logging information in a window-based output screen.

NOTE A singleton instance means only one instance of the class in question is available per JVM instance. Thus, only one instance of the WindowHandler will be available per JVM instance.

The WindowHandler class has a private configure() method that reads the configuration information for this particular Handler from the default JDK logging configuration file located in "/jre/lib/logging.properties". It reads the configuration information with the help of the java.util.logging.LogManager class. The WindowHandler class relies on the following configuration properties:

- level

- filter

- formatter

These properties should be defined in the configuration file in the following key-value fashion:

```
sam.logging.handler.WindowHandler.level = some value
sam.logging.handler.WindowHandler.filter = some value
sam.logging.handler.WindowHandler.formatter = some value
```

NOTE   It is not mandatory that WindowHandler should read the configuration from the default JDK configuration file. In fact, we may define the configuration in a separate configuration file and pass it to the runtime. We have explored this concept in the "File-Based Configuration" section. The intention here is to show that it is also possible to change the default configuration file to accommodate our own configuration. Don't forget to keep a backup in situations like these!!!

If no configuration information is defined, then the level property is set to Level.INFO, which acts as the threshold level for this Handler. Only LogRecord objects with levels greater than or equal to the WindowHandler level will be processed. If no filter property is defined, the filter setting gets set to no filter and if no formatter property is set, then the default formatter is set to java.util.logging.SimpleFormatter.

The abstract methods close() and flush() are implemented as do-nothing methods, as there is no stream associated with this WindowHandler object. Inside the publish() method, we obtain the logging information formatted with the associated Formatter object by calling the format() method of the Formatter class. This performs the formatting of the logging information and any localization to be done and returns formatted logging information to the WindowHandler class. The WindowHandler class then calls the showInfo() method of the LogWindow class to print the message to the output window.

Two other interesting methods you should know about are makeFilter() and makeFormatter(). The makeFilter() method tries to load and instantiate the Filter specified in the configuration. If it fails, it prints a failure message to the console. The makeFormatter() method attempts to load and instantiate any Formatter specified in the configuration file. If it fails, then it sets SimpleFormatter as the default Formatter.

Listing 4-4, CustomHandlerDemo.java, is a demo program that will use the WindowHandler object to publish logging information.

Listing 4-4. CustomHandlerDemo.java

```java
package sam.logging.handler;
import java.util.logging.*;

public class CustomHandlerDemo
{
 private WindowHandler handler = null;
 private Logger logger = null;

 public CustomHandlerDemo()
 {
  handler = WindowHandler.getInstance();
  //obtaining a logger instance and setting the handler
  logger = Logger.getLogger("sam.logging.handler");
  logger.addHandler(handler);
 }
 /**
  *This method publishes the log message
  */
 public void logMessage()
 {
  logger.info("Hello from WindowHandler...");
 }


 public static void main(String args[])
 {
  //logging with the help of a logger
  CustomHandlerDemo demo = new CustomHandlerDemo();
  demo.logMessage();
  //using the handler.publish() to log
  WindowHandler h = WindowHandler.getInstance();
  LogRecord r = new LogRecord(Level.WARNING, "The Handler publish method...");
  h.publish(r);
 }
}
```

This demo program demonstrates two uses of the WindowHandler. First, it obtains a Logger instance with the package name sam.logging.handler, sets the Handler object associated with the Logger as the WindowHandler instance, and then uses the info() method of the Logger to log the message. The Logger will internally create a LogRecord object with the given message and with the level as Level.INFO (as the method invoked was logger.info()) and pass the LogRecord object to the WindowHandler to publish.

The second way is to obtain the singleton reference of the WindowHandler object, create a LogRecord object with the appropriate level, and then call the publish() method of the WindowHandler to print the message to the window. The preceding program will print messages in the order shown in Figure 4-1 to the output window.

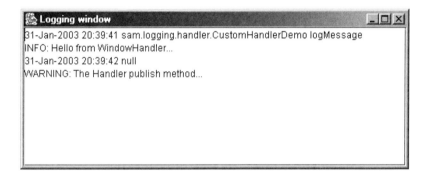

Figure 4-1. The custom logging window

 CAUTION Although it is perfectly feasible to create a LogRecord object and directly call the publish() method of the Handler class, this is not the best practice. It is advisable to use a Logger object to publish any logging information.

To alter the behavior of the WindowHandler object, we can change the parameters of the WindowHandler object by either changing the configuration file or programmatically setting the parameters. For example, if we change the formatter property to java.util.logging.XMLFormatter, then the output in the logging window will be XML formatted. Figure 4-2 shows the output in XML format.

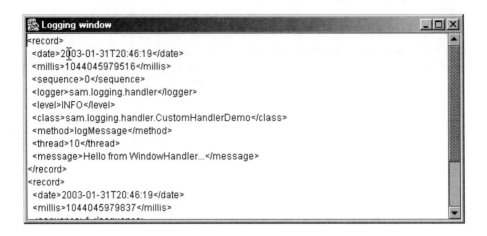

Figure 4-2. The logging output in XML format

Remote Logging

In the client-server application scenario, often logging information needs to be distributed across different machines. Imagine a situation where you are running several different RMI components on different machines. Each application can have independent message logs, but you may like to get all the log information in a central place from where you can better manage the system. In such cases, you will need to pass back and forth the logging information from the client or component machines to a central place.

Ideally for a Java-based application, the central logging location would also run a Java RMI application accepting different logging information from different components, logging them with appropriate formatting, and sending them to the desired destination. With the JDK 1.4 logging API, this flexibility is achievable only by using the java.util.logging.LogRecord object, which is serializable.

There are two possible ways to use the serializable LogRecord objects to achieve remote logging. First, different components within the application will have to encapsulate the logging information in LogRecord objects and serialize them to the listening RMI component in the desired remote location. Secondly, we can develop a custom Handler object that will take care of the RMI part of the logging. By attaching this custom Handler to the obtained Logger object in the application component, we can achieve the desired remote logging. With the help of the following sample programs in the following sections, we will see how the remote logging mechanism works within the JDK 1.4 logging framework.

Remote Logging Server

Listing 4-5, RemoteLoggingServer.java, is a Java RMI–based remote logging server component that listens to any incoming logging request and then logs it on the server machine.

Listing 4-5. RemoteLoggingServer.java

```
package sam.logging.rmi;
import java.rmi.RemoteException;
import java.rmi.server.UnicastRemoteObject;
import java.rmi.Naming;
import java.util.logging.LogManager;
import java.util.logging.LogRecord;
import java.util.logging.Logger;
import java.util.logging.Level;
import java.util.logging.FileHandler;
public class RemoteLoggingServer extends UnicastRemoteObject
implements Logging {
    private Logger logger = null;
    private FileHandler handler = null;
    private String defaultPattern = null;
    private String defaultAppend = null;
    private String defaultLevel = null;
    private LogManager manager = LogManager.getLogManager();;

    public RemoteLoggingServer() throws RemoteException {
        super();

        defaultPattern =
manager.getProperty("java.util.logging.FileHandler.pattern");
        defaultAppend =
manager.getProperty("java.util.logging.FileHandler.append");
        setLoggerConfig(defaultPattern, new
Boolean(defaultAppend).booleanValue());
    }
    /**
     * constructor with the file handler pattern and append mode
     */
```

```java
            public RemoteLoggingServer(String pattern, boolean append) throws
        RemoteException {
                super();
                setLoggerConfig(pattern, append);

            }

            private void setLoggerConfig(String pattern, boolean append) {
                try {
                    //obtain a package specific logger
                    logger = Logger.getLogger("sam.logging.rmi");
                    //create the file handler with the given pattern
                    handler = new FileHandler(pattern, append);
                    //associate the handler with the logger
                    logger.addHandler(handler);

                    //setting the level of the logger via remote handler property
                    defaultLevel =
        manager.getProperty(RemoteLoggingServer.class.getName()+".level");

        logger.setLevel(Level.parse(defaultLevel!=null?defaultLevel:"INFO"));

                    //debug messages
                    logger.info("started with logging level: "+logger.getLevel());

                }catch(Exception e) {
                    System.out.println(e.toString());
                    System.exit(1);
                }
            }


            /**
             * This method is the core method which publishes the logging
             * information to the desired file.
             */
            public void logMessage(LogRecord record) throws RemoteException {
                try {
                    //logging the message
                    logger.log(record);
                }catch(Exception e) {
                    throw new RemoteException(e.toString());
                }
            }
```

```java
    public static void main(String args[]) {
        //pattern to store in the current directory in log0.out,log1.out etc.
        String pattern = "log%u.out";
        boolean append = true;
        RemoteLoggingServer server = null;
        try {
            server = new RemoteLoggingServer();
            Naming.bind("rmi://oemcomputer/LoggingServer", server);
            System.out.println("Server started...");
        }catch(Exception re) {
            re.printStackTrace();
        }
    }
}
```

The `RemoteLoggingServer` component is a simple RMI server-side component that implements an interface named `Logging`, declared as shown here:

```java
package sam.logging.rmi;

import java.rmi.Remote;
import java.rmi.RemoteException;
import java.util.logging.LogRecord;

public interface Logging extends Remote
{
   public void logMessage(LogRecord record) throws RemoteException;
}
```

The `RemoteLoggingServer` class provides an implementation of the `logMessage()` remote method in which it basically publishes the logging information to the specified destination with the help of the associated `Handler` object. The `Handler` object attached to the `RemoteLoggingServer` component is a `java.util.logging.FileHandler` object. The `FileHandler` uses a default append property to decide whether to append the logging information to the specified logging file; it also uses as a default pattern of `%h/java%u.log`, which means the logging information will be stored in a sequential series of files such as "java0.log", "java1.log", etc., in the system's "user.home" directory. The location and structure of the logging file can be changed at startup by passing a different pattern from the `main()` method of the component to the constructor of the `RemoteLoggingServer` component. The `RemoteLoggingServer` component obtains the `level` property from the configuration file by reading the `sam.logging.rmi.RemoteLoggingServer.level` property. At startup the component is bound to the registry with the name "LoggingServer" and listens to the RMI default port 1099:

```
Naming.bind("rmi://oemcomputer/LoggingServer", server);
```

where oemcomputer is the name of the remote machine. As a normal RMI development procedure, make sure you generate the Stubs and Skeletons of the RemoteLoggingServer component, and set the classpath environment variable to include all the required classes.

As per the Java 2 requirement, the RMISecurityManager requires a policy file to be passed to the Java runtime. This policy file describes permissions for class(es) to be able to access certain remote objects. We will define a policy file, "myPolicy.txt", to grant permission to all classes.

```
grant
{
 //allow permission to everything
     permission java.security.AllPermission;
};
```

At this point, we need to start the rmiregistry and then start the RemoteLoggingServer with the following command:

```
java -Djava.security.policy=myPolicy.txt sam.logging.rmi.RemoteLoggingServer
```

NOTE As per Java 2, the SecurityManager needs to be configured properly in order to perform RMI operation to any remote machine. The simplest way to achieve this to write a custom policy file and pass it to the Java runtime. For example, "myPolicy.txt", the sample policy file used for this example, grants permission to all requests. In theory, granting permission to all requests is not the best practice. You need to consult RMI books to learn more about policy files. For the time being, we are granting permission to all requests.

The RemoteLoggingServer component is now up and running to receive any logging request.

Remote Logging Handler

Listing 4-6, RemoteHandler.java, creates a custom Handler object to delegate logging activity to the remote logging server developed in Listing 4-5.

Listing 4-6. RemoteHandler.java

```
package sam.logging.handler;

import java.util.logging.*;
import java.rmi.Naming;
import java.rmi.Remote;
import java.rmi.RemoteException;
import sam.logging.rmi.*;

public class RemoteHandler extends Handler {
    private static RemoteHandler handler = null;
    private Logging remoteLogger = null;
    private LogManager manager = null;
    private RemoteHandler(String serverName) {
        config();
        try {
            //obtain the remote server reference
            remoteLogger = (Logging)Naming.lookup(serverName);
        }catch(Exception re) {
            re.printStackTrace();
            System.exit(1);
        }
    }

    private void config() {
        manager = LogManager.getLogManager();

setLevel(Level.parse(
manager.getProperty("sam.logging.handler.RemoteHandler.level")));
    }

    /**
     * This method returns a singleton instance of the
     * present Handler object.
     *@param serverName name of the remote server
     *@return RemoteHandler object
     */
```

```
            public static synchronized RemoteHandler getInstance(String serverName) {
                if(handler ==null) {
                    handler = new RemoteHandler(serverName);
                }
                return handler;
            }
            /**
             * This is the overridden publish() method
             */
            public synchronized void publish(LogRecord record) {
                try {
                    remoteLogger.logMessage(record);
                }catch(RemoteException re) {
                    reportError(null, re, ErrorManager.WRITE_FAILURE);
                }
            }
            //overridden close() and publish() methods
            public void close(){ };
            public void flush(){ };
        }
```

The RemoteHandler object described in Listing 4-6 is a singleton. We need to ensure that we only obtain the reference to the RemoteLoggingServer component once and use the same reference throughout the application context to perform remote logging. The remote reference to RemoteLoggingServer is obtained in the private constructor of the RemoteHandler class. The client to this program is prohibited from invoking the constructor directly to create a new instance of it. Alternatively, RemoteHandler provides the following static method:

```
public static synchronized RemoteHandler getInstance(String serverName)
```

which returns an already existing instance of the RemoteHandler object or creates a new one and returns that. The constructor calls a private method, config(), to configure the initialization parameters for the Handler by reading the logging configuration file properties via the LogManager.

The RemoteHandler class extends the abstract base class java.util.logging.Handler. The overridden publish() method of the RemoteHandler class uses the remote reference of the RemoteLoggingServer object and passes the LogRecord object to the remote logMessage() method to publish the logging information. The publish() method of the RemoteHandler is synchronized to make it thread-safe.

Remote Logging Client

Listing 4-7, RemoteLoggingDemo, is a client program that uses the RemoteHandler object developed in Listing 4-6 to enable remote logging. This application makes use of the RemoteHandler object to log information to a remote machine.

Listing 4-7. RemoteHandlerDemo.java

```
package sam.logging.handler;

import java.util.logging.*;
public class RemoteHandlerDemo
{
 private Logger logger = null;
 private RemoteHandler handler = null;

 public RemoteHandlerDemo()
 {
  logger = Logger.getLogger("sam.logging.handler");
  handler = RemoteHandler.getInstance("LoggingServer");
  logger.addHandler(handler);
 }

 public void logMessage()
 {
  LogRecord record = new LogRecord(Level.SEVERE, "Severe message....");
  logger.log(record);
 }

 public static void main(String args[])
 {
  RemoteHandlerDemo demo = new RemoteHandlerDemo();
  demo.logMessage();
 }
}
```

The RemoteHandlerDemo class is a very simple class that obtains a package-specific logger, obtains an instance of the RemoteHandler object, and attaches the RemoteHandler to the logger as the preferred Handler. It then creates a simple LogRecord object and logs the message to the remote location. Although the logging activity is carried out remotely, the applications need *not* know any details about the remote objects or how it is done. In that sense, the application carries on using the normal logging activity, and the custom RemoteHandler takes care of the rest.

Logging in Practice

Let's consider an application scenario in which several components are distributed across different machines in order to implement an employee data management system. Imagine that one of the components is a Java RMI component that reads XML employee data stored in a file local to the machine on which the RMI program is running. There is also an application component client to the RMI program that obtains the XML-formatted employee information from the RMI component, parses the data, and inserts the data into a database.

The information being accessed and stored to the database is critical to the functioning of the employee management system. We need to maintain traces of user activity with the data and log every success and failure in the whole process. Also, it will be useful to provide users with information about their activity. The client program executes on a completely different machine in a separate JVM environment interacting with RMI components and the database. Hence, it is required that the client program should produce traces of its activity in the client environment. In order to achieve a centralized control system, critical logging information would also need to be passed to the remote logging component, which will log the information to a predefined destination.

The diagram in Figure 4-3 presents the overall architecture of the system.

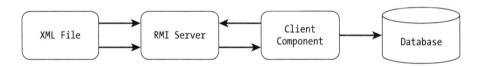

Figure 4-3. The employee data management architecture

In a nutshell, the implemented system will perform the following operations:

- The RMI server component will read the XML employee data.

- The server component implements a logging mechanism that stores the logging information to a predefined destination.

- The client component will obtain the employee data by invoking a remote method on the RMI server component.

- The client component will store the data in the database via JDBC.

- The client component will produce its own debug trace to a small Java window. The client component will also pass critical logging information to a remote logging server.

- The remote logging server is a separate RMI component that will store the logging information in XML format.

The different components involved in the whole system are as follows:

- The `Employee` object

- The remote server interface

- The remote server component

- The remote logging server

- The RMI manager component

- The client component

Figure 4-4 presents the UML diagram for these components. The diagram explains how these components are related to one another and how the objects interact.

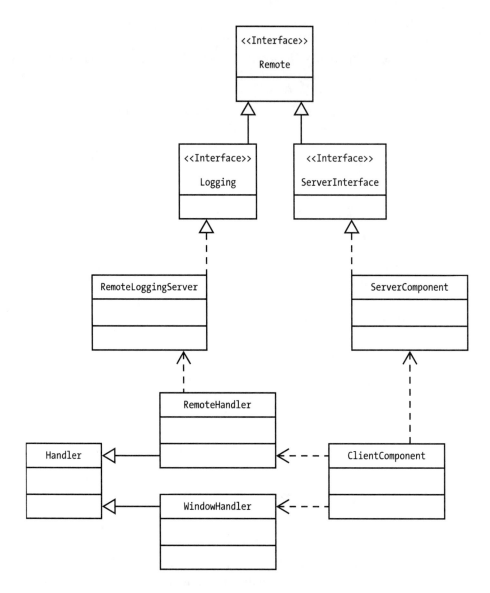

Figure 4-4. UML diagram for the components

Employee Object

Listing 4-8, Employee.java, is a business object that represents employee data. This class is a Java Bean. As the Employee object is used for the RMI, it implements the java.io.Serializable interface to make it possible to transport logging information over the RMI protocol.

Listing 4-8. Employee.java

```
package com.apress.business;

public class Employee implements java.io.Serializable{

    /** Holds value of property name. */
    private String name;

    /** Holds value of property age. */
    private int age;

    /** Holds value of property department. */
    private String department;

    /** Holds value of property code. */
    private int code;

    /** Creates a new instance of Employee */
    public Employee() {
    }

    /** Getter for property name.
     * @return Value of property name.
     */
    public String getName() {
        return this.name;
    }

    /** Setter for property name.
     * @param name New value of property name.
     */
    public void setName(String name) {
        this.name = name;
    }
```

```java
        /** Getter for property age.
         * @return Value of property age.
         */
        public int getAge() {
            return this.age;
        }
        
        /** Setter for property age.
         * @param age New value of property age.
         */
        public void setAge(int age) {
            this.age = age;
        }
        
        /** Getter for property department.
         * @return Value of property department.
         */
        public String getDepartment() {
            return this.department;
        }
        
        /** Setter for property department.
         * @param department New value of property department.
         */
        public void setDepartment(String department) {
            this.department = department;
        }
        
        /** Getter for property code.
         * @return Value of property code.
         */
        public int getCode() {
            return this.code;
        }
        
        /** Setter for property code.
         * @param code New value of property code.
         */
        public void setCode(int code) {
            this.code = code;
        }
        
    }
```

Remote Server Interface

Listing 4-9, `ServerInterface.java`, defines the remote interface for the server component responsible for reading the XML employee data. It defines a single remote method, `readDocument(String docId)`. The defined method throws a `java.rmi.RemoteException` in accordance with the Java RMI specification if there is a problem.

Listing 4-9. ServerInterface.java

```
package com.apress.server;
import java.rmi.Remote;
import java.rmi.RemoteException;
import java.util.List;
public interface ServerInterface extends Remote
{
    public List readDocument(String docId) throws RemoteException
        }
```

Remote Server Component

Listing 4-10, `ServerComponent.java`, is the implementation of the remote `ServerInterface` and provides implementation for the only declared remote method, `readDocument(String docID)`. It parses the specified XML file and creates a `java.util.List` of `Employee` objects and returns the `List` object back to the caller. It also has its own logging enabled—it does so by obtaining a separate `Logger` with the namespace "com.apress.server" and using a `FileHandler` to publish the logging information. The `FileHandler` is initialized with the pattern %h/employeeLog%g.out, which means the log files will be created in the "user.home" directory with the name "employeeLog(n).out" where "n" represents the unique ID.

Listing 4-10. ServerComponent.java

```
package com.apress.server;

import java.rmi.server.UnicastRemoteObject;
import java.rmi.Naming;
import java.rmi.RemoteException;
import java.io.File;
import java.util.Vector;
import java.util.List;
import java.util.Iterator;
import java.io.IOException;
```

```java
import org.jdom.Document;
import org.jdom.input.SAXBuilder;
import org.jdom.JDOMException;
import org.jdom.Element;
import java.util.logging.*;
import com.apress.business.Employee;

public class ServerComponent extends UnicastRemoteObject
implements ServerInterface{

    private Document doc = null;
    private SAXBuilder builder = null;
    private Vector empList = null;
    private Logger logger = null;
    private FileHandler handler = null;
    /** Creates a new instance of ServerComponent */
    public ServerComponent() throws RemoteException {
        super();
        builder = new SAXBuilder();
        empList = new Vector();

        try {
            //obtain a logger instance
            logger = Logger.getLogger("com.apress.server");
            //creating a FileHandler object with pattern
            handler = new FileHandler("%h/employeeLog%g.out");
            //setting the handler to the logger
            logger.addHandler(handler);
        }catch(IOException ioe) {
            ioe.printStackTrace();
        }
    }
    /**
     * This method reads the specified XML document from the current working
     * directory. It creates a list of Employee objects out of the XML data
     * file and returns it to the caller.
     * @param docId the name of the XML document file
     * @return the list of the Employee object
     * @exception RemoteException in case there is a problem in
     * reading the file
     */
```

```java
    public List readDocument(String docId) throws RemoteException {
        logger.entering("com.apress.server.ServerComponent", "readDocument");
        String name= null;
        String code=null;
        String dept = null;
        String age = null;
        try {
            //obtaining a DOM instance from the document
            doc = builder.build(new File(docId));
            //finding the root element
            Element root = doc.getRootElement();
            //getting all the children
            List list = root.getChildren();
            Iterator iterator = list.iterator();
            //iterating through the records and creating the Employee objects
            while(iterator.hasNext()) {
                Element element = (Element)iterator.next();
                name = element.getChildText("name");
                code = element.getChildText("code");
                dept = element.getChildText("dept");
                age = element.getChildText("age");
                Employee emp = new Employee();
                emp.setName(name);
                emp.setCode(Integer.parseInt(code));
                emp.setAge(Integer.parseInt(age));
                emp.setDepartment(dept);
                empList.add(emp);
            }
        }catch(JDOMException jdome) {
         logger.severe("Exception in parsing the
XML file: "+jdome.toString());
        }
        logger.exiting("com.apress.server.ServerComponent", "readDocument");

        return empList;
    }

}
```

Remote Logging Server

For this example, we are going to use the remote logging server component we developed in Listing 4-5. We will view the data reader RMI component developed in the previous section and the remote logging server as a combined entity. Accordingly, we will create a RMI manager service that will manage both of these RMI components.

The RMIManager

Listing 4-11, RMIManager.java, is a simple utility that manages two remote services for RemoteLoggingServer and ServerComponent. It can start the services by binding them to the rmiregistry or stop the services by unbinding them from the rmiregistry, depending on whether the command line option "start" or "stop" has been passed to it.

Listing 4-11. RMIManager.java

```
package com.apress.server;

import java.rmi.registry.*;
import java.rmi.Naming;
import sam.logging.rmi.RemoteLoggingServer;
public class RMIManager {

    /** Creates a new instance of RMIManager */
    public RMIManager() {
    }

    /**
     * @param args the command line arguments
     */
    public static void main(String[] args) {
        try {
            if(args[0].equalsIgnoreCase("start")) {
                //binding the services by creating a registry
                //at port 1099(default)
                Registry reg = LocateRegistry.createRegistry(1099);
                Naming.rebind("rmi://oemcomputer/AppServer",
new ServerComponent());
                Naming.rebind("rmi://oemcomputer/LoggingServer",
```

```
                new RemoteLoggingServer());
                    System.out.println("AppServer started...");
                }else if(args[0].equalsIgnoreCase("stop")) {
                    //unbinding the services
                    Naming.unbind("rmi://oemcomputer/AppServer");
                    Naming.unbind("rmi://oemcomputer/LoggingServer");
                    System.exit(1);
                }

        }catch(Exception e) {
            System.out.println(e.toString());
        }
    }

}
```

Client Component

Listing 4-12, ClientComponent.java, is the client program that will use the RMI component to receive the employee data and write the required information to the database. It is mainly responsible for the following:

- First, it obtains a reference to the remote server component and obtains the List of the Employee objects to be inserted into the database.

- It obtains a JDBC connection to a specified database and inserts the data to the database table(s).

- It obtains the database configuration parameters from a configuration file passed to the Java runtime as a command line option.

- It obtains a reference to the remote logging server component, which is responsible for receiving logging information and publishing it to the specified destination.

- It also publishes the client-side logging information to a small Java window.

Listing 4-12. ClientComponent.java

```java
package com.apress.db;

import java.sql.*;
import java.util.Properties;
import java.io.FileInputStream;
import java.io.FileNotFoundException;
import java.io.IOException;
import java.util.List;
import java.util.Iterator;
import java.util.logging.*;
import java.rmi.Naming;
import java.rmi.NotBoundException;
import java.rmi.RemoteException;
import com.apress.business.Employee;
import com.apress.server.ServerInterface;
import sam.logging.handler.RemoteHandler;
import sam.logging.handler.WindowHandler;

public class ClientComponent {

    private String driverName = null;
    private String jdbcURL = null;
    private String userName = null;
    private String password = null;
    private Properties props = null;
    private Logger logger = null;
    private RemoteHandler remoteHandler = null;
    private WindowHandler windowHandler = null;
    private ServerInterface server = null;

    /** Creates a new instance of ClientComponent */
    public ClientComponent(String propFile) {
        props = new Properties();
        try {
            props.load(new FileInputStream(propFile));
            driverName = props.getProperty("DriverName");
            jdbcURL = props.getProperty("URL");
            userName = props.getProperty("userName");
            password = props.getProperty("Password");
            System.out.println("driver name: "+driverName);
            System.out.println("url: "+jdbcURL);
            System.out.println("user name: "+userName);
            System.out.println("password: "+password);
```

```java
            //obtain the reference to the rmi server
            server= (ServerInterface)
Naming.lookup("rmi://oemcomputer/AppServer");

            //obtain an instance of the logger
            logger = Logger.getLogger("com.apress.db");
            //obtain an instance of the remote handler
            //talking to the logging server named LoggingServer
            remoteHandler=
RemoteHandler.getInstance("rmi://oemcomputer/LoggingServer");
            //getting an instance of the window handler
            windowHandler = WindowHandler.getInstance();
            //adding the remote handler to the logger
            logger.addHandler(remoteHandler);
            //adding the window handler to the logger
            logger.addHandler(windowHandler);
            //set the logger level the same as the handler level
            logger.setLevel(remoteHandler.getLevel());

            //configuration done
            logger.config("client configuration done...");
        }catch(FileNotFoundException fnfe) {
            fnfe.printStackTrace();
            System.out.println("Could not find the properties
file: "+propFile);
            System.exit(1);
        }catch(IOException ioe) {
            ioe.printStackTrace();
            System.out.println("Problem in reading the
prop file: "+propFile);
            System.exit(1);
        }catch(NotBoundException re)
        {
            logger.severe("servert named AppServer is
not bound "+re.toString());
        }

    }
```

```java
        //private helper method for obtaining a connection
        private Connection makeConnection()throws SQLException {
            Connection conn = null;
            try {
                Class.forName(driverName);
                conn = DriverManager.getConnection(jdbcURL, userName, password);
            }catch(ClassNotFoundException cnfe) {
                System.out.println("Class not found: "+driverName);
                System.exit(1);
            }catch(SQLException sqle) {
                throw sqle;
            }
            System.out.println("evaluation: "+(logger.getLevel().intValue()<Level.INFO.intValue()));
            logger.info("Connection obtained as: "+conn);
            return conn;
        }

         //private method for closing the connection
        private void closeConnection(Connection conn) {
            try {
                if(conn !=null)
                    conn.close();
            }catch(SQLException sqle) {
                //WARNING
                logger.warning("Could not close the connection..");
            }
            logger.info("connection closed..");
        }

        /**
         * This is a private method responsible for writing the
         * employee object datato the database.
         * @param conn the Connection object
         * @param employee the Employee object
         * @exception SQLException is thrown in case there is a problem
         */
        private void insertData(Connection conn, Employee employee)
    throws SQLException {
            logger.entering(ClientComponent.class.getName(), "insertData()");
            Statement stmt =null;
            StringBuffer queryString = new StringBuffer("INSERT INTO
    EMPLOYEE VALUES(");
```

```java
    try {
        stmt = conn.createStatement();
        queryString.append(employee.getCode());
        queryString.append(",'");
        queryString.append(employee.getName());
        queryString.append("','");
        queryString.append(employee.getDepartment());
        queryString.append("',");
        queryString.append(employee.getAge());
        queryString.append(")");

        logger.info("The queryString is ; "+queryString.toString());
        stmt.execute(queryString.toString());
        logger.fine("inserted data..");
        conn.commit();
        stmt.close();
    }catch(SQLException sqle) {
        throw sqle;
    }

    logger.exiting(ClientComponent.class.getName(), "insertData()");

}

/**
 * This method is responsible for obtaining the employee data
   from the specified
 * file and writing it to the database
 * @param docId the document name in the remote place containing
 * the XML data.
 */
public void setEmployeeData(String docId) throws SQLException {
    Connection conn = null;
    List empList = null;
    Iterator iterator = null;
    logger.entering(ClientComponent.class.getName()
```

```
                , "setEmployeeData()");
            try {
                    conn = makeConnection();
                    empList = server.readDocument(docId);
                    iterator = empList.iterator();
                    while(iterator.hasNext())
                    {
                        Employee emp = (Employee)iterator.next();
                        insertData(conn, emp);
                    }
                    logger.info("Job done...");
            }catch(SQLException sqle) {
                    logger.severe("SQL problem: "+sqle.toString());
            }catch(RemoteException re)
            {
                    logger.severe("Remote exception in invoking the
    method readDocument() "+re.toString());
            }finally {
                    closeConnection(conn);
            }
                logger.exiting(ClientComponent.class.getName(), "setEmployeeData()");

        }
        /**
         * @param args the command line arguments
         */
        public static void main(String[] args) {
            String propFile = args[0];
            String fileName = args[1];
            ClientComponent comp = new ClientComponent(propFile);
            try {
                comp.setEmployeeData("employee.xml");
            }catch(SQLException sqle) {
                sqle.printStackTrace();
            }


        }

    }
```

The `ClientComponent` obtains its own named logger with the namespace "com.apress.client" and attaches two separate `Handlers` for logging information to a remote place and to a small Java window on the client machine.

Creating the Employee Data File

Now we are ready to execute our little demo application. Let's create a small XML file, as shown in Listing 4-13, containing the employee data.

Listing 4-13. employee.xml

```xml
<record>
<employee>
 <code>100</code>
 <name>Sam</name>
 <dept>Dev</dept>
 <age>22</age>
</employee>
<employee>
 <code>101</code>
 <name>paul</name>
 <dept>Dev</dept>
 <age>38</age>
</employee>
<employee>
 <code>102</code>
 <name>derek</name>
 <dept>Sales</dept>
 <age>43</age>
</employee>
</record>
```

Configuring the Database

The previous program will require a table called EMPLOYEE to be defined in a database. The following SQL command will create this table with "CODE" being the primary key.

```
CREATE TABLE EMPLOYEE("CODE" NUMBER NOT NULL,"NAME" VARCHAR(10)
NOT NULL,"DEPT" VARCHAR(10) NOT NULL, "AGE" NUMBER NOT NULL,
PRIMARY KEY("CODE"));
```

The following configuration file, "db.properties", will pass the database connection parameters to the `ClientComponent` at startup:

```
DriverName=sun.jdbc.odbc.JdbcOdbcDriver
URL=jdbc:odbc:dbdef
userName=system
Password=manager
```

As we are using JDBC-ODBC driver for this simple example, we need to create a Data Source Name (DNS) with the name "dbdef" and configure it to point to the right data source.

Starting Up the Server

We need to generate the `Stub` and `Skeleton` classes for the server component. This can be done by the following command:

```
rmic com.apress.server.ServerComponent
```

We can start the server component by executing the `RMIManager` class:

```
java com.apress.server.RMIManager start
```

Running the Client

You probably have noticed that we are using the `RemoteHandler` and `WindowHandler` objects developed in Chapter 2. Both these `Handlers` have the ability to read the initialization parameters from the configuration file specified via the command line option -Djava.util.logging.config.file or from the default JDK "logging.properties" configuration file. We can design a custom configuration file with the following entry, setting the level used by the `RemoteHandler` and the `WindowHandler`:

```
############################################################
# RemoteHandler configuration
# This is a custom handler developed to enable remote logging
############################################################
sam.logging.handler.RemoteHandler.level=FINEST

############################################################
#WindowHandler configuration
#This is a custom handler which passes the logging info
#to a Java based logging window
############################################################
sam.logging.handler.WindowHandler.level = FINEST
```

Extending the Logging Framework

The `ClientComponent` is designed to acquire the database connection properties from a configuration file and also the name of the employee data XML file in the remote server as a command line option. The "db.properties" file specified previously defines the database connection properties, and we pass "employee.xml" as the name of the remote file from which to obtain the employee data.

```
Java -Djava.util.logging.config.file=/your-path/config.properties
com.apress.db.ClientComponent /your-path/db.properties employee.xml
```

The logging information related to the `ClientComponent` will appear in a small Java window as shown in Figure 4-5.

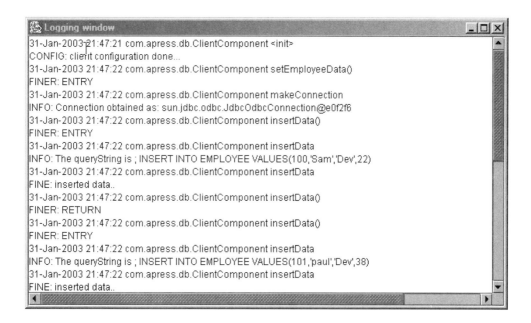

Figure 4-5. Logging information in the client-side logging window

On the server side, the `ServerComponent` will store its own logging information as well as the logging information being passed from the `ClientComponent`. The `ServerComponent`, as discussed earlier, has its own logging enabled with a `FileHandler` object that has the fixed pattern `%h/employeeLog%g.out`. Hence, the `ServerComponent` logging information will be located in the "user.home" directory under the names `employeeLog0.out`, `employeeLog1.out`, etc. On the other hand, the `RemoteLoggingServer` is responsible for configuring the location for the remote logging information enabled by any client application using the `RemoteHandler`. If no pattern is specified with `RemoteLoggingServer`, the default `FileHandler` pattern is used.

We can limit the amount of information being printed in any of the logging destinations by changing the level associated with the Handler. For example, in the ClientComponent JVM, if we change the level of the WindowHandler to Level.INFO, then we will see the logging information being printed as shown in Figure 4-6.

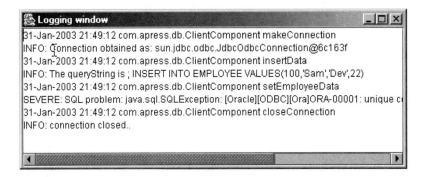

Figure 4-6. The logging information in the client-side logging window

Clearly, changing the level has reduced the amount of information. The log is now more readable. But notice that we have achieved this by merely changing the configuration file—this is the beauty of having a configurable logging API like the JDK 1.4 logging API.

Conclusion

In the previous chapters, we have examined the architecture, use, and extension of the JDK 1.4 logging API. We have also seen one practical example of how the logging API can be very useful in tracing and debugging applications. The flexibility of publishing log messages when needed and the granularity of our choices means a great deal to application developers and administrators. Beginning in the next chapter, we will explore in similar detail log4j, another popular Java-based logging API from Apache.

CHAPTER 5

Understanding Apache log4j

THE APACHE LOG4J implementation is a highly scalable, robust, and versatile logging framework. This API simplifies the writing of logging code within an application, yet allows the flexibility of controlling logging activity from an external configuration file. It also allows us to publish logging information to desired granularity depending on the detail of the logging information suitable to each application.

We can tailor the granularity of logging activity suitable for the development phase or the deployment phase of an application without having to change the source code. It is possible to switch over to a different logging behavior by only changing a few configuration parameters.

Apache log4j is also capable of publishing logging information to various destinations such as files, consoles, and NT event logs. Moreover, logging information can even be distributed over Java Message Service (JMS) or JDBC, or can be output to a TCP/IP socket. This API lets us take logging information and publish or print it in different formats and layouts that are human readable and reusable by any error handling and analyzer program at a future date. The scalability aspect of log4j allows developers to enhance the capability of logging by creating new logging destinations and unique formats and layouts, which is done by extending the existing framework.

Although the application of the log4j framework is easy, it demands certain methods and practices be adopted for the best possible results. In this chapter, we will discuss the overall architecture of the log4j framework and different objects involved within the API, and examine in detail the application and usage of the core logging objects. This chapter uses the Apache log4j version 1.2.6 release as the basis for the concepts and examples presented herein. Although the subsequent releases of log4j will incorporate more features, the basic concepts discussed in this book will remain unchanged and will prove useful to mastering any subsequent release.

Installing log4j

Apache log4j is an open-source project from Apache group. You need to meet the following criteria to successfully install and use log4j:

- Get the latest version of the log4j binary distribution from http://jakarta.apache.org. The examples and concepts in this book are based on the log4j version 1.2.6 release. You may obtain any later version of log4j, if available, and still be able to follow the examples in this book.

- Apache log4j is JDK 1.1.x compatible. Make sure you have the appropriate JDK version downloaded to your machine.

- You need a JAXP-compatible XML parser to use log4j. Make sure you have "Xerces.jar" installed on your machine.

- The e-mail–based logging feature in log4j requires the Java Mail API ("mail.jar") to be installed in your machine. Apache log4j is tested against version 1.2 of the Java Mail API.

- The Java Mail API will also require the JavaBeans Activation Framework ("activation.jar") be installed in your machine.

- The JMS-compatible features of log4j will require that JMS is installed on your machine as well as JNDI.

Once you have acquired and installed all the required .jar files, you must make sure that all these resources are available within the classpath of the Java runtime.

Overview of the log4j Architecture

The architecture of the log4j API is layered. Each layer consists of different objects performing different tasks. The top layer captures the logging information, the middle layer is involved in analyzing and authorizing the logging information, and the bottom layer is responsible for formatting and publishing the logging information to a destination. In essence, log4j consists of three types of primary objects:

- Logger: The Logger object (formerly known as the Category object in releases prior to log4j 1.2) is responsible for capturing logging information. Logger objects are stored in a namespace hierarchy.

- Appender: The Appender object is responsible for publishing logging information to various preferred destinations. Each Appender object will have at least one target destination attached to it. For example, a ConsoleAppender object is capable of printing logging information to a console.

- Layout: The Layout object is used to format logging information in different styles. Appender objects utilize Layout objects before publishing logging information. Layout objects play an important role in publishing logging information in a way that is human readable and reusable.

The preceding core objects are central to the architecture of log4j. Apart from them, there are several auxiliary objects that are plug and play to any layer of the API. These objects help manage the different Logger objects active within an application and fine-tune the logging process.

Next, let's go over the principal auxiliary objects in the log4j framework that play a vital role in the logging framework:

- Level: The Level object, previously referred to as the Priority object, defines the granularity and priority of any logging information. Each piece of logging information is accompanied with its appropriate Level object, which tells the Logger object about the priority of the information. There are seven levels of logging defined within the API: OFF, DEBUG, INFO, ERROR, WARN, FATAL, and ALL. Each level defined has a unique integer value associated with it.

- Filter: The Filter object is used to analyze logging information and make further decisions on whether that information should be logged or not. In the log4j context, Appender objects can have several Filter objects associated with them. If logging information is passed to a particular Appender object, all the Filter objects associated with that Appender need to approve the logging information before it can be published to the preferred destination attached to the Appender. Filter objects are very helpful in filtering out unwanted logging information based on any application-specific criteria.

- ObjectRenderer: The ObjectRenderer object is specialized in providing a String representation of different objects passed to the logging framework. More precisely, when the application passes a custom Object to the logging framework, the logging framework will use the corresponding ObjectRenderer to obtain a String representation of the passed Object. This is used by Layout objects to prepare the final logging information.

- LogManager: The LogManager object performs the management of the logging framework. It is responsible for reading the initial configuration parameters from a system-wide configuration file or a configuration class. Each Logger instance created with a namespace within an application is stored in a namespace hierarchy by the LogManager. When we try to obtain the reference named logger, the LogManager class returns the already created instance of it, or else creates a new instance of the named logger, stores it in a repository for future reference, and returns the new instance to the caller application.

Now that we have seen the log4j core components, it is time to briefly discuss how they interact with each other. The central part of the log4j framework is the Logger object. An application instantiates a named Logger instance and passes different logging information to it. A Logger object has a designated Level object associated with it. The Logger object provides several logging methods that are capable of logging information categorized into different levels.

A Logger only logs the messages with Levels equal to or greater than its assigned Level or else rejects the logging request. Once the Level condition has been met, the Logger object passes the logging information to all its associated Appender objects and also to all the Appender objects associated to its parent Logger, recursively up the logging hierarchy.

Similar to Logger objects, Appender objects can also have threshold Levels attached to them. The logging information is validated against the threshold Level attached to the Appender. If the log message has a Level equal to or greater than the threshold Level, the logging message is passed to the next stage. The Appender objects then look for any Filter object associated with them. If there are any, the logging information is passed through all the Filter objects in a chain. Once a message is approved by all the Filter objects, the Appender then utilizes any Layout object associated with it to format the message, and finally it publishes the logging information to the preferred destination. Figure 5-1 depicts the overall flow of the log4j logging architecture in a UML sequence diagram.

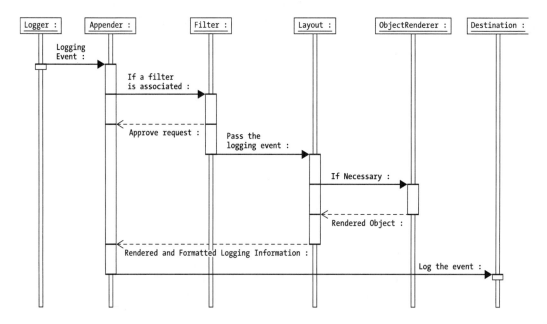

Figure 5-1. Overview of the log4j framework

If you have gone through the JDK 1.4 logging API discussion in Chapters 2 through 4, you might be wondering about the similarities and the differences between these two logging APIs. On the surface, the architecture of both APIs look strikingly similar. However, subtle but vital differences exist between these two APIS, which we will discuss in Chapter 10.

Configuring log4j

Before we can use log4j in an application, we need to configure log4j in an application-specific manner. Configuring log4j typically involves assigning `Level`, defining `Appender`, and specifying `Layout` objects. The configuration information is conventionally defined within a properties file in a key-value pattern. It is also possible to define the log4j configuration in an XML format, which we will discuss later in this section. By default, the `LogManager` class will look for a file named "log4j.properties" in the classpath used for loading the log4j classes.

Using an external configuration file as a means to control logging behavior is a particularly useful feature, because it requires no source code change to switch to a completely different logging scheme.

Listing 5-1 shows a simple log4j configuration. It defines the level and appender for the root logger.

Listing 5-1. Example log4j Configuration File

```
#set the level of the root logger to DEBUG and set its appender
as an appender named X
log4j.rootLogger = DEBUG, X

#set the appender named X to be a console appender
log4j.appender.X=org.apache.log4j.ConsoleAppender

#set the layout for the appender X
log4j.appender.X.layout=org.apache.log4j.PatternLayout
log4j.appender.X.layout.conversionPattern=%m%n
```

The preceding configuration defines the level of the root logger as DEBUG and specifies the appender to use as X. Next, we define the appender X as referencing the `org.apache.log4j.ConsoleAppender` object and specify the layout of the appender as `org.apache.log4j.PatternLayout`. A `PatternLayout` also requires a conversion pattern or a format to be supplied. We supply the conversion pattern %m%n in this case, which means the logging message will be printed followed by a newline character. It is possible to define much more complicated and descriptive conversion patterns, which we will discuss in detail in Chapter 6.

NOTE Within the conversion pattern, %m represents the message string and %n represents a newline character. We will learn more about these conversion patterns in Chapter 6.

A more complex configuration can attach multiple appenders to a particular logger. Each appender in turn can have a different layout, and that layout can have a conversion pattern associated with it. Listing 5-2 is an example of a more complex configuration file.

Listing 5-2. Complex log4j Configuration File

```
# define the root logger with two appenders writing to console and file
log4j.rootLogger = DEBUG, CONSOLE, FILE

#define your own logger named com.foo
log4j.logger.com.foo=com.foo.MyLogger
#assign appender to your own logger
log4j.logger.com.foo.appender=FILE

#define the appender named FILE
log4j.appender.FILE=org.apache.log4j.FileAppender
log4j.appender.FILE.File=${user.home}/log.out

#define the appender named CONSOLE
log4j.appender.CONSOLE=org.apache.log4j.ConsoleAppender
log4j.appender.CONSOLE.conversionPattern=%m%n
```

This configuration file defines the root logger as having level DEBUG and attaches two appenders named CONSOLE and FILE to it. We define one of our own custom loggers with the name com.foo and define the Java class file representing the custom logger. We then attach an appender named FILE to the custom logger. The appender FILE is defined as org.apache.log4j.FileAppender. The FILE appender writes to a file named "log.out" located in the user.home system path. It is important to note that log4j supports UNIX-style variable substitution such as ${variableName}. The variable name defined is considered the key and first searched in the system properties. If not found, the log4j framework then looks for the value for the variable in the properties file being parsed. The CONSOLE appender is then assigned to the org.apache.log4j.ConsoleAppender and the conversion pattern defined is %m%n, which means the printed logging message will be followed by a newline character.

XML-Style Configuration

With log4j, it is also possible to define configuration parameters in an XML file and pass that file to the application at startup to configure different logging components. The XML configuration follows a document type definition (DTD) named "log4j.dtd". The configuration parameters and values are described in tag formats. For example, the configuration information listed in Listing 5-1 can be defined in XML format as follows:

```xml
<?xml version="1.0" encoding="UTF-8" ?>
<!DOCTYPE log4j:configuration SYSTEM "log4j.dtd">
<log4j:configuration>
  <root>
    <priority value ="debug" />
    <appender-ref ref="X"/>
  </root>
  <appender name="X" class="org.apache.log4j.ConsoleAppender">
    <param name="conversionPattern" value="%m%n"/>
  </appender>
</log4j:configuration>
```

Both the XML-style configuration and properties-style configuration are quite effective in configuring log4j. Both are flexible and good styles of configuration. However, it seems that a few components in log4j such as `Filter`, `AsyncAppender`, etc., can only be configured through XML-style configuration. It seems that log4j is evolving from properties-style configuration towards XML-style configuration, and gradually it will embrace XML-style configuration as the standard. For the time being, we need to master both of these configuration styles.

Default Initialization

In general, log4j makes no assumption about the environment it is running in. Therefore, it is the application developer's responsibility to configure log4j. Configuring log4j essentially means specifying loggers, appenders, layouts, etc. The `LogManager` class performs the initialization operation at startup only once through a class-level `static` initializer block. The default initialization operation essentially consists of the following steps:

1. The `LogManager` class looks for the system property `log4j.configuration`.

2. If the `log4j.configuration` property is not defined, then it tries to look for a resource named `log4j.properties` in the application classpath.

3. It then attempts to convert the defined configuration resource string to an URL object. If the resource string cannot be converted into a valid java.net.URL object, then a java.net.MalformedURLException is thrown.

4. If no resource can be found, then the initialization is aborted.

5. If the resource is found and if it is a normal Java properties-style file containing configuration information in a key-value format, then the org.apache.log4j.PropertyConfigurator class is used to parse the configuration file. If the configuration file is an XML file, then the org.apache.log4j.xml.DOMConfigurator class is used to parse the XML file and initialize the logging objects.

It is also possible to avoid the default initialization classes such as LogManager and write your own configuration class. The custom configuration class can be specified as a log4j.configurationClass to the Java runtime at application startup. Any custom configuration class by default should implement the org.apache.log4j.spi.Configurator interface.

For example, we can pass the configuration file and configuration class respectively to the Java runtime with the following commands:

```
java -Dlog4j.configuration=config file yourApp
java -Dlog4j.configurationClass=config class yourApp
```

Creating a Configuration File

We will now see how to write a small program that will print very basic logging information with the help of a Logger object. We will create our own configuration properties file as defined in Listing 5-3, give it the name "log4j.properties", and pass it to the Java runtime as a system property.

Listing 5-3. log4j.properties

```
#set the level of the root logger to DEBUG (the lowest level) and set its appender
#as an appender named X
log4j.rootLogger = DEBUG, X

#set your own logger
log4j.logger.com.apress.logging.log4j=DEBUG,X

#set the appender named X to be a console appender
log4j.appender.X=org.apache.log4j.ConsoleAppender
```

```
#set the layout for the appender X
log4j.appender.X.layout=org.apache.log4j.PatternLayout
log4j.appender.X.layout.conversionPattern=%p-%m%n
```

In this configuration file, we have defined our own logger, com.apress.logging.log4j, and assigned it the level DEBUG and the appender X. The appender X is again defined to be a org.apache.log4j.ConsoleAppender with a conversion pattern of %m%n, which means the logging message will be followed by a newline character and printed to its default output stream, System.out. The %p sign will print the level of the logging message as a part of the output.

The program in Listing 5-4, SimpleLogging.java, is intended to print a simple debugging message. The main point to take away is that the Logger will be configured through the "log4j.properties" file defined earlier in Listing 5-3.

Listing 5-4. SimpleLogging.java

```
package com.apress.logging.log4j;

import org.apache.log4j.*;

public class SimpleLogging {
    /** Creates a new instance of SimpleLogging */
    public SimpleLogging() {
    }

    /**
     * @param args the command line arguments
     */
    public static void main(String[] args) {
        Logger logger =
Logger.getLogger(SimpleLogging.class.getPackage().getName());
        logger.info("Hello this is an info message");
    }
}
```

One important item to note in this simple program is how we obtain the Logger object reference. We create a logger with a namespace the same as the package name of the class, which in this case is com.apress.logging.log4j. The strategy for creating a logger namespace will be discussed in detail later in the "Logger Object" section. For the time being, it is enough to notice that in the configuration file we have also created a logger with the same name as the package name (com.apress.logging.log4j) of the SimpleLogging class. Once the logger is obtained, we then call the info() method on the Logger object to print the message.

Running the Program

We are now ready to run this program. It is important to make sure the classpath system variable contains all the classes as well as the "log4j.properties" file. We can then run the program with the following command by passing the name of the configuration file to load as a system parameter:

```
java -Dlog4j.configuration=log4j.properties com.apress.logging.log4j.SimpleLogging
```

The appender attached to the obtained logger is org.apache.log4j.ConsoleAppender. Hence, the program in Listing 5-4 will print the following message to the console:

```
INFO-Hello this is an info message
INFO-Hello this is an info message
```

You may be wondering why the same information is printed twice. This leads to another interesting point about the Logger object hierarchy, which we will discuss in great detail in the Logger section. The simple answer is that the message is printed twice because the message is propagated to the named logger and also to the root logger for handling. Both loggers have printed the message through their respective appenders.

Apache log4j also allows us to configure the logging framework programmatically without specifying any system property. As mentioned earlier, the properties-style configuration files are parsed with the org.apache.log4j.PropertyConfigurator object; we can use the same object within an application to read and parse the configuration file. For example, in the program in Listing 5-4, we could have used the following to configure the logging framework:

```
public static void main(String args[])
{
    PropertyConfigurator.configure(args[0]);
}
```

where args[0] is the name of the configuration file supplied as a command line parameter. This will also configure the framework correctly by reading any configuration file specified. The only important thing to note about this method is that ideally the configuration should be loaded at the entry point of the application such as in the main() method. Otherwise, the application might be loading the configuration information several times and slow down performance.

In a more simplistic situation, the Logger object can assume a very basic configuration through the org.apache.log4j.BasicConfigurator class.

```
BasicConfigurator.configure()
```

This instruction configures the root logger to a level of DEBUG and assigns `org.apache.log4j.ConsoleAppender` as default appender with the conversion pattern `%-4r[%t]%-5p%c%x - %m%n`. By default, log4j is configured to propagate the logging request up through the logger hierarchy. If we use the default setting in an application, and we obtain our own named logger but do not use any external configuration file to configure it, then it will automatically inherit and use the properties of the root logger set by the `BasicConfigurator`.

Dynamic Loading of Configuration

If we are configuring the logging framework with an external configuration file, one frustrating thing we may encounter is having to restart the application every time we change the properties file. To avoid this, both the `PropertyConfigurator` and the `DOMConfigurator` classes can implement dynamic loading of the configuration file. This is demonstrated in the following methods in both configuration classes:

```
public void configureAndWatch(String filename, long delay);
public void configureAndWatch(String filename);
```

These methods use another helper class, `org.apache.log4j.helpers.FileWatchDog`, that determines if the configuration file exists. If the file exists, it then creates a separate thread and searches for any modification in the file after a specified interval or after a default interval of 60 seconds. If the configuration file is modified, then the configuration is reread to configure the logging framework.

This property becomes very useful in the context of server-based applications, where taking any Web site down may not be desired, yet we need to change the application's logging configuration.

NOTE From this point on, we will be using the "log4j.properties" configuration file listed in Listing 5-3 for all future examples created in this chapter. This is because we will be using the same package structure for all the examples and thereby the same named logger. Any extra configuration information mentioned in relevant sections, such as our discussion on attaching different appenders, will have to be included in the "log4j.properties", if not mentioned otherwise.

Configuring log4j with Servlet

The use of log4j is not restricted to standalone applications, and it can be widely applied to any type of application deployment environment. One of the most frequently encountered server-based deployment environments is the Web server and servlet environment. Listing 5-5, LoggingServlet.java, shows a simple servlet to demonstrate the use of log4j within the Web server environment.

NOTE To compile the Java servlet program, you need a 1.x version of servlet.jar in your classpath. If you are using Tomcat as explained in this example, you will find "servlet.jar" in the /lib directory of the Tomcat installation.

Listing 5-5. LoggingServlet.java

```
import javax.servlet.*;
import javax.servlet.http.*;
import java.io.PrintWriter;
import java.io.IOException;
import org.apache.log4j.*;

public class LoggingServlet extends HttpServlet {
    private static Logger logger =
Logger.getLogger(LoggingServlet.class);

    public void doPost(HttpServletRequest req, HttpServletResponse res)
                    throws IOException, ServletException
    {
        logger.info("invoked the LoggingServlet...");
        PrintWriter writer = res.getWriter();
        writer.println("Check your web server console...");
        writer.flush();
        writer.close();
    }

}
```

Next, we will write a small HTML file to invoke this servlet:

```
<html>
<body>
<h1>Please enter value and press submit</h1>
<form method="POST"
action="http://localhost:8080/logdemo/servlet/LoggingServlet">
<input type=submit value=Invoke>
</bodY>
</html>
```

Notice that the form named "action" is pointing to the `LoggingServlet`, which is executed in a host named "localhost" that listens to port 8080. This is the default port for the HTTP request.

Within the servlet we obtain a `Logger` instance, and within the `doPost()` method we use the `Logger.info()` method to print the logging information. To make the logging work properly, we need to configure log4j for the Web server environment we are using. We will take a look at how to do this using the Tomcat Web server configuration as an example in the next section.

Setting Up Tomcat

In this section, we will demonstrate the use of the Tomcat 3.2.1 Web server configuration under the Windows operating system. You can easily figure out the corresponding files in the UNIX environment to configure Tomcat.

NOTE Tomcat is an open-source servlet engine from Apache, rather than a full-scale Web server. Tomcat can also be integrated with the Apache Web server. Although we are using Tomcat for the examples in this book, you can experiment with other Web servers that support Java servlets.

First build the example servlet along with the HTML file into a .war file and deploy the servlet into a folder named "logdemo" under your default Tomcat directory. After deploying the servlet successfully, you should be able to see your HTML file by entering your Web server URL in the browser window (e.g., `http://localhost:8080/logdemo/logging.html`).

NOTE To build a .war file, we need to use ANT with a custom build script. A .war file, or Web application archive, is a variant of the .jar file that is used by Tomcat for Web application deployment. Consult some ANT documentation for details on building applications with ANT. Once we have created the .war file, we need to drop it in the "/webapps" folder of the Tomcat installation. Once we restart Tomcat, it will automatically extract the files from within the .war file.

There are basically two ways to configure log4j to work with Tomcat, and these are described next.

Configuring Through a System Parameter

The log4j configuration within the Tomcat environment is not a difficult one. By following the steps described here, we can set up Tomcat to use log4j:

1. We can pass the "log4j.properties" file as a system variable to the execution environment of the tomcat.

2. Go to the "tomcat.bat" file in "%TOMCAT_HOME%\bin".

3. Add an entry to set the CLASSPATH variable pointing to the directory containing the "log4j.properties" file. For example, in the following example configuration:

   ```
   set CP=%CP%;C:\Jakarta-tomcat-3.2.1\webapps\logdemo\
   ```

4. we would add an entry to the "tomcat.bat" file as follows:

   ```
   set TOMCAT_OPTS=-Dlog4j.configuration=log4j.properties
   ```

5. Start up Tomcat, and it will load the "log4j.properties" file and use it to print log4j logging information.

Configuring Through the Servlet Initialization

Apache log4j can be configured at initialization of the servlet by passing it the name of the properties file through the application-specific "web.xml" file.

1. Go to the "logdemo/WEB-INF" folder of Tomcat.

2. Open the "web.xml" file and enter the following servlet configuration:

```xml
<servlet>
  <servlet-name>LoggingServlet</servlet-name>
  <servlet-class>LoggingServlet.class</servlet-class>

  <init-param>
  <param-name>log4j-conf</param-name>
  <param-value>log4j.properties</param-value>
  </init-param>

  <load-on-startup>1</load-on-startup>
</servlet>
```

3. Override the init() method in the LoggingServlet as follows:

```java
public void init()throws ServletException
{
    super.init();
    String configFile = getInitParameter("log4j-conf");
    PropertyConfigurator.configure(configFile);
}
```

4. Start up Tomcat, and the LoggingServlet will configure it through the "log4j.properties" file.

Once we invoke the LoggingServlet from the HTML page, we can see the following output in the Tomcat console:

invoked the LoggingServlet...

NOTE We can redirect logging information anywhere we would like to by changing the log4j configuration file.

We have now finished looking at the various aspects of configuring log4j. Starting with the next section, we will explore different log4j objects in detail.

Level Object

The `org.apache.log4j.Level` object replaces the `org.apache.log4j.Priority` object in previous versions of log4j. It denotes the priority or severity associated with a logging message. A `Logger` and `Appender` can have threshold levels associated with them. Logging messages get filtered according to how their levels compare to those of both the `Logger` and `Appender` objects. Hence, it is possible to turn off or on a certain level of logging by changing the levels associated with the `Logger` and these objects. The `Level` class defines the following levels:

- *ALL (lowest):* This level has the lowest possible rank and turns on the logging of all logging information.

- *DEBUG:* This level is used to print debugging information helpful in the development stage.

- *INFO:* This level is used to print informational messages that help us to determine the flow of control within an application.

- *ERROR:* This level is used for printing error-related messages.

- *WARN:* This level is used for printing information related to some faulty and unexpected behavior of the system that needs immediate attention to forestall malfunctioning of the application.

- *FATAL:* This level is used to print system-critical information about problems that are causing the application to crash.

- *OFF (highest):* This is the highest level, and using this level turns off all the logging information printing.

The levels have unique integer values attached to them and can be arranged from lowest to highest value as follows:

ALL<DEBUG<INFO<WARN<ERROR<FATAL<OFF

Logger Object

The `Logger` object is the main object that an application developer uses to log any message. Once the logging information is passed to a logger, the rest is done behind the scenes. `Logger` objects only encapsulate logging messages and do not have any knowledge about the destination or the formatting of those messages. This is where the `Appender` and `Layout` objects come into picture, as we will see later in this chapter.

The Logger objects acting within a particular instance of an application follow a parent-child hierarchy. To illustrate this concept, consider Figure 5-2.

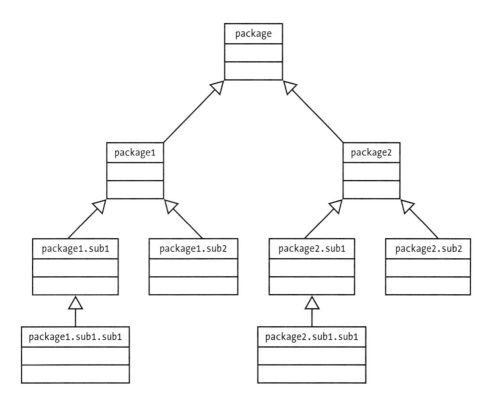

Figure 5-2. The parent-child relationship of Logger objects

At the top of the hierarchy exists a root logger. The root logger exists outside the scope of any custom logger hierarchy that we may come up with. It always exists as the root logger for all possible logger hierarchies, and it has no namespace. All the other application-specific Logger objects are child objects to the root logger. The parent-child relationship of loggers signifies the dependency and the separation of the loggers acting within the same application. It means that a child logger can inherit properties of its parent logger recursively up the tree. Typically, a child logger will inherit the following properties from its parent logger(s):

- Level: If the child logger has no explicit tree level specified, it will use the level of its immediate parent or the first proper level it finds recursively up the hierarchy.

- Appender: If there is no appender attached to a logger, then it uses the appender of its immediate parent logger or the first appender it finds recursively up the tree.

- ResourceBundle: ResourceBundles are key-value pattern properties files used for the localization of logging messages. A child logger also inherits any ResourceBundle specified with its parent logger.

This hierarchical relationship also means that when a child logger is using the properties of its parent logger, any change to the property of the parent logger will affect the behavior of the child logger. Changes to properties of child loggers, on the other hand, do not affect parent loggers. This parent-child relationship is dictated by the additivity property in the context of log4j.

By default, Logger objects have the additivity flag set to true. The additivity property can be disabled for a child logger by setting the additivity flag to false, in which case it will not inherit any of the parent logger's properties. This is controlled by the following method in the Logger object:

```
public boolean setAdditivity(boolean value)
```

or by setting the configuration as:

```
log4j.logger.loggerName.additivity=false
```

We can use various convenience methods of the Logger object to create new named loggers, obtain an existing named logger, and log messages at various levels of priority. The Logger class does not allow us to instantiate a new Logger instance, rather it provides two static methods for obtaining a Logger object instance:

```
public static Logger getRootLogger();
public static Logger getLogger(String name);
```

The first of these methods returns the root logger of the application instance. As said before, the root logger always exists and does not have a name. Any other named Logger object instance is obtained through the second method by passing the name of the logger. The name of the logger can be any arbitrary string. To make application logging more effective and self-explanatory, the naming of loggers plays an important role. Generally speaking, a Logger object should be given a name corresponding to the package it belongs to or a fully qualified class name from which the Logger instance is created. Again, this name can be strongly typed as a string containing the name of the package or the class. But a more flexible way of doing so is as depicted in the following example (which was also presented earlier in Listing 5-4):

```
Logger logger = Logger.getLogger(SimpleLogging.class.getPackage().getName());
```

This approach is refactoring proof in the sense that in the future if for any reason we decide to change the package structure, the logging code need not change. Clearly, you can see the benefit of this approach, as opposed to strongly typing the logger name, which is unlikely to render much benefit to the application.

NOTE   *Refactoring* is the process of improving the internal design of the code without affecting the external behavior of the code.

When a new `Logger` instance is created, the `LogManager` stores the instance in namespace storage with the namespace as the key. If during the course of the application we try to create the same `Logger` instance again, the existing instance is returned. In a real-life application, we would probably *not* use the root logger, but instead obtain our own named loggers. All the named loggers by default inherit the properties from the root logger recursively.

Logging Information

Once we obtain an instance of a named logger, we can use several methods of the logger to log messages. The `Logger` class has the following methods for printing the logging information. We have to remember that the `Logger` class inherits all these methods from the previous `Category` class. The methods inherited from the `Category` class will sometimes refer to another historic class, `Priority`, which is now replaced by the `Level` class. We can interchange the use of `Category` with `Logger` and `Priority` with `Level` without affecting any application integrity.

NOTE   As the `Logger` object has replaced the previous `Category` object, so too have some methods in the `Category` object been deprecated. We have to be cautious in using those methods and possibly avoid using any method directly from the `Category` class.

Level-Based Logging Methods

The methods listed in Table 5-1 are level-based logging methods in the sense that each method assigns a particular level to the message being logged.

Table 5-1. Logging Methods in the Logger Class

Method	Description
public void debug(Object message);	This method prints messages with the level Level.DEBUG.
public void error(Object message);	This method prints messages with the level Level.ERROR.
public void fatal(Object message);	This method prints messages with the level Level.FATAL.
public void info(Object message);	This method prints messages with the level Level.INFO.
public void warn(Object message);	This method prints messages with the level Level.WARN.

A similar set of methods exists with the message and an instance of the java.lang.Throwable object. The Throwable object denotes the error condition that should be logged and contains the stack trace of the application. The Throwable instance can be null. This set of methods helps us log any particularly erroneous situation arising within the application, and the stack trace enables us to determine the exact location of the error.

Localized Logging

One thing that makes the Java language so flexible is its localization feature. Apache log4j uses this feature to publish localized logging messages, which means application logging becomes language independent. This is done through a java.util.ResourceBundle object and by attaching separate locale-specific message properties files to the application.

The java.util.ResourceBundle is a technique to make our program language independent. With this technique at the simplest level, we use certain keys within our program. These keys map to certain messages (values) and are defined within a properties file. The ResourceBundle properties files are locale specific. For example, we can define messages in English and German in two separate properties files named "MyResources_en.properties" and "MyResources_de.properties". In the program we can use the ResourceBundle object with the name MyResource.properties. In a situation where the locale requires German, our program will automatically pick up the resource named MyResources_de.properties.

The `ResourceBundle` is specified by invoking the method `Logger.setResourceBundle(ResourceBundle name)`. It can also be set via the configuration file as follows:

`log4j.logger.loggerName.resourceBundle=resourceBundle name`

The `ResourceBundle` loads the locale-specific properties file containing the message key and the localized message value, which the application uses to publish messages. The `Logger` class provides the following methods for localized logging, and they accept the `Priority` or `Level` object of the logging message, the localization key, and a `Throwable` instance:

```
public void 17dlog(Priority p, String key, Throwable t);
public void 17dlog(Priority p, String key, Object params[], Throwable t);
```

The first method is a straightforward one. It looks for the localized message with "key" as the localization key. If the key cannot fetch any value from the `ResourceBundle`, then the key itself is used as the message string. The second method accepts an array of `Object`, which contains all the parameters to be localized. The formatting pattern is obtained that matches the key, and all the parameters passed in the array are localized using the `java.text.MessageFormat.format(String, Object[])` method.

Generic Logging

The `Logger` class also allows us to use generic logging methods in situations where the level of logging is not predefined. The following sets of methods are generic logging methods:

```
public void log(Priority p, Object message);
public void log(Priority p, Object message, Throwable t);
public void log(String fqcn, Priority p, Object message, Throwable t);
```

The first two methods are obvious in the sense that they accept the logging level and the message object as the argument and optionally a `java.lang.Throwable` instance. The last method is the most generic one, and it takes an extra argument, `fqcn`, which is the fully qualified name of the caller class. The generic logging methods are rarely used directly from an application. But any wrapper class in the `Logger` class may tend to use these generic methods internally to print logging information.

All the preceding methods accept a `java.lang.Object` as a parameter, which is the message to be printed. This potentially can represent any arbitrary object. The

Logger object passes this object to the associated Appender object(s), and Appender objects in turn pass the message to the Layout objects. The Layout objects will interpret the object and render it into a human-readable format. We will discuss this process with the help of org.apache.log4j.or.ObjectRenderer in Chapter 6.

Configuration Methods

The Logger class offers a couple of methods to configure the Logger instance. These methods can add or remove Appenders and can set the Level of the Logger instance.

```
public void addAppender(Appender appender)
public void removeAppender(Appender appender)
public void removeAppender(String name)
public void removeAllAppenders()
public void setLevel(Level level)
```

All these methods are very much self-explanatory. We must be careful in using these methods, as they override the default configuration.

CAUTION   You should not directly use these methods to set the configuration information, as doing so pretty much hard codes the configuration parameters with the source code. A better approach is to configure the Logger with the external configuration file.

Conditions of Successful Logging

Use of the logging methods does not guarantee that logging information will be published. Logging information is filtered through at various layers before it gets printed to a preferred destination, as you may recall from the discussion in the "Overview of the log4j Architecture" section. With respect to Logger, the main filtering happens at the logging levels. As discussed earlier, a logger will have its own level or will inherit the level of its immediate parent up in the logger hierarchy recursively. Any logging information will only be approved by a logger if and only if the level p associated with the logging message is equal to or greater than the level q assigned to the logger. In other words, if $p >= q$ is satisfied, the logger will approve the message and pass it on to the associated Appender objects.

Thus, if a Logger has a default level of WARN, any attempt to do logging with the info() method will not produce any logging information.

A Logger Example

The program shown in Listing 5-6, `LoggerDemo.java`, will demonstrate the basic logging methods and also experiment with localizing the logging information.

Listing 5-6. LoggerDemo.java

```java
package com.apress.logging.log4j;

import org.apache.log4j.*;

/** This class demonstrates the basic use of Logger class methods
 */
public class LoggerDemo {

    private static Logger logger =
Logger.getLogger(LoggerDemo.class.getPackage().getName());

    /** Creates a new instance of LoggerDemo */
    public LoggerDemo(String rbName) {
        //setting the use of parent handler to false
        logger.setAdditivity(false);
        logger.debug("Set the parent additivity to false...");
        logger.setResourceBundle(java.util.ResourceBundle.getBundle(rbName));
        logger.debug("Set the resource bundle...");

    }

    /** demonstrates the basic level based logging methods
     * @param name name to say hello to
     */
    public void doLogging(String name) {
        logger.debug("Entered the doLogging method..");
        String str = "Hello ";
        String output = null;

        if(name == null) {
            output = "Anonymous";
            logger.warn("No name passed, set to anonymous...");
        }else {
            output = str.concat(name);
            logger.info("Constructed the string object..."+output);
        }
```

```
        logger.info("printing the message...");
        logger.debug("Exiting the doLogging method...");
    }

    /** demonstrates the localized logging methods
     */
    public void doLocalizedLogging() {

        logger.l7dlog(Level.DEBUG, "Entry", null);
        logger.l7dlog(Level.DEBUG, "Exit", null);
    }

    public static void main(String args[]) {
        String name = args[0];
        String rbName = args[1];
        LoggerDemo demo = new LoggerDemo(rbName);
        demo.doLogging(name);
        demo.doLocalizedLogging();
    }
}
```

To execute this program, we use the same "log4j.properties" file described in Listing 5-3. First, we obtain a Logger instance with the name of the package of the LoggerDemo class as a class variable. In the constructor, we set the additivity property of this logger to false, which means that this logger will not forward any logging requests to its immediate parent logger. Next, we set the ResourceBundle for this logger, which will be used for the localization of the logging information. The doLogging() method uses several logging methods from the Logger class. Logging information with less severity is printed with the debug() method, and other important messages are printed with the info() and warn() methods of the Logger class.

The doLocalizedLogging() method simply prints two messages to demonstrate how a message passed to the logging methods is interpreted as the localization key and the corresponding message value is printed. Consider the following "logging_fr.properties" file containing the localization key and value:

Entry=Entrer
Exit=Sortir

When the l7dlog() method is called by passing the messages "Entry" and "Exit" respectively, the log4j framework looks into "logging_fr.properties" and prints the corresponding values as the logging information.

If we execute the program with the following command:

```
java -Dlog4j.configuration=log4j.properties
com.apress.logging.log4j.LoggerDemo sam logging_fr
```

we will see the following information being printed in the console:

```
DEBUG - Set the parent additivity to false...
DEBUG - Set the resource bundle...
DEBUG - Entered the doLogging method..
INFO - Constructed the string object...Hello sam
INFO - printing the message...
DEBUG - Exiting the doLogging method...
DEBUG - Entrer
DEBUG - Sortir
```

Notice that the last two lines of the logging message are printed as localized messages. The information with the level DEBUG is only intended to be printed during development to provide a better understanding of the control flow of the application. We can easily turn off DEBUG-level messages by changing the level in the "log4j.properties" file as follows:

```
log4j.logger.com.apress.logging.log4j=INFO,X
```

With the new level set to INFO, the logger will only print messages with a priority equal to or greater than INFO. If we reexecute the program with the preceding settings, we will see the following output to the console:

```
INFO - Constructed the string object...Hello sam
INFO - printing the message...
```

Notice that DEBUG-level messages are omitted this time.

LogManager Object

The `org.apache.log4j.LogManager` class manages the creation and storage of each named logger created from within an application. Internally it uses another helper class, `org.apache.log4j.Hierarchy`, to store the reference of each `Logger` object created. The hierarchy is such that every child logger created will have a pointer to its parent logger, but a parent logger will not have any reference to its child logger. Also, log4j does not restrict application developers from instantiating a child logger before its parent. In such scenarios, the child logger instance is created, and in the `Hierarchy` class it is stored with an empty node for the future assignment of a parent logger whenever it is created.

Application developers normally do not have to bother about using the `Hierarchy` class. Instead, they use the convenience methods provided by the `LogManager` and `Logger` classes to create and obtain any named logger. It is also interesting to note that when we change the property of any existing named logger, a new instance is never created. The existing reference is obtained from the `Hierarchy` class, and the properties are changed to that reference. This is the reason why methods in the `Logger` class such as

```
public void addAppender(Appender appender)
```

are `synchronized` in order to make sure that two threads do not operate on the same instance of a named logger at the same time.

The `LogManager` class provides the useful methods described in Table 5-2.

Table 5-2. Methods in the LogManager Class

Method	Description
`public static Enumeration getCurrentLoggers();`	This method returns an enumeration of the existing named loggers.
`public static Logger exists(String name);`	This method checks for the existence of a particular named logger.
`public static Logger getLogger(String name);`	This method obtains an existing named logger.

In the next section, we will explore the other aspects of log4j that help us deal with client-specific logging information.

Nested Diagnostic Context (NDC)

Logging is most useful in complex distributed applications. The majority of real-life complex distributed systems are multithreaded. A good example of such is a Web application written with Java servlet technology. Each servlet handles multiple clients at the same time, yet the logging code written within the servlet is the same. It is almost always required that the logging output of one client be differentiated from another. One approach is to execute a different logging thread per client. But this solution may not always be ideal. Another less complex approach may be to uniquely stamp each logging output with some client-specific information. This is where the *Nested Diagnostic Context* (NDC) comes into the picture.

The `NDC` class in log4j has the methods listed in Table 5-3 to manage the information in the `NDC` stack.

Table 5-3. Methods in the NDC Class

Method	Description
public static void pop();	This method is called when exiting a context.
public static void push(String message);	This method adds the diagnostic context for the current thread.
public static void remove();	This method is called when exiting a thread. It removes the diagnostic context for the particular thread.

Notice that all the methods in the NDC class are static. The NDC is managed per thread as a stack of contextual information. It is important to make sure that the remove() method of NDC is called when leaving the run() method of a thread. This ensures the garbage collection of the thread. Interestingly, a thread can inherit the NDC from another thread by calling the inherit(Stack stack) method of the NDC class. This is very useful when we want to compare the contextual information of two different threads.

Message Diagnostic Context (MDC)

The *Message Diagnostic Context* (MDC) is a mechanism to store client-specific data, using the java.util.Map format. The key of this Map can be replaced by its value in the conversion pattern specified with the Layout object used with an appender. The MDC class provides the methods in Table 5-4 to manipulate the key and the value stored within the Map.

Table 5-4. Methods in the MDC Class

Method	Description
public static Object get(String key);	This method retrieves the Object stored against the key.
public static void put(String key, Object o);	This method stores the Object o against the key.
public static void remove(String key)	This method removes the mapping of any Object with the key.

The following example will help illustrate the concepts associated with the MDC and NDC objects in a much clearer way. Imagine that we have a Java servlet program that is multithreaded and handles multiple clients at the same time. We might wish to stamp each logging output with some client-specific information such as the client's IP address. Let's modify the LoggingServlet.java (shown previously in Listing 5-5) to use MDC and NDC in order to separate out each logging output for each client request. To start, insert the following code within the doPost() method:

```java
public void doPost(HttpServletRequest req, HttpServletResponse res)
                  throws IOException, ServletException
{
    String remoteAddress = req.getRemoteAddr();
    String remoteHost = req.getRemoteHost();

    //pushing to NDC
    NDC.push(remoteHost);
    //mapping in MDC
    MDC.put("remoteAddress", remoteAddress);
    logger.info("invoked the LoggingServlet...");
    PrintWriter writer = res.getWriter();
    writer.println("Check your web server console...");
    writer.flush();
    writer.close();
}
```

In the preceding piece of code, we obtain the remote host name and the remote host address. The NDC contains the remote host name and the MDC contains the remote host address. Now we will modify the "log4j.properties" file as follows to change the conversion pattern used by the appender to display the MDC and NDC information:

```
log4j.appender.X.layout.conversionPattern=%x -%X{remoteAddress} %m%n
```

The %x displays the NDC information and %X{variable name} displays the MDC information. Note that the variable name specified within the MDC pattern has to match the variable name assigned within the code. Now the logging output will contain the NDC and MDC information as follows:

```
hostname1 - host address1 invoked the LoggingServlet...
hostname2 - host address2 invoked the LoggingServlet...
```

It is evident how useful the NDC and MDC information can be to distinguish the logging output although the same information is being printed.

Appender Object

The ability to filter logging information and using different methods in the Logger class is a great feature for application developers. But the Logger itself is not capable of printing logging messages. It does so with the help of Appender objects. Appender objects are primarily responsible for printing logging messages to different destinations such as consoles, files, sockets, NT event logs, etc. Occasionally, Appender objects can have Filter objects associated with them to make further decisions about the logging of a particular message.

The writing of information to the preferred destination attached to any particular appender can be synchronous or asynchronous depending on how the application developer uses the appender. It is a major benefit that Appender objects are quite flexible in terms of destination of the logging information. It is possible to create Appender objects to write to a database and JMS in order to achieve a distributed logging framework. We will discuss in this section the normal Appender objects capable of handling logging information within the same JVM context; the relevant distributed logging Appender objects appear later in Chapter 7. In the context of log4j, the class diagram in Figure 5-3 depicts the relationship of Appender objects and how they are organized.

Each Appender object has different properties associated with it, and these properties indicate the behavior of that object. In general, Appender objects will have the following properties:

- layout: Each Appender object needs to know how to format the logging information passed to it. It uses the Layout objects and the conversion pattern associated with them to format the logging information.

- target: Each Appender object will have a target destination attached to it. The target may be a console, a file, or other item depending on the appender.

- level: Each Appender object can have a threshold Level associated with it. Logging information is compared with the threshold level, and if the logging request level is equal to or greater than this threshold, the logging information is processed further; otherwise it is ignored.

- filter: It is possible to attach Filter objects to Appenders. The Filter objects can analyze logging information beyond level matching and decide whether logging requests should be handled by a particular Appender or ignored.

Depending on the type of Appender object, each Appender can have other special attributes. We will discuss each Appender object in upcoming sections, but first we will take a look at adding Appender objects to Logger objects.

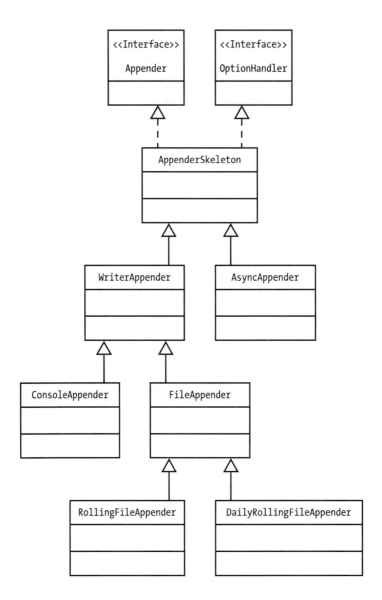

Figure 5-3. The Appender class hierarchy in log4j

Adding Appenders to Loggers

Logger objects require one or more Appender objects to be associated with them in order to print logging information to a particular destination. We can add an Appender object to a Logger with the following method:

```
public void addAppender(Appender appender);
```

or by including the following setting in the configuration file:

```
log4j.logger.loggerName.appender=appenderName
```

The addAppender() method adds an Appender to the Logger object. It is possible to add many Appender objects to a logger, each printing logging information to separate destinations. But there is an important point to be noted about adding Appenders to loggers: Appenders are additive. Each logging request to a logger will be forwarded to all the Appender objects associated with it and also to all the Appender objects associated with its parent loggers up in the logger hierarchy.

If you recall the discussion about the logger hierarchy in the "Logger Object" section, you have probably figure out that you can turn the additivity feature off by setting the additivity flag to false, which is done by calling the setAdditivity(Boolean flag). If the additivity flag is set to false, the logging information will only be forwarded to the Appender objects associated with a particular Logger object.

A Better Way of Adding Appenders to Loggers

Although it is perfectly feasible to add Appender objects with the addAppender() method of the Logger class, this hard codes the Logger and Appender relationship; as a result, future changes to this relationship mean changing the code, recompiling it, and then redeploying it. To avoid this undesirable situation, it is recommended you associate Appenders to Loggers via configuration properties.

Referring back to the "log4j.properties" configuration file (Listing 5-1), note that we have attached a ConsoleAppender to the root logger. In real life, this approach is much more flexible and maintainable, as the configuration can be changed when needed without changing the code (and even without redeploying the application if we have included ConfigureAndWatch with the Configurator classes).

Logger to Appender Collaboration

So far we have seen how Logger objects encapsulate logging information and how different Appender objects are capable of printing logging information to different destinations. But how do Logger objects pass logging information to Appender objects? Creating an intermediate link object named LoggingEvent does the trick. The org.apache.log4j.spi.LoggingEvent class encapsulates all the relevant logging information such as the fully qualified name of the caller class, the level of the logging message, the message itself, the Logger instance, the timestamp, and optionally a java.lang.Throwable instance. Before proceeding to hand over the logging request to any associated `Appender`, the `Logger` creates an instance of the `LoggingEvent` object with the logging-related information.

The `Logger` object then calls the `doAppend(LoggingEvent event)` method of the `Appender` objects. Notice from the `Appender` class diagram shown earlier in Figure 5-3 that all the `Appender` objects inherit from the base class `AppenderSkeleton`. The `doAppend()` method is in reality implemented within the `AppenderSkeleton` class and inherited by all other `Appender` objects. It is important to note that the `doAppend()` method is `synchronized`, which means publishing of the logging event happens in a synchronous manner. Therefore, log4j is thread-safe.

The `doAppend()` method performs some crucial checks on the logging request such as comparing the requested logging level with the threshold level of any `Appender` associated with the `Logger`, checking if the `Appender` is open, and also checking any associated `Filter` object with the `Appender`. If it finds a `Filter` object, it invokes that `Filter` object to make further decisions about the logging request. Once approved, the `append()` method of the associated subclass `Appender` object takes over and publishes the logging information.

WriterAppender

`WriterAppender` is a high-level `Appender` object that extends the `org.apache.log4j.AppenderSkeleton` object and writes logging information to a `java.io.Writer` object or `java.io.OutputStream` object depending on whether the application developer using this appender has set the target to either a `Writer` object or an `OutputStream` object. The `WriterAppender` class can have the following properties:

- `immediateFlush`: This property indicates if the output stream should be flushed each time there is a request to write certain logging information. By default, this option is set to `true`. If the flag is set to `false`, then the underlying stream can defer the writing of logging information to physical media to a later time

- `encoding`: It is possible to use any encoding scheme for writing logging information. By default, `WriterAppender` uses the system-specific encoding scheme.

- `threshold`: This denotes the cutoff level of logging for `WriterAppender`. Any logging request with a level below this level will be ignored. There is no threshold level set as default, which means that level filtering is not active for this `Appender` object.

- `target`: This specifies any `java.io.Writer` object or `java.io.OutputStream` object.

NOTE Flushing the stream for every logging request is costly and can slow up performance by 10 to 20 percent, but it guarantees that all the information is logged. If the immediateFlush property is set to false, then there is chance that some logging information will be missing if there is an arbitrary exit from the application or the application crashes.

The WriterAppender class has the constructors shown in Table 5-5.

Table 5-5. Constructors in the WriterAppender Class

Constructor	Description
public WriterAppender();	This is the default constructor.
public WriterAppender(Layout layout, OutputStream os)	This constructor accepts a given Layout and constructs an OutputStreamWriter object with the given OutputStream.
public WriterAppender(Layout layout, Writer writer)	This constructor accepts the given Layout and the output destination as the Writer object.

The principal method in the WriterAppender class is

public void append(LoggingEvent event);

This serves as the entry point for this WriterAppender. Whenever a logging request is made via the append() method, it invokes the protected boolean checkEntryConditions () method to check if the conditions for logging are valid. It also checks if there is a set output target and a layout attached to it. If these conditions are not met, then the writing operation returns and prints the appropriate error message to the console. Remember that threshold-level checking and any filtering of the logging request through any of the associated Filter objects has already been done by the base class, AppenderSkeleton, before the request has been delegated to any particular Appender object. Otherwise, if everything is appropriate, it proceeds to write the logging information to the associated target.

WriterAppender again has two subclasses, ConsoleAppender and FileAppender, which write to a console and any file object respectively. In real life, we will hardly use WriterAppender directly. Instead, we will use one of the subclasses as described next.

153

ConsoleAppender

org.apache.log4j.ConsoleAppender is a very simple class designed to write logging information to either System.out or System.err. It extends the org.apache.log4j.WriterAppender class. Any logging application intended to print logging information to a console should use this Appender. Interestingly, it overrides the closeWriter() method from its superclass, WriterAppender, and does nothing, as the console stream should not be closed. It has the following properties:

- immediateFlush: This flag is by default set to true, which results in the console stream being flushed with each logging output request.

- encoding: It is possible to use any character encoding scheme, but the default is the platform-specific encoding scheme.

- threshold: This is the cutoff logging level. Any logging request with a level below the threshold will be ignored. There is no default threshold level specified.

- target: The target destination of the logging output—either System.out or System.err. The default is System.out.

FileAppender

org.apache.log4j.FileAppender extends the org.apache.log4j.WriterAppender class and provides the facility to write logging information to a file. FileAppender is flexible in terms of how information should be logged to the destination file. It can enable buffered writing, append or overwrite information to the same file, and roll the filenames depending on data and time. It has the following properties:

- immediateFlush: This flag is by default set to true, which results in the output stream to the file being flushed with each append operation.

- encoding: It is possible to use any character encoding scheme, but the default is the platform-specific encoding scheme.

- threshold: This is the cutoff logging level. Any logging request with a level below the threshold will be ignored. There is no default threshold level specified.

- fileName: The name of the file to which the logging information will be written. The filename can be specified with a UNIX-style variable name such as ${user.home}/log.out, which means the location of the file "log.out" should be in the system-specific "user.home" directory.

- fileAppend: This is by default set to true, which results in the logging information being appended to the end of the same file.

- bufferedIO: This flag indicates whether we need buffered writing enabled. It is set to false by default.

- bufferSize: If bufferedI/O is enabled, this indicates the buffer size.

Table 5-6 lists the constructors for the FileAppender class.

Table 5-6. Constructors in the FileAppender Class

Constructor	Description
public FileAppender()	The default constructor
public FileAppender(Layout layout, String fileName);	The constructor with the layout information and the name of the file
public FileAppender(Layout layout, String fileName, boolean append);	Same as the previous constructor, with an additional Boolean flag for append mode.
public FileAppender(Layout layout, String fileName, boolean append, boolean bufferedIO, int bufferSize);	Constructor with all the parameters set

FileAppender delegates the printing of logging information to its superclass, WriterAppender. Interestingly, it sets the Writer object of the WriterAppender to a custom writer, org.apache.log4j.helpers.QuietWriter. The QuietWriter is a normal java.io.Writer except that it does not throw any exception if there is a problem in I/O operation. Instead, it passes the problem to an org.apache.log4j.spi.ErrorHandler type of object. The ErrorHandler is declared as an interface; one concrete implementation of this interface is org.apache.log4j.helpers.OnlyOnceErrorHandler. The OnlyOnceErrorHandler only logs the first error message to System.err and silently ignores the rest. This is helpful to avoid flooding of the logging destination with error messages.

The configuration parameters of the FileAppender class can be set via the methods inherited from the AppenderSkeleton class. However, as mentioned previously, this ties up the code with the configuration information. It is recommended that you separate the configuration information from the source code and specify this information through the configuration file settings. For example, a configuration file can set the FileAppender-specific configuration information in the following manner:

```
log4j.appender.dest = org.apache.log4j.FileAppender
#set the name of the file
log4j.appender.dest.File=${user.home}/log.out
#setting the immediate flush to true (default)
log4j.appender.dest.ImmediateFlush=true
#setting the threshold
log4j.appender.dest.Threshold=ERROR
#setting the append to false, overwrite
log4j.appender.dest.Append=false
```

This configuration file configures an appender named `dest`. The appender `dest` is set to be a `FileAppender` object. The configuration file then sets different properties for this `FileAppender` object.

RollingFileAppender

`org.apache.log4j.RollingFileAppender` extends the `FileAppender` class. It writes the log information to a specified file, but writes, or *rolls over*, to a secondary file when the primary file reaches a certain size. The `RollingFileAppender` has the following properties in addition to all the properties inherited from the `FileAppender` class.

- `maxFileSize`: This is the critical size of the file above which the file will be rolled. The default maximum file size is 10MB.

- `maxBackupIndex`: This property denotes the number of backup files to be created. It defaults to one backup file.

The `RollingFileAppender` class has the constructors listed in Table 5-7.

Table 5-7. Constructors in the RollingFileAppender Class

Constructor	Description
`public RollingFileAppender()`	This is the default constructor, which internally calls the default constructor of the `FileAppender` class.
`public RollingFileAppender(Layout layout, String fileName) throws IOException`	This constructor instantiates the `FileAppender` object with the given filename. By default, it will append the log information to the given file.
`public RollingFileAppender(Layout layout, String fileName, boolean append) throws IOException`	This constructor accepts the `Layout`, the filename and the `append` property. If the `append` property is `true`, it appends the log information to the file until it reaches the maximum size.

The `RollingFileAppender` class has several useful methods to control its behavior, and these appear in Table 5-8.

Table 5-8. Methods in the RollingFileAppender Class

Method	Description
`public void rollOver()`	This method performs the usual rollover operation. The rollover operation is activated when the maximum file size is reached or can be forced at any stage of the operation by the application developer. When called: If the `maxBackupIndex` is >0, then the file "log.1" is renamed as "log.2" and so on for keeping backups. The "log.1" file is then closed, and a new file "log.2" is opened to log the next bit of information. If the `maxBackupIndex` = 0; then the log file is truncated as soon as the maximum file size is reached with no backup file created.
`public void setMaxBackupIndex(int maxBackupIndex)`	This method, which takes a positive value, sets the maximum backup index after which the oldest backup file will be erased. If set to zero, no backup file will be created.
`public void setMaxFileSize(long size)`	This method is the same as the previous method, except it accepts the file size as a long value.
`public void setMaxFileSize(String size)`	This method takes the maximum file size after which the file will be rolled over. We can specify the file size with the suffix "KB", "MB", etc. to indicate kilobytes and megabytes. For example, we can specify a 20-megabyte file size with "20MB".
`public void subAppend(LoggingEvent event)`	This is the overridden method from the superclass `WriterAppender`, and it implements the bulk of the writing to a rolling file.

The following properties file demonstrates how to configure the `RollingFileAppender` properties:

```
log4j.appender.dest = org.apache.log4j.RollingFileAppender
#set the name of the file
log4j.appender.dest.File=${user.home}/log.out
#setting the immediate flush to true (default)
log4j.appender.dest.ImmediateFlush=true
#setting the threshold
log4j.appender.dest.Threshold=ERROR
#setting the append to false, overwrite
log4j.appender.dest.Append=false
#set the maximum file size before roll over
log4j.appender.dest.MaxFileSize=10KB
#set the backup index
log4j.appender.dest.MaxBackupIndex=2
```

This configuration file defines a `RollingFileAppender` named `dest`. It then sets the other configuration parameters for this appender.

DailyRollingFileAppender

Size-based rolling of log files is good for managing a huge amount of logging data and spreading it across multiple files. But in real life, when applications are running day after day, we need to implement some daily-based logging capacity. The `org.apache.log4j.DailyRollingFileAppender` object does this for us. It extends the `FileAppender` class and inherits all its properties. The rolling of the file is accomplished with a `DatePattern` configuration parameter. `DatePattern` indicates when to roll over the file and the naming convention to be followed. For example, a `DailyRollingFileAppender` configured with the `DatePattern '.' yyyy-MM-dd` will end up in log files being renamed as "log.out-2002-09-17" on September 17, 2002, at midnight and the logging will continue to a file named "log.out".

`DatePattern` follows the `java.text.SimpleDateFormat` object formatting style. It is possible to define the exact date and time of file rolling through `DatePattern`. Table 5-9 demonstrates how `DatePattern` is used to control the rollover schedule assuming that the log filename is set to "log.out".

NOTE Do not use ":" anywhere in `DatePattern`. The ":" character is used to specify a protocol, which is not exactly what we want to do with date formats.

Table 5-9. DatePattern Conventions

DatePattern	Rollover Schedule	Example
`'.' yyyy-MM`	Roll over at the end of each month and beginning of the next month	The log file will be rolled over to "log.out-2002-05" on May 31, 2002, and similarly will be rolled over to "log.out.2002-09" on September 30, 2002.
`'.' yyyy-MM-dd`	Roll over at midnight each day	On September 30, 2002, at midnight, the "log.out" file will be rolled over to "log.out.2002-09-30".
`'.' yyyy-MM-dd-a`	Roll over at midday and midnight of each day	On September, 30, 2002, at midday, the "log.out" file will be rolled over to "log.out-2002-09-30-AM", and at midnight that file will in turn be rolled over to "log.out.2002-09-30-PM".
`'.' yyyy-MM-dd-HH`	Roll over at the top of every hour.	On September 30, 2002, at 10:00:000 hour, the "log.out" file will be rolled over to "log.out.2002-09-30-09". Notice that it is prefixed with the previous hour.
`'.' yyyy-MM-dd-HH-mm`	Roll over at every minute.	On September 30, 2002 at 10:20:000, the "log.out" file will be rolled over to "log.out.2002-09-30-10-19".
`'.' yyyy-ww`	Roll over on the first day of each week depending upon the locale	If the first day of the week is Monday, then at midnight on Sunday, December 28, the "log.out" file will be rolled over to "log.out.2002-52".

The `DailyRollingFilteAppender` has two constructors. The first is a do-nothing default constructor:

```
public void DailyRollingFileAppender()
```

The second, shown in the following line of code, accepts the `Layout`, the filename, and the `DatePattern` to be used for the rollover:

```
public void DailyRollingFileAppender(Layout layout, String fileName,
String datePattern)
```

The `subAppend(LoggingEvent event)` method is overridden from the `WriterAppender` class, and it implements the daily rolling activity.

As we can see, the `DailyRollingFileAppender` is a very powerful mechanism to obtain fine-grained control over the logging process. In real life, how the logging information is organized is as equally important as which information is logged. The `DailyRollingFileAppender` can prove very helpful in publishing logging information on an hourly, daily, and monthly basis, which helps analyze application performance to a great extent without your having to deal with too much or too old information.

The following properties file demonstrates how to configure a `DailyRollingFileAppender`:

```
log4j.appender.dest = org.apache.log4j.DailyRollingFileAppender
#set the name of the file
log4j.appender.dest.File=${user.home}/log.out
#setting the immediate flush to true (default)
log4j.appender.dest.ImmediateFlush=true
#setting the threshold
log4j.appender.dest.Threshold=ERROR
#setting the append to false, overwrite
log4j.appender.dest.Append=false
#set the DatePattern
log4j.appender.dest.DatePattern='.' yyyy-MM-dd
```

This configuration file defines the configuration parameters for a `DailyRollingFileAppender` object. The `DatePattern` conversion pattern will follow the convention defined in Table 5-9.

File-Based Logging Example

The program shown later in this section, FileBasedLoggingDemo.java, will demonstrate how the different file-based Appender objects handle logging information. We have seen that the file-based Appender objects can write data to a file and roll the logging output file daily or after a specified period. In order to demonstrate how different files are rolled, in the following example we will see how to create a thread that will log messages to the file in a repeated manner. We will also see how to create a configuration file defining all the required logger, appender, and layout information. The properties file "file_logging.properties", which appears in Listing 5-7, defines the properties required for this file-based logging example.

Listing 5-7. file_logging.properties

```
#set the level of the root logger to DEBUG (the lowest level)
#and set its appenders named DEBUG and CONSOLE
log4j.rootLogger = DEBUG, CONSOLE

#set your own logger
log4j.logger.com.apress.logging.log4j=DEBUG, FILE,ROLLING, DAILY

#set the appender CONSOLE
log4j.appender.CONSOLE=org.apache.log4j.ConsoleAppender

#set the appender FILE
log4j.appender.FILE=org.apache.log4j.FileAppender
log4j.appender.FILE.File=${user.home}/out.log

#set the appender ROLLING
log4j.appender.ROLLING=org.apache.log4j.RollingFileAppender
log4j.appender.ROLLING.File=${user.home}/rolling.log
log4j.appender.ROLLING.MaxFileSize=1KB

#set the appender DAILY
log4j.appender.DAILY=org.apache.log4j.DailyRollingFileAppender
log4j.appender.DAILY.File=${user.home}/daily.log
log4j.appender.DAILY.DatePattern='.' yyyy-MM-dd-HH-mm

#set the layout for the appenders
log4j.appender.CONSOLE.layout=org.apache.log4j.PatternLayout
log4j.appender.CONSOLE.layout.conversionPattern=%p - %m%n

log4j.appender.FILE.layout=org.apache.log4j.PatternLayout
log4j.appender.FILE.layout.conversionPattern=%p - %m%n
```

```
log4j.appender.ROLLING.layout=org.apache.log4j.PatternLayout
log4j.appender.ROLLING.layout.conversionPattern=%p - %m%n

log4j.appender.DAILY.layout=org.apache.log4j.PatternLayout
log4j.appender.DAILY.layout.conversionPattern=%p - %m%n
```

The destination files are defined in the configuration file "file_logging.properties", and the location of the files is defined by ${user.home}, which means the log files will be created in the location user.home system property.

Now that we have seen the properties required for the file-based logging example, let's take a look at FileBasedLoggingDemo.java, shown in Listing 5-8.

Listing 5-8. FileBasedLoggingDemo.java

```
package com.apress.logging.log4j;

import org.apache.log4j.*;

public class FileBasedLoggingDemo implements Runnable{

    private static Logger logger =
Logger.getLogger(FileBasedLoggingDemo.class.getPackage().getName());
    /** Creates a new instance of FileBasedLoggingDemo */
    public FileBasedLoggingDemo()
    {
    }

    /** This method is called by the application. This method creates
     * a new thread to start logging
     */
    public void doLogging()
    {
        Thread t = new Thread(this);
        t.start();
    }


    /** The thread's run() method, which does repeated logging
     * at an interval of 60secs.
     */
    public void run()
    {
        int count=1;
        while(true) {
            //logging information
```

```
            try {
                logger.debug("Logging the information..."+count);
                Thread.sleep(60*1000);
                count++;
            }catch(Exception e) {
                logger.warn("Exception occured", e);
            }
        }
    }
    /** the main method
     */
    public static void main(String args[])
    {
        FileBasedLoggingDemo demo = new FileBasedLoggingDemo();
        demo.doLogging();
    }
}
```

This program will publish logging information to three different files—"out.log", "rolling.log", and "daily.log"—through three different appenders—FILE, ROLLING, and DAILY, respectively. The `DailyRollingFileAppender` is configured to log information and roll at every minute. All the appenders have the `append` property set to `true` and will append any logging message to the same file until the rollover criteria is reached. When executed, this program will create files like the following in the location defined by the `user.home` system property:

Filename	Description
daily.log. 2002-09-30-21-35	Logged on September 30, 2002 at 21:35
daily.log. 2002-09-30-21-36	Logged on September 30, 2002 at 21:36
out.log	Normal log file
rolling.log	Initial rolling file
rolling.log.1	Rollover file once the maximum file size is reached

AsyncAppender

When an application produces a huge amount of logging information, it may be critical to produce logging messages asynchronously, which might improve performance by a considerable amount. As mentioned in our discussion of the previous `Appender` objects, the `doAppend()` method is `synchronized`. This might reduce performance when thousands of `Logger` objects are trying to use the same `Appender` object to print logging information. The `AsyncAppender` object uses a bounded buffer to store logging events. Once the size limit of the buffer is reached, the logging events are dispatched to specific `Appender` objects. It is possible to attach multiple `Appender` objects to `AsyncAppender`. The `AsyncAppender` object uses a separate thread for each `LoggingEvent` object contained in the buffer.

The `org.apache.log4j.AysncAppender` class extends the `org.apache.log4j.AppenderSkeleton` class and also implements an interface, `org.apache.log4j.spi.AppenderAttachable`. The interface `AppenderAttachable` defines a set of methods that any object accepting an `Appender` object should implement. The set of methods includes those for attaching and removing `Appender` objects to the class. By default, the `AsyncAppender`'s buffer size can contain 128 `LoggingEvent` objects. Until release 1.2.6 of log4j, `AsyncAppender` could only be configured by `DOMConfigurator` through an XML-style configuration file.

Listing 5-9 demonstrates the XML configuration file for `AsyncAppender`. The configuration defines a `ConsoleAppender` as the target `Appender` for the defined `AsyncAppender`. The `ConsoleAppender` is given a `PatternLayout` with a conversion pattern to format the logging message. The named logger `com.apress.logging.log4j` and the root logger both use the appender named `ASYNC` to implement asynchronous logging.

Listing 5-9. async.xml

```
<?xml version="1.0" encoding="UTF-8"?>
<!DOCTYPE log4j:configuration SYSTEM "log4j.dtd">

<log4j:configuration xmlns:log4j="http://jakarta.apache.org/log4j/"
debug="true">

  <appender name="ASYNC" class="org.apache.log4j.AsyncAppender">
        <appender-ref ref="CONSOLE"/>
  </appender>

  <appender name="CONSOLE" class="org.apache.log4j.ConsoleAppender">
   <layout class="org.apache.log4j.PatternLayout">
        <param name="ConversionPattern"
                        value="%d %-5p [%t]  - %m%n"/>
   </layout>
  </appender>
       <logger name="com.apress.logging.log4j" additivity="false">
                <level value="debug"/>
                <appender-ref ref="ASYNC"/>
          </logger>
```

```
  <root>
   <priority value="debug"/>
   <appender-ref ref="ASYNC"/>
  </root>
</log4j:configuration>
```

The program in Listing 5-10, AsyncLogging.java, uses the "async.xml" file defined in Listing 5-9 as its configuration source. This example simply sets the buffer size for the AsyncAppender being used to 4. The AsyncAppender will not print any message so long as the number of logging events is less than the buffer size. Once the number of logging events exceeds the buffer size, the buffer is flushed and all the messages will be printed.

Listing 5-10. AsyncLogging.java

```
package com.apress.logging.log4j;

import org.apache.log4j.*;
import org.apache.log4j.xml.DOMConfigurator;
public class AsyncLogging
{

    //private static Logger logger
    Logger.getLogger(AsyncLogging.class.getPackage().getName());
        private AsyncAppender asyncAppender = null;
    private ConsoleAppender consoleAppender = null;

    /** Creates a new instance of AsyncLogging */
    public AsyncLogging()
    {

        try {
            logger.setAdditivity(false);
            asyncAppender =
(AsyncAppender)logger.getRootLogger().getAppender("ASYNC");
            asyncAppender.setBufferSize(4);
        }catch(Exception e) {
            System.out.println("error: "+e.toString());
        }

    }

    /** This method simply logs the messages
     */
```

```
    public void doLogging()
    {
        logger.debug("Hello 1");
        logger.debug("Hello 2");
        logger.debug("Hello 3");
        //logger.debug("Hello 4");
        //logger.debug("Hello 5");
    }

    /** the main method
     */
    public static void main(String args[])
    {
        AsyncLogging demo = new AsyncLogging();
        demo.doLogging();
    }
}
```

Executing this program will not produce any logging messages, as the buffer size for the `AsyncAppender` is set to 4, and we are only logging 3 events. If we uncomment the two other logging events, numbered 4 and 5, and we will see these messages printed in the console as follows:

```
2002-10-13 14:05:34,198 DEBUG [main]  - Hello 1
2002-10-13 14:05:34,218 DEBUG [main]  - Hello 2
2002-10-13 14:05:34,218 DEBUG [main]  - Hello 3
2002-10-13 14:05:34,218 DEBUG [main]  - Hello 4
2002-10-13 14:05:34,218 DEBUG [main]  - Hello 5
```

Filter Object

The process of making decisions about printing the logging information associated with each logging request is known as filtering. The decision whether to accept or reject a particular logging request can be taken at several stages of the whole logging process. Typically, the application developer can decide whether to log certain information and reject the rest. From the point of view of log4j, the filtering of log requests can be based on the level or any other application-specific criteria.

The `Filter` objects help to filter logging requests by analyzing the information encapsulated within the `LoggingEvent` object. `org.apache.log4j.spi.Filter` is an abstract class and the base class for all other `Filter` objects that can be present within the log4j framework. It defines an abstract method, `public int decide(LoggingEvent event)`, that is overridden by all the `Filter` subclasses. The `decide()` method does the analysis on the LoggingEvent object and returns an integer value indicating the result of the analysis. The Filter objects are organized in a linear chain in a sequential manner, and they are invoked sequentially. It is possible to add or remove any Filter object from the chain.

The filtering process within log4j typically follows these steps:

1. The application makes a logging request by invoking one of the logging methods of the Logger object.

2. The Logger object internally constructs a LoggingEvent object by encapsulating the logging message and other logging-related information.

3. The Logger object then passes the LoggingEvent object to any Appender object associated with it.

4. The Appender object then passes the LoggingEvent object to any of the Filter objects associated with it.

5. The Filter objects decide on the validity of the logging request based on any predefined criteria and return an integer value indicating the result of the analysis. Each Filter object can possibly return three integer values:

    • If the integer value DENY is returned, then the logging request is stopped without passing it to any other Filter object in the chain.

    • If the integer value ACCEPT is returned, the logging request is accepted, and logging information is published without consulting any other Filter in the chain.

    • If the integer value NEUTRAL is returned, the next Filter in the chain is consulted.

6. If there are no more Filter objects in the chain, then the log event is logged.

The Filter objects are configurable only through DOMConfigurator. However, the PropertyConfigurator object does not support DOMConfigurator at the moment, which means these objects can only be configured through an XML configuration file instead of a properties-style configuration file. But it is possible to instantiate a Filter object and add it to the filter chain using the addFilter(Filter filter) method of any Appender object.

In the "A Complete Example" section, we will see an example of using log4j in a real-life application. In the example, we will all also see how custom `Filter` objects can be used effectively to achieve desired logging activity.

Layout Object

As we have learned in the previous sections, `Logger` objects and `Appender` objects are the heart and soul of the log4j framework. Those objects capture the logging request and encapsulate the logging information, and are capable of sending the logging output to various destinations. But in order to convert logging information to any human-readable pattern, `Appender` objects use `Layout` objects to format the logging information. The layout of the logging information is quite important in the light of future analysis of this information. We will discuss in great detail the different `Layout` objects available in log4j in Chapter 6.

ObjectRenderer

The logging information that we intend to publish can be of various types and in various formats. Typically, in an object-oriented application where several objects hold data and interact with each other, more often than not we need to publish whole objects and their contents in a human-readable format. Inspecting the current status of the object and the attribute values a particular object holds makes it easier to understand how that object is behaving in response to certain messages sent to it and possible to define the corrective actions required in case it is not behaving appropriately.

In the context of log4j, a `Logger` class has several logging methods, all of which can accept an `Object` argument as the logging message. This `Object` argument can be a simple `String` representing the exact text information we wish to publish or a custom `Object` such as a `Customer`, a `Person`, etc. When we pass a custom `Object` to be logged, the intention is to publish the state and the content of the object. The `org.apache.log4j.or.ObjectRenderer` interface defines the way to associate any `ObjectRenderer` with any `Object` and obtain a `String` representation of the content of the object.

`Layout` objects call the `ObjectRenderer` to obtain a `String` representation of the `Object` content before they attempt to format the `Object` argument passed to the `Logger`. If the message argument is passed to the `Logger` is a `String`, no `ObjectRenderer` is required to convert the message, and the `Layout` object processes the message.

The `ObjectRenderer` objects can only be configured with `DOMConfigurator` and thereby can be defined in an XML-style configuration file. The configuration information of a `ObjectRenderer` defines the rendering class, which is an implementation of the `org.apache.log4j.or.ObjectRenderer` interface, and also defines the rendered class, which is the custom `Object` that needs to be rendered as a `String` representation. The section "A Complete Example" will demonstrate the use of a custom `ObjectRenderer`.

A Complete log4j Example

To reinforce the concepts we have discussed thus far, let's consider an application dealing with several customer orders. The application processes the orders and sends appropriate responses back to the customers. All the orders processed by the system are logged and can be used for future reference. Let's also assume that the system requires flexibility in terms of logging such that it can decide to log only orders with product codes falling within a certain range. The application will typically pass to the logging framework the order information to be printed. From a design point of view, the application will need to keep the logging methods generic and will have configurable appenders, filters, layouts, etc.

The application will use certain `Logger(s)`, each of which will have its own set of appenders, filters, and layouts. It will be possible to change logging behavior completely by switching the `Logger` being used or by changing the associated appenders, filters, and layouts. This design will offer more flexibility for and maintainability of the system. From the logging point of view, this system will need the following objects to be in place:

- `CustomerOrder`: This object will hold the basic information about the order each customer is placing.

- `OrderRenderer`: This object is capable of rendering the `CustomerOrder` object as a `String` representation.

- `ProductFilter`: This object is capable of filtering the logging information based on a predefined product code range.

Listing 5-11, `CustomerOrder.java`, represents the business object holding the customer order information.

Listing 5-11. CustomerOrder.java

```java
package com.apress.business;

public class CustomerOrder {

    /** Holds value of property productName. */
    private String productName;

    /** Holds value of property productCode. */
    private int productCode;

    /** Holds value of property productPrice. */
    private int productPrice;

    /** Creates a new instance of CustomerOrder */
    public CustomerOrder() {
    }

    public CustomerOrder(String name, int code, int price)
    {
        this.productCode = code;
        this.productPrice = price;
        this.productName = name;
    }


    /** Getter for property productName.
     * @return Value of property productName.
     */
    public String getProductName() {
        return this.productName;
    }

    /** Setter for property productName.
     * @param productName New value of property productName.
     */
    public void setProductName(String productName) {
        this.productName = productName;
    }

    /** Getter for property productCode.
     * @return Value of property productCode.
     */
```

```java
    public int getProductCode() {
        return this.productCode;
    }

    /** Setter for property productCode.
     * @param productCode New value of property productCode.
     */
    public void setProductCode(int productCode) {
        this.productCode = productCode;
    }

    /** Getter for property productPrice.
     * @return Value of property productPrice.
     */
    public int getProductPrice() {
        return this.productPrice;
    }

    /** Setter for property productPrice.
     * @param productPrice New value of property productPrice.
     */
    public void setProductPrice(int productPrice) {
        this.productPrice = productPrice;
    }
}
```

The program in Listing 5-12, ProductFilter.java, demonstrates the custom Filter object. The ProductFilter object overrides the decide(LoggingEvent event) method from the Filter class and inspects the product code of the CustomerOrder. If the product code is greater than 100, ProductFilter accepts the logging request or else denies it. If the object passed to ProductFilter is not an instance of the CustomerOrder, it remains neutral and allows the framework to invoke the next filter in the chain.

Listing 5-12. ProductFilter.java

```java
package com.apress.logging.log4j.filter;

import org.apache.log4j.spi.Filter;
import org.apache.log4j.spi.LoggingEvent;
import com.apress.business.CustomerOrder;

public class ProductFilter extends Filter
{
```

```java
/** Creates a new instance of ProductFilter */
public ProductFilter() {
}

public int decide(LoggingEvent event)
{
    int result=this.ACCEPT;
    //obtaining the message object passed through Logger
    Object message = event.getMessage();
    //checking if the message object is of correct type
    if(message instanceof CustomerOrder)
    {
        CustomerOrder order = (CustomerOrder)message;
        int productCode = order.getProductCode();
        //checking for the product code greater than 100 only
        if(productCode<100)
        {
            result = this.DENY;
        }
    }else
    {
        //this filter can ignore this, pass to next filter
        result = this.NEUTRAL;
    }

    return result;
    }
}
```

Once the `ProductFilter` approves the logging request, the logging event is passed to the associated `Appender` object. The `Appender` object will then pass the event to the associated `Layout` object, which then tries to render the logging message object into a `String` representation before formatting it according to any conversion pattern. In order for the `Layout` objects to successfully render the message, we need to have an `ObjectRenderer` for the `CustomerOrder` object. The program in Listing 5-13, `OrderRenderer.java`, implements the `ObjectRenderer` interface and provides an implementation of the `doRender(Object obj)` method. To keep the example simple, it returns a hyphen-separated list of the attribute values of the `CustomerOrder` object.

Listing 5-13. OrderRenderer.java

```java
package com.apress.logging.log4j.renderer;

import org.apache.log4j.or.ObjectRenderer;
import com.apress.business.CustomerOrder;

public class OrderRenderer implements ObjectRenderer
{
    private static final String separator = "-";

    /** Creates a new instance of OrderRenderer */
    public OrderRenderer() {
    }

    public String doRender(Object obj)
    {
        StringBuffer buffer = new StringBuffer(50);
        CustomerOrder order = null;
        String productName = null;
        int productCode = 0;
        int productPrice = 0;
        //check if the instance is of correct type CustomerOrder
        if(obj instanceof CustomerOrder)
        {
            order = (CustomerOrder)obj;
            productName = order.getProductName();
            productCode = order.getProductCode();
            productPrice = order.getProductPrice();

            buffer.append(productName);
            buffer.append(separator);
            buffer.append(new Integer(productCode).toString());
            buffer.append(separator);
            buffer.append(new Integer(productPrice).toString());
        }

        return buffer.toString();
    }
}
```

Now, once we have all the objects ready, we need to pass the object hierarchy to the log4j framework. As discussed before, the `ObjectRenderer` can only be configured through `DOMConfigurator`, and we will define the logger configuration through an XML-style configuration file. Listing 5-14 shows the configuration file used for this example, "filter_properties.xml".

Listing 5-14. filter_properties.xml

```xml
<?xml version="1.0" encoding="UTF-8"?>
<!DOCTYPE log4j:configuration SYSTEM "log4j.dtd">

<log4j:configuration xmlns:log4j="http://jakarta.apache.org/log4j/">

 <renderer renderedClass="com.apress.business.CustomerOrder"
renderingClass="com.apress.logging.log4j.renderer.OrderRenderer">
 </renderer>

 <appender name="A1" class="org.apache.log4j.ConsoleAppender">

   <layout class="org.apache.log4j.PatternLayout">
     <param name="ConversionPattern" value="%t %-5p %c{2} - %m%n"/>
   </layout>
   <filter class="com.apress.logging.log4j.filter.ProductFilter"/>
 </appender>

 <logger name="com.apress.logging.log4j">
   <level value="debug"/>
   <appender-ref ref="A1"/>
 </logger>
</log4j:configuration>
```

Finally, Listing 5-15 presents a sample application to demonstrate the filtering of the log messages and rendering of the `CustomerOrder` object.

Listing 5-15. ProductFilterDemo.java

```java
package com.apress.logging.log4j;

import org.apache.log4j.Logger;
import com.apress.business.CustomerOrder;
import com.apress.logging.log4j.filter.ProductFilter;
import com.apress.logging.log4j.renderer.OrderRenderer;
public class ProductFilterDemo
```

```
{
    private static Logger logger =
Logger.getLogger(ProductFilterDemo.class.getPackage().getName());

    /** Creates a new instance of ProductFilterDemo */
    public ProductFilterDemo() {
    }

    public void processOrder(CustomerOrder order)
    {
        logger.info(order);
    }

    public static void main(String args[])
    {
        CustomerOrder order1 = new CustomerOrder("Beer", 101, 20);
        CustomerOrder order2 = new CustomerOrder("Lemonade", 95, 10);
        CustomerOrder order3 = new CustomerOrder("Chocolate", 223, 5);

        ProductFilterDemo demo = new ProductFilterDemo();
        demo.processOrder(order1);
        demo.processOrder(order2);
        demo.processOrder(order3);
    }

}
```

This application creates three different `CustomerOrder` objects with different product names, product codes, and product prices. The `processOrder()` method simply logs the `CustomerOrder` object passed to it. With the `ProductFilter` object in place, executing the application in Listing 5-15 will result in the following log messages being printed, excluding any having product codes below 100:

```
main INFO  logging.log4j - Beer-101-20
main INFO  logging.log4j - Chocolate-223-5
```

Conclusion

In this chapter, we have examined the various key objects in the log4j framework and also explored how these objects interact to capture, filter, and produce logging information to various destinations. Besides the key objects, log4j involves many more auxiliary objects that help handle the logging information. In the next chapter, we will learn about different `Layout` objects in log4j.

CHAPTER 6

Formatting Logging Information in log4j

IN THE PREVIOUS CHAPTER, we discussed the core objects in the log4j API, and learned how they interact with each other to produce flexible logging messages. We saw that the initiation of a logging process starts with Logger objects. The encapsulated logging information is passed to Appender objects, and Appender objects use Layout objects to format the logging information in a human-readable way before publishing the logging information to a destination.

How logging information is structured is very important. In a real-life application, logging information constitutes more than just debugging messages—it can contain vital data about software modules, how they are interacting with each other, and other useful information. This information can be reused to maintain and debug the application modules. Often it may be necessary to post logging information to another error processing program running on a remote machine. In such scenarios, it becomes important to agree on a structure for the logging information. This is where Layout objects come into the picture.

Apache log4j provides various Layout objects, each of which can format logging data according to various layouts. It is also possible to create an application-specific Layout object that formats logging data in an application-specific way. In this chapter, we will examine the various Layout objects within log4j and learn how to use them within an application.

The Layout Hierarchy

The structure of logging information can vary in terms of the message content, the type of content, and the way the information is presented. But in abstract terms, all logging information can be organized into a header, body, and footer. The header may present an introduction to the message; the body contains the logging information; and the footer section can contain some hint about the content of the message. You can see how this resembles the physical documents that people deal with everyday. Bearing this idea in mind, log4j provides an abstract class called Layout that offers a skeleton implementation of all the common operations. All other individual Layout objects are basically subtypes of this abstract superclass.

Individual Layout objects differ in the styles they use to format the logging information passed to them. These individual Layout objects inherit all the common operations from their abstract superclass and implement their own formatting methods. They may optionally override and provide their own implementation of any method in the base class. Figure 6-1 depicts the class diagram of different Layout objects within the log4j API.

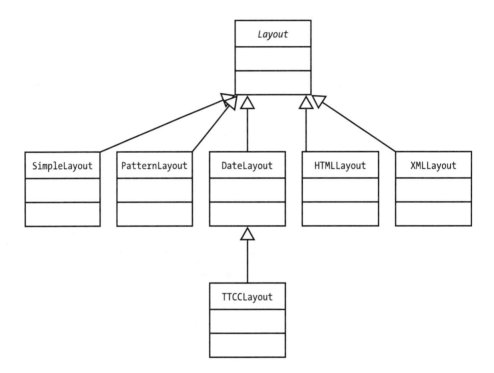

Figure 6-1. The Layout object hierarchy

All Layout objects receive a LoggingEvent object from the Appender objects. The Layout objects then retrieve the message argument from the LoggingEvent and apply the appropriate ObjectRenderer to obtain the String representation of the message, as discussed in the previous chapter.

The Layout Objects in log4j

The top-level class in the hierarchy is the abstract class org.apache.log4j.Layout. This is the base class for all other Layout classes in the log4j API. This class provides a skeleton implementation of all the common operations across all other Layout objects and declares two abstract methods, listed in Table 6-1, specifically for the subclasses to override.

Table 6-1. Abstract Methods in the Layout Class

Method	Description
`public abstract boolean ignoresThrowable()`	This method indicates whether the logging information handles any `java.lang.Throwable` object passed to it as a part of the logging event. If the `Layout` object handles the `Throwable` object, then the `Layout` object does not ignore it, and returns `false`.
`public abstract String format(LoggingEvent event)`	Individual layout subclasses will implement this method for layout-specific formatting.

Apart from these `abstract` methods, the `Layout` class provides concrete implementation for the methods listed in Table 6-2.

Table 6-2. Other Methods in the Layout Class

Method	Description
`public String getContentType()`	Returns the content-type used by the `Layout` objects. The base class returns text/plain as the default content-type.
`public String getFooter()`	Specifies the footer information of the logging message.
`public String getHeader()`	Specifies the header information of the logging message.

Each subclass can return class-specific information by overriding the concrete implementation of these methods.

As the `Layout` class is defined `abstract` within an application, we never use this class directly; instead, we work with its subclasses.

SimpleLayout Object

`org.apache.log4j.SimpleLayout` provides a very basic structure for the logging message. It includes only the level of the logging information and the logging message itself. As we saw in the previous chapter, the `LoggingEvent` object can contain other information related to the logging activity, such as the time, thread, location information, etc., and producing all this information can clutter the logging output.

It can be a painstaking process to cull the necessary information from the large amount of information that is contained within a logging event. In this case, SimpleLayout proves very useful for publishing quick debugging-style messages.

In short, the SimpleLayout object performs the following actions:

- It formats the LoggingEvent object by only including the level information and the message and ignores all other information.

- It does not handle the java.lang.Throwable instance passed through the logging event, and the ignoresThrowable() method returns true.

An example message formatted with SimpleLayout can look like the following:

INFO - "A Message"

The structure of the formatting is the level information, followed by a hyphen sign (-), and the logging message.

NOTE As SimpleLayout is a closed system, there is no configuration parameter for this layout. This object always formats the logging information the same way, with the same style.

TTCCLayout Object

TTCCLayout is much more effective in a multiuser environment than the other Layout objects. Before moving on to the other Layout objects available within log4j API, we will see how log4j handles the multiuser logging environment through TTCCLayout.

The formatting style adopted by the SimpleLayout object is very simplistic. In some cases it might prove useful, and in other cases we may want to publish more detailed information about the logging event. Particularly in multithreaded applications, where multiple clients are accessing the same application module, it is important to publish the time of logging, the active thread, etc., to distinguish between two separate client activities. One other technique to differentiate between each client is the *Nested Diagnostic Context* (NDC). All this information can be put into the LoggingEvent object before passing it to the Layout objects.

org.apache.log4j.TTCCLayout does the job of presenting detailed information about a logging event. It extends the org.apache.log4j.helpers.DateLayout class. Typically, it contains the following information as part of the logging message:

- *Thread:* The invoking thread.

- *Time:* The time in terms of number of milliseconds elapsed since the application was started.

- *Category:* The category or the logger used to create this logging event.

- *Context:* The NDC information. This information is not automatically included in the LoggingEvent object. We have to deliberately include this information in the LoggingEvent as explained in the previous chapter. Thus, this parameter is optional output from TTCCLayout in the sense that it might not display any NDC data, although the NDC setting is enabled in case the LoggingEvent does not contain any NDC data.

NOTE The TTCCLayout object ignores any java.lang.Throwable instance passed to the LoggingEvent.

We will now see how to write a simple program to illustrate the formatting provided by the TTCCLayout object. For the sake of completeness, we will first configure the logger used in this example programmatically, and also configure it through a configuration file later in this section.

To perform the programmatic configuration, we will obtain an instance of a named Logger and attach a ConsoleAppender to the logger instance. To format the logging message, we will also attach a TTCCLayout object to the ConsoleAppender. In this example, we will instantiate a TTCCLayout object with the yyyy-MM-dd date pattern. This will cause the date to be formatted as "2002-10-20", for example. In the computeSquareRoot() method, we will create one NDC, and the String value of the double argument will be passed to it. After computing the square root, we will print the square root value with the logger.info() method. Now that we have discussed the particulars of the example demonstrating TTCCLayout, let's take a look at the code as presented in Listing 6-1, LayoutDemo.java.

Listing 6-1. LayoutDemo.java

```
package com.apress.logging.log4j;

import org.apache.log4j.Logger;
import org.apache.log4j.ConsoleAppender;
import org.apache.log4j.TTCCLayout;
import org.apache.log4j.NDC;
```

```java
public class LayoutDemo
{
    private static Logger logger =
Logger.getLogger(LayoutDemo.class.getPackage().getName());
    private ConsoleAppender appender = null;
    private TTCCLayout layout = null;

    /** Creates a new instance of LayoutDemo */
    public LayoutDemo()
    {
        //set the parent additivity to false
        logger.setAdditivity(false);

         //initialize the layout
        layout = new TTCCLayout("yyyy-MM-dd");

        //initialize the console appender with the layout
        appender = new ConsoleAppender(layout,"System.out");

        //adding the console appender to the logger
        logger.addAppender(appender);

    }

    public void computeSquareRoot(double number)
    {
        NDC.push(new Double(number).toString());
        double sqrt = Math.sqrt(number);
        logger.info("The sqrt value: "+sqrt);
        NDC.pop();

    }

    public static void main(String args[])
    {
        LayoutDemo demo = new LayoutDemo();
        demo.computeSquareRoot(22);
        demo.computeSquareRoot(44);
    }
}
```

NOTE Notice the use of NDC.push() in the beginning of the computeSquareRoot() method and NDC.pop() before leaving the computeSquareRoot() method.

Executing this program will produce the following output to System.out in a console:

```
2002-10-17 [main] INFO com.apress.logging.log4j 44.0 - The sqrt value: 6.6332495807108
```

The output can be divided into the parts described in Table 6-3.

Table 6-3. TTCCLayout Formatting Structure

Information	Meaning
2002-10-17	The date of the logging activity (Time elapsed from the start of the application can also be displayed.)
[main]	The thread invoking the logging request
INFO	The logging level
com.apress.logging.log4j	The name of the logger
44.00	The NDC value
-	The separator
The sqrt value...	The logging message

As is evident from the structure of the logging information, TTCCLayout has seven constituents for the logging information it publishes. The appearance of each constituent in the final logging information depends on whether the information has been supplied as a part of the LoggingEvent object to the TTCCLayout object. The TTCCLayout object controls the appearance of the different parts of the logging messages through the bean properties listed in Table 6-4.

Table 6-4. Bean Properties in the TTCCLayout Class

Bean Property	Method	Description	Default
categoryPrefixing	setCategoryPrefixing(boolean)	Specifies whether the name of the category or the logger should be a part of the logging information	Defaults to true
contextPrinting	setContextPrinting(boolean)	Specifies whether the NDC should be a part of the logging information	Defaults to true
threadPrinting	setThreadPrinting(boolean)	Specifies whether the thread information should be a part of the logging information	Defaults to true

As the TTCCLayout class is a direct subclass of DateLayout, it also inherits the bean properties listed in Table 6-5 from the DateLayout class.

Table 6-5. Bean Properties Inherited from DateLayout

Bean Property	Method	Description	Default
dateFormat	setDateFormat(String)	Sets the date format to be used in Java SimpleDateFormat style (e.g., yyyy-MM-dd) or one of the strings NULL, RELATIVE, DATE, ABSOLUTE, or ISO8601	Defaults to RELATIVE
timeZone	setTimeZone(String)	Time zone specified in the java.util.TimeZone.getTimeZone(String) method (e.g., GMT-8:00)	Defaults to nothing

The log4j Layout objects can also be configured through configuration files by setting the bean property values. For example, Listing 6-2 demonstrates how to use a configuration file, "ttcc.properties", in this example to re-create the logger and layout configuration created programmatically in Listing 6-1.

Listing 6-2. ttcc.properties

```
#configuring the root logger
log4j.rootLogger=DEBUG,CONSOLE

#configuring the named logger
log4j.logger.com.apress.logging.log4j=DEBUG, CONSOLE

#configuring the appender CONSOLE
log4j.appender.CONSOLE=org.apache.log4j.ConsoleAppender
log4j.appender.CONSOLE.layout=org.apache.log4j.TTCCLayout

#configuring the layout TTCCLayout
log4j.appender.CONSOLE.layout.ThreadPrinting=false
og4j.appender.CONSOLE.layout.ContextPrinting=false
log4j.appender.CONSOLE.layout.CategoryPrefixing=false
log4j.appender.CONSOLE.layout.DateFormat=RELATIVE
```

NOTE While executing the program with this configuration file, please remember to turn off the configuration code in the constructor of the program. It makes no sense to do the same configuration in two places.

In this configuration, we disable the ThreadPrinting and ContextPrinting bean properties. As mentioned in Table 6-5, the DateFormat bean property defaults to RELATIVE, which means this program will print the time elapsed in milliseconds since the program has started.

Executing the example program in Listing 6-1 with this configuration file will result in displaying the following logging information in the console:

```
40 INFO 22.0 - The sqrt value: 4.69041575982343
50 INFO 44.0 - The sqrt value: 6.6332495807108
```

Notice the thread and the NDC information are now not displayed as a part of the logging information, as we have disabled the ContextPrinting property.

CAUTION Do not use the same TTCCLayout instance in two different Appender objects. This is not thread-safe.

DateLayout Object

As we have seen in the previous section, the TTCCLayout class uses another class, DateLayout, to format its date- and timestamp-related information. DateLayout is an abstract class that extends the org.apache.log4j.Layout class. It is also a convenience class for handling all date-related formatting tasks, and it accepts a LoggingEvent object and a date format to format the timestamp included in the LoggingEvent object.

The DateLayout class has the bean properties listed in Table 6-6 for setting the parameters of date-related formatting tasks.

Table 6-6. Bean Properties in the DateLayout Class

Bean Property	Method	Description	Default
dateFormat	setDateFormat(String)	Sets the date format to be used in Java SimpleDateFormat style (e.g., yyyy-MM-dd) or one of the strings NULL, RELATIVE, DATE, ABSOLUTE, or ISO8601	Defaults to RELATIVE
timeZone	setTimeZone(String)	Time zone specified in java.util.TimeZone.getTimeZone(String) method (e.g., GMT-8:00)	Defaults to nothing

The date formats used with DateLayout have the properties listed in Table 6-7.

Table 6-7. Date Formats in the DateLayout Class

Date Format	Meaning
NULL	No date or time is displayed.
RELATIVE	Displays the time elapsed after the application was started.
DATE	Formats the date with the dd MMM YYYY HH:mm:ss,SSS pattern—for example, 10 Oct 2002 15:30:39,450. The final SSS represents the time elapsed after the application was started.

Table 6-7. Date Formats in the DateLayout Class (Continued)

Date Format	Meaning
ABSOLUTE	Formats a date with the HH:mm:ss,SSS pattern—for example, 10:49:33, 459. The final SSS represents the time elapsed after the application was started.
ISO8601	Formats a date with the YYYY-mm-dd HH:mm:ss,SSS pattern—for example, 2002-10-20 10:49:33,459.

Any Layout object we want to format and publish the date and timestamp information related to logging could potentially use this class to do the formatting of this type of information.

HTMLLayout Object

The goal of a well-designed system is to make users comfortable with how information is presented to them. In this respect, your application might need to produce logging information in a nice HTML-formatted file. org.apache.log4j.HTMLLayout is an object dedicated to formatting logging information in HTML.

The HTMLLayout class extends the abstract org.apache.log4j.Layout class and overrides the format() method from its base class to provide HTML-style formatting. This is a very simple Layout object that has the configurable bean properties listed in Table 6-8.

Table 6-8. Bean Properties in HTMLLayout

Bean Property	Method	Description	Default
contentType	setContentType(String)	Sets the content type of the HTML content.	Defaults to "text/html"
locationInfo	setLocationInfo(String)	Sets the location information for the logging event.	Defaults to false
title	setTitle(String)	Sets the title for the HTML content.	Defaults to "Log4j Log Messages"

The `HTMLLayout` object includes the following as a part of the logging information it displays:

- The time elapsed from the start of the application before a particular logging event was generated

- The name of the thread that invoked the logging request

- The level associated with this logging request

- The name of the logger

- The optional location information for the program file and the line number from which this logging was invoked

- The logging message

- The `NDC` information

- Any exception that is generated in the application and needs to be logged (This is due to the object being able to handle a `java.lang.Throwable` instance.)

To demonstrate the formatting capability of the `HTMLLayout` object, we will use the same program presented in Listing 6-1, but pass a different configuration file to configure the logger with `HTMLLayout`. Listing 6-3 describes this configuration file, "html.properties".

Listing 6-3. html.properties

```
#configuring the custom logger
log4j.logger.com.apress.logging.log4j=DEBUG,FILE

log4j.appender.FILE=org.apache.log4j.FileAppender
log4j.appender.FILE.File=htmlLayout.html

log4j.appender.FILE.layout=org.apache.log4j.HTMLLayout
log4j.appender.FILE.layout.Title=HTML Layout Demo
log4j.appender.FILE.layout.LocationInfo=true
```

In the configuration file, we assign the `FileAppender` object the filename "htmlLayout.html", and the logging information will be written to this file. The file will be created in the path from which you run the application. The `FileAppender` in turn uses `HTMLLayout` to format the logging information. The `HTMLLayout` object has its bean properties `LocationInfo` set to `true` and `Title` set to "HTML Layout Demo".

Executing the program with this configuration file will create the "htmlLayout.html" file containing all the logging information. Figure 6-2 shows this HTML file.

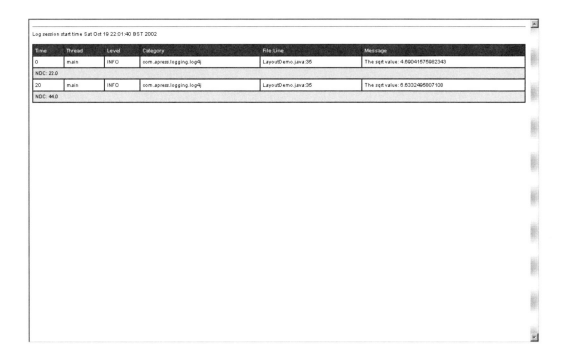

Figure 6-2. The HTML file produced with HTMLLayout

A Caution About Using HTMLLayout

Our discussion of `HTMLLayout` is not quite finished without a quick look at a possible problem with the source file that was generated in the previous example. If we open this file, we will see the HTML code shown in Listing 6-4.

Listing 6-4. The HTML Source Code Produced by HTMLLayout

```
<!DOCTYPE HTML PUBLIC "-//W3C//DTD HTML 4.01 Transitional//EN"
"http://www.w3.org/TR/html4/loose.dtd">
<html>
<head>
<title>Log4J Log Messages</title>
<style type="text/css">
<!--
body, table {font-family: arial,sans-serif; font-size: x-small;}
th {background: #336699; color: #FFFFFF; text-align: left;}
-->
</style>
</head>
<body bgcolor="#FFFFFF" topmargin="6" leftmargin="6">
<hr size="1" noshade>
Log session start time Sat Oct 19 22:01:40 BST 2002<br>
<br>
<table cellspacing="0" cellpadding="4" border="1" bordercolor="#224466"
width="100%">
<tr>
<th>Time</th>
<th>Thread</th>
<th>Level</th>
<th>Category</th>
<th>File:Line</th>
<th>Message</th>
</tr>

<tr>
<td>0</td>
<td title="main thread">main</td>
<td title="Level">INFO</td>
<td title="com.apress.logging.log4j category">com.apress.logging.log4j</td>
<td>LayoutDemo.java:35</td>
<td title="Message">The sqrt value: 4.69041575982343</td>
</tr>
<tr><td bgcolor="#EEEEEE" style="font-size : xx-small;" colspan="6"
title="Nested Diagnostic Context">NDC: 22.0</td></tr>
```

```
<tr>
<td>20</td>
<td title="main thread">main</td>
<td title="Level">INFO</td>
<td title="com.apress.logging.log4j category">com.apress.logging.log4j</td>
<td>LayoutDemo.java:35</td>
<td title="Message">The sqrt value: 6.6332495807108</td>
</tr>
<tr><td bgcolor="#EEEEEE" style="font-size : xx-small;" colspan="6"
title="Nested Diagnostic Context">NDC: 44.0</td></tr>
```

Notice that the header information contains the `<html>` and the `<body>` tags, but the footer for the `</body>` and `</html>` tags is completely missing. Clearly, this is not a well-formed HTML file. Some browsers might allow us to use this style of HTML source, but some may not. The question is, why is the footer (i.e., the closing tags) missing?

The answer lies in when the `getFooter()` method of the `HTMLLayout` is called. As it stands at the moment in version 1.2.6 of log4j, the `getFooter()` method of any `Layout` object is called when the `close()` method of the related `Appender` object is called. This may or may not be a small bug in the API, depending on how the application is performing the logging activity.

Imagine an application module that is a server component handling multiple client calls. For every call we want to write down the logging information to an HTML file. We want the header to be included only once when the `HTMLLayout` object is initialized. This is done in the `setWriter()` method of `HTMLLayout` at initialization. Now the issue is when we want to write the footer. Certainly not after every bit of logging information is appended to the file. Hang on—we might want this to happen if for every logging request we want to open a new file and close the file after the logging is over. In this situation, we will be perfectly fine if we call the `getFooter()` method after every logging request is formatted. But in normal scenarios, if we want to include all the logging information in a single file or to be more strict, and that file contains logging information for more than one logging request, we cannot append the footer information every time.

Clearly, the best place to call the `getFooter()` is when the `Appender` objects themselves are no longer needed. For this situation, when we exit our server component (such as the `destroy()` method in a servlet), we would call the `LogManager.shutdown()` method to close all the `Appender` objects. This ensures that the footer is written to the end of the HTML file produced.

In this particular example, in the `computeSquareRoot()` method just before leaving the method, if we call

```
LogManager.shutDown()
```

we would see that the footer information is included in the final HTML file. This may not be the ideal situation, but this is how we have to deal with it at the moment.

XMLLayout Object

Logging information in HTML format is nice and user friendly, but not precisely reusable. The data is structured but *not* in a descriptive way. HTML-style logging information is not portable across multiple application modules. To render logging information in XML format, which is portable, log4j provides the org.apache.log4j.xml.XMLLayout object.

The XMLLayout object may include the following items from LoggingEvent in the final output:

- The logger name

- The timestamp

- The level associated with the logging request

- The invoking thread name

- The logging message

- The NDC information

- The java.lang.Throwable instance included within the LoggingEvent

- The location info for the logging request (By default, the location info feature is turned off.)

XMLLayout follows the document type definition contained in the "log4j.dtd" file to create the XML output. It is important to note that the final output is *not* a well-formed XML file. It may sound surprising, but the purpose of this object is to produce logging information as a series of <log4j:event> elements. The final output then can be referenced as an entity to another proper XML file.

 NOTE Please refer to the "log4j.dtd" file that comes with the Apache log4j binary distribution.

To illustrate this concept, let's again reuse the program in Listing 6-1 with the configuration file for XMLLayout, "xml.properties", defined in Listing 6-5.

Listing 6-5. xml.properties

```
#configuring the custom logger
log4j.logger.com.apress.logging.log4j=DEBUG,FILE

log4j.appender.FILE=org.apache.log4j.FileAppender
log4j.appender.FILE.File=xmlLayout.xml

log4j.appender.FILE.layout=org.apache.log4j.xml.XMLLayout
log4j.appender.FILE.layout.LocationInfo=true
```

The configuration uses a `FileAppender` along with `XMLLayout` to format the logging information.

Executing the program with this configuration file will write the formatted logging information to the "xmlLayout.xml" file. The content of the file looks similar to the following:

```
<log4j:event logger="com.apress.logging.log4j" timestamp="1035061552691"
level="INFO" thread="main">
<log4j:message><![CDATA[The sqrt value: 4.69041575982343]]></log4j:message>
<log4j:NDC><![CDATA[22.0]]></log4j:NDC>
<log4j:locationInfo class="com.apress.logging.log4j.LayoutDemo"
method="computeSquareRoot" file="LayoutDemo.java" line="35"/>
</log4j:event>

<log4j:event logger="com.apress.logging.log4j" timestamp="1035061552711"
level="INFO" thread="main">
<log4j:message><![CDATA[The sqrt value: 6.6332495807108]]></log4j:message>
<log4j:NDC><![CDATA[44.0]]></log4j:NDC>
<log4j:locationInfo class="com.apress.logging.log4j.LayoutDemo"
method="computeSquareRoot" file="LayoutDemo.java" line="35"/>
</log4j:event>
```

As is evident, the XML output is a series of `<log4j:event>` elements containing other child elements to present the logging information. The code snippet described next shows how to include this information in a well-formed XML file:

```
<?xml version="1.0" ?>

<!DOCTYPE log4j:eventSet SYSTEM "log4j.dtd" [<!ENTITY logEntity SYSTEM
"xmlLayout.xml">]>

<log4j:eventSet version="1.2" xmlns:log4j="http://jakarta.apache.org/log4j/">
  &logEntity;
</log4j:eventSet>
```

At first sight, this might seem confusing. But the rationale behind this is it makes the Layout object rendering the logging message into XML format and the Appender object using this Layout independent of each other.

To further illustrate, let's say that you are writing a custom appender. You want the appender to include your company information header with every logging output. You also want the logging information to be published in XML format. In such scenarios, you will override the doAppend() method in your custom appender to write the logging information into a XML file. Also, you can include a standard header containing your company information and can still use the existing XMLLayout object to format the logging information in its own style. You can then include a reference to the file that the XMLLayout object produced as an external ENTITY within your overall XML file. Clearly, you have achieved the flexibility of including the XML logging information produced by the XMLLayout object as an ELEMENT of any other XML content.

PatternLayout Object

Formatting any piece of information means giving it a pattern that is understandable and recognizable by some external entity. By providing a pattern to the logging information, that information will be recognized by a human or a program. A pattern further means that if the module producing the logging information and a module receiving the information agrees on a pattern beforehand, that information can be processed. This is where PatternLayout becomes useful.

org.apache.log4j.PatternLayout extends the base abstract class Layout and overrides the format() method to structure logging information according to a supplied pattern. We can supply the pattern either through a configuration file or programmatically. The PatternLayout object has the bean property listed in Table 6-9.

Table 6-9. Bean Property in PatternLayout

Bean Property	Method	Description	Default
conversionPattern	setConversionPattern()	Sets the conversion pattern	Defaults to %r [%t] %p %c %x - %m%n

PatternLayout can include all the information within the LoggingEvent object in the final message. The list of items that it can handle is presented in Table 6-10. Notice the exception is the java.lang.Throwable instance.

PatternLayout formats the logging information against a given pattern. The pattern supplied essentially dictates the following items:

- The formatting information is dictated by *format modifiers*.

- The information to be displayed is dictated by *conversion characters*.

Table 6-10 displays all the conversion characters that can be used with PatternLayout.

Table 6-10. The Conversion Characters for PatternLayout

Conversion Character	Meaning
c	The Logger used to invoke this logging request. This can optionally take a precision specifier. For instance, in our example the Logger name is com.apress.logging.log4. With a precision specifier c{2}, the logger will be printed as "logging.log4j". Notice that only the corresponding number of elements from the right-hand side are included in the final output.
C	The fully qualified name of the Logger invoking this logging request. This can also accept a precision specifier as describe with conversion character c. Generating the fully qualified name of the logger can be very slow.
d	The date of the logging request. This can also take an optional date specifier. For example, %d{yyyy-MM-dd} will print the date in year-month-day format. If no date format is specified, this uses the ISO8601 format defined within log4j. As the performance of java.text.SimpleDateFormat is quite poor, for better results use the DateFormat objects provided with the log4j API.
F	The name of the file from which the logging request was issued.
l	The location information. This information can be quite useful when dealing with any exception stack trace. However, generating this information with log4j can be quite slow. A trade-off has to be made before this feature is used.
L	The line number in the program file from which the logging request was issued.

Table 6-10. The Conversion Characters for PatternLayout (Continued)

Conversion Character	Meaning
m	The logging message.
M	The method in the program from which the logging request was issued.
n	Platform-dependent line separator.
p	The level associated with the logging request.
r	The RELATIVE date format displaying the number of milliseconds elapsed from the start of the application before this logging request was issued.
t	The invoking thread.
x	The NDC information.
X	The MDC information. The X conversion character is followed by the key for the MDC. For example, X{clientIP} will print the information stored in the MDC against the key clientIP.
%	The literal percent sign. %% will print a % sign.

The format modifiers used along with PatternLayout are described in Table 6-11.

Table 6-11. Format Modifiers Used in PatternLayout

Modifiers	Left Justified	Minimum Width	Maximum Width	Meaning
%10c	No	10 characters	None	Displays the logger name. If the name is less than 10 characters, then padding is applied to the left side.
%-10c	Yes	10 characters	None	Displays the logger name. If the name is less than 10 characters, then padding is applied to the right side.
%.20c	No	None	20 characters	Displays the logger name. If the name is more than 20 characters, then it is truncated from the beginning.

Table 6-11. Format Modifiers Used in PatternLayout (Continued)

Modifiers	Left Justified	Minimum Width	Maximum Width	Meaning
%20.30c	No	20 characters	30 characters	Displays the logger name. If the name is less than the minimum width (20 chars), then padding is applied to the left side; if the name is more than 30 characters, then it is truncated from the beginning.
%-20.30c	Yes	20 characters	30 characters	Displays the logger name. If the name is shorter than 20 characters, then padding is applied to the right side to keep it left justified. If the name is longer than 30 characters, then it is truncated from the beginning.

To illustrate the power of the conversion patterns, let's try to use LayoutDemo.java (Listing 6-1) and pass it the following configuration file. The configuration will specify PatternLayout as the Layout object used with the ConsoleAppender, and we will pass an appropriate conversion pattern to PatternLayout.

```
#configuring the custom logger
log4j.logger.com.apress.logging.log4j=DEBUG,CONSOLE

log4j.appender.CONSOLE=org.apache.log4j.ConsoleAppender

log4j.appender.CONSOLE.layout=org.apache.log4j.PatternLayout
log4j.appender.CONSOLE.layout.ConversionPattern=%d{yyyy-MM-dd}-%t-%x-%-5p-%-10c:%m%n
```

Executing the program with this configuration file will produce the following output to the console:

```
2002-10-20-main-22.0-INFO -com.apress.logging.log4j:The sqrt value:
4.69041575982343
2002-10-20-main-44.0-INFO -com.apress.logging.log4j:The sqrt value:
6.6332495807108
```

Now that you have an understanding of conversion patterns, you should be able to tell that the conversion pattern %r [%t] %p %c %x - %m%n means nothing other than TTCCLayout.

Conclusion

In this chapter, we have discussed in detail how each Layout object behaves and how these objects can be configured through a configuration file. The log4j API provides a comprehensive set of Layout objects, which is sufficient for most applications. If your application needs a more sophisticated Layout object, you need to create one for yourself. We will see how to write a new Layout object in Chapter 8. In the next chapter, we will continue our discussion of log4j by examining how we can deliver logging information in the arena of distributed computing.

CHAPTER 7
Advanced Logging with log4j

THIS CHAPTER IS DEDICATED to the advanced topics of logging with log4j API. Writing logging information to a console or to a file is limited in terms of flexibility and reuse. The logging information printed to a console is pretty volatile and likely to disappear once the application exits its present running instance. Therefore, the console-based logging information is more suitable for development-stage debugging messages.

On the other hand, logging information printed to a file local to the system is inefficient because it is hardly accessible to other applications that might be able to use the same logging information. It is going to be extra work to make this information accessible to the other application modules.

Although an important point of logging is to enable remote debugging and socket management of application modules, it is equally important to make the logging data accessible to remote application modules. Sometimes, the nature of logging data is sensitive, and it may be required to maintain the history of the logging information in a database. In other scenarios, when we want to process any sensitive logging data in real time, we might want to post the data over a TCP/IP socket to another server component ready to respond to the information sent to it. Also, it is possible that we might need to maintain an order-processing system, where certain customer-specific logging information is e-mailed to respective customers. These are few of the many possibilities that we may want to implement with logging information.

Arguably, in most of the normal application scenarios, file-based logging proves sufficient. However, in a distributed computing scenario, situations may arise in which we might need distributed logging functionality. In such situations, the power of log4j enables us to make best of its logging features.

The log4j API handles many of the situations discussed by providing different `Appender` objects. The list may not be exhaustive and may not cater to every situation that can arise specific to different applications, but it is sufficient for most common application scenarios. In case an application needs something different, the API provides a flexible design for us to integrate custom objects within the API or extend the existing framework to suit an application's specific needs.

In this chapter, we will discuss how to distribute and store logging data in the following ways:

- Writing logging information to a database

- Distributing logging data using Java Message Service (JMS)

- Distributing logging data over Simple Mail Transfer Protocol (SMTP)

- Sending logging data over a TCP/IP socket

- Using Telnet protocol to upload logging data to a remote machine

- Storing logging data in OS-specific event logs

In the next few sections, we will discuss one by one the different Appender objects provided within the log4j API and how they accomplish the task of managing and distributing logging data.

A Sample Advanced Logging Application

We will first create a simple program that we will use throughout this chapter to demonstrate the capabilities of different advanced Appender objects. The program obtains a named logger instance, com.apress.logging.log4j. The deposit() and withdraw() methods deposit and withdraw some money to and from an account. The amount deposited gets added to the balance. The withdraw() method allows withdrawing only if there are sufficient funds available and then deducts the amount withdrawn from the current balance. If the balance is not enough, this program will print a message to the user.

The application logs activities for both these methods and uses the user name as the NDC information. The application also logs both the success and failure of each operation. Listing 7-1, AdvancedLogging.java, is an example implementation of the described business process.

Listing 7-1. AdvancedLogging.java

```
package com.apress.logging.log4j;

import org.apache.log4j.Logger;
import org.apache.log4j.NDC;
```

```java
public class AdvancedLogging
{
    private static Logger logger =
Logger.getLogger(AdvancedLogging.class.getPackage().getName());
    private  String userName = null;
    private double balance;
    
    /** Creates a new instance of AdvancedLogging */
    public AdvancedLogging(String user)
    {
        this.userName = user;
    }
    /**
     *Deposit some amount
     */
    public void deposit(double amount)
    {
        NDC.push(userName);
        balance += amount;
        logger.info("Deposited "+amount+" new balance: "+balance);
        NDC.pop();
    }
    /**
     *withdraw some amount
     */
    public void withdraw(double amount)
    {
        NDC.push(userName);
        if(balance>=amount)
        {
            balance -= amount;
            logger.info("Withdrawn "+amount+" new balance: "+balance);
        }else
        {
            System.out.println("Not enough balance");
            logger.error("Failed to withdraw: balance: "+balance+" attempted withdraw: "+amount);
        }
        NDC.pop();
    }
```

```
    public static void main(String args[])
    {
        AdvancedLogging demo = new AdvancedLogging("sam");
        demo.depositBalance(100.50);
        demo.withDraw(80);
        demo.withDraw(50);
    }
}
```

Logging to a Database with JDBCAppender

It is often a good practice to store the required logging data in a database. This serves two purposes: First, the data is persisted, and second, the data can be accessed and analyzed by the applications residing outside the domain of the application being logged.

The log4j API provides the org.apache.log4j.jdbc.JDBCAppender object, which is capable of putting logging information in a specified database. It does simplistic jobs such as opening a database connection by reading JDBC connection parameters passed to it, writing the data to one or more tables following a specified SQL statement, and closing the connection. We can extend the functionality of the JDBCAppender object to meet our needs. At the present moment, JDBCAppender operates in the following manner:

- It has a buffered implementation. The logging events passed to it are stored in a buffer of a predefined size. Once the maximum size of the buffer is reached, the buffer is flushed, and the data is written to the table, following the specified SQL statement.

- It opens a single connection to the database and maintains the connection until the appender is closed.

- As the SQL operation can be INSERT, UPDATE, or DELETE for a particular record, JDBCAppender cleverly uses the executeUpdate() method of the java.sql.Statement object. This gives the flexibility to execute any type of SQL statement. The decision whether to insert, update, or delete a particular logging record is up to the application developer to decide and is specified by the SQL statement in the configuration file. JDBCAppender will make no decision regarding the nature of the SQL statement. It merely executes the SQL statement passed to it.

- Although JDBCAppender does not decide the nature of the SQL statement to be executed, it is responsible for maintaining the integrity of the logging event that is being logged. The methods in JDBCAppender are not synchronized to keep its performance intact. This can potentially create a problem of data integrity. Before all the elements of the buffer are written to the database, another logging request might arrive. The buffer will get the new logging event appended to it. Recognizing this new data in the buffer, JDBCAppender will again try to iterate through the buffer to write all the elements in it to the database. This can lead to attempting to write duplicate data in the database, which will surely result in database error.

- To avoid the problem just mentioned, after each element of the buffer is written to the database, JDBCAppender stores it in a secondary buffer. In the end, it compares the primary buffer with the elements in the secondary buffer, and removes from the primary buffer all the elements that are present in the secondary buffer. This ensures that no duplicate element is retained in the primary buffer.

- JDBCAppender provides a close() method to release any database resource obtained. In theory, the close() method can be called at any time in an application's lifetime. Moreover, when the application terminates by calling the LogManager.shutdown() method, the close() method of every appender active in the system is called. This might result in a loss of data if the close() method is called before a JDBCAppender instance can finish its writing operation. To make sure that data is not lost, the close() method in the JDBCAppender flushes the primary buffer to ensure that the data already in the buffer gets written to the database.

Configuring JDBCAppender

Before we proceed to an example of JDBCAppender in action, it is important to first understand how to configure JDBCAppender objects. JDBCAppender has the configurable bean properties listed in Table 7-1.

Table 7-1. Bean Properties in the JDBCAppender Class

Bean Property	Method	Description	Default
bufferSize	setBufferSize(int)	Sets the buffer size	Default size is 1.
driver	setDriver(String)	Sets the driver class to the specified string	If no driver class is specified, defaults to "sun.jdbc.odbc.JdbcOdbcDriver".
layout	setLayout(String)	Sets the layout to be used	Defaults to org.apache.log4j.PatternLayout.
password	setPassword(String)	Sets the password against the user name specified to obtain a connection to the database	User must specify a valid password to access the database.
URL	setURL(String)	Sets the JDBC URL	Defaults to some arbitrary value. User must specify a proper JDBC URL.
user	setUser(String)	Sets the user name to be used to obtain a connection to the specified database	User must specify a valid user name to access the database.

Creating a Table for Storing Logging Information

Listing 7-2 describes the SQL statement to create a table named LOGGING_DATA to store logging information.

Listing 7-2. SQL for Creating the LOGGING_DATA Table

```
CREATE TABLE LOGGING_DATA
("USER_ID" VARCHAR2(10) NOT NULL,
"DATE" VARCHAR2(10) NOT NULL,
"LOGGER" VARCHAR2(50) NOT NULL,
"LEVEL" VARCHAR2(10) NOT NULL,
"MESSAGE" VARCHAR2(1000) NOT NULL)
```

Configuration File for Using with JDBCAppender

Listing 7-3, "jdbc.properties", describes the configuration file we will be using to log messages to a database table.

Listing 7-3. jdbc.properties

```
#configuring the custom logger
log4j.logger.com.apress.logging.log4j=DEBUG,DB

log4j.appender.DB=org.apache.log4j.jdbc.JDBCAppender
log4j.appender.DB.URL=jdbc:odbc:dbdef
log4j.appender.DB.user=system
log4j.appender.DB.password=manager
log4j.appender.DB.sql=INSERT INTO LOGGING_DATA VALUES('%x','%d{yyyy-MM-dd}','%C','%p','%m')
```

In the configuration file we assign a level of DEBUG and a `JDBCAppender` to the named logger `com.apress.logging.log4j`. The `JDBCAppender` object is given the following configuration parameters:

- Database URL to connect to is `jdbc:odbc:dbdef`, where `dbdef` is the name of the database we are connecting to.

- The user ID to connect to the database is `system` and the password is `manager`.

- The SQL to execute is an INSERT statement with the table name LOGGING_DATA and values to be entered into the table. Notice that the values are specified following a `PatternLayout` (refer to the previous chapter for details on `PatternLayout` objects). The values specified follow the same order as the table columns and inserts the `NDC`, the date of logging, the fully qualified name of the logger, the level of logging, and finally the logging message itself.

Executing this program with the "jdbc.properties" file as the configuration file will write the data to the database. Figure 7-1 presents an HTML report of the data stored in the table LOGGING_DATA.

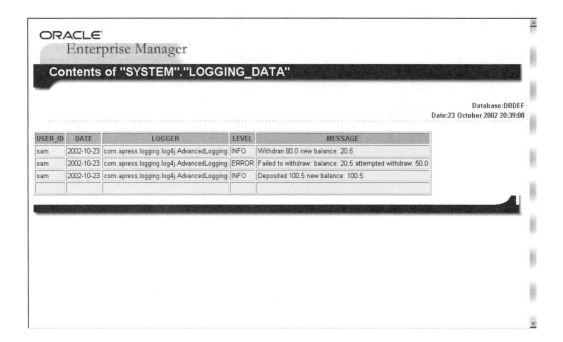

Figure 7-1. The LOGGING_DATA table

Perhaps you have noticed that no JDBC programming has to be done to write the data to the database. It is all done within JDBCAppender. Also, notice this example demonstrates the power of log4j in that the destination of the logging information can be changed by merely changing the configuration file passed to it, requiring no code change at all.

Extending JDBCAppender

JDBCAppender is good enough to perform simple SQL operations. It reads the SQL query and other JDBC-related parameters from a configuration file and executes the SQL operation. One of the prime factors for SQL optimization is the ability to execute dynamic SQL queries. In Java language, the dynamic SQL is handled through java.sql.PreparedStatement interface-type objects. If you are familiar with JDBC programming, you will know how to use the PreparedStatement object. JDBCAppender on its own does *not* use the PreparedStatement object to handle database-related operations.

It is possible to extend the functionality of JDBCAppender by subclassing it. We will take a look at an example of customizing JDBCAppender by giving it the flexibility to work with PreparedStatement objects. We will accept the following configuration parameters at initialization, in addition to the configuration parameters standard to JDBCAppender:

- sqlString: The SQL string representing the dynamic SQL construct. This is similar to the constructs used by the PreparedStatement objects in JDBC.

- values: Once the PreparedStatement object is constructed, we need to set the values for different columns. The values will contain different aspects of the logging information in a PatternLayout construct. For example, %p-%m will be converted to a string in the form of LEVEL-MESSAGE.

NOTE We are going to reuse the database table LOGGING_DATA as described in Listing 7-2 in the upcoming example.

We will now write a sample custom Appender object that performs a JDBC operation. At startup, this Appender object will get initialized through the bean property values specified in the configuration file passed to the log4j runtime. The CustomJDBCAppender object inherits all the properties and a few methods from its base class JDBCAppender. Specifically, it overrides only the following methods from the JDBCAppender class:

- execute(String sql): This method is overridden to use a PreparedStatement object.

- doAppend(LoggingEvent event): This method is overridden to perform the normal appender activity.

The CustomJDBCAppender provides its own methods to set and retrieve the bean properties specific to it. One important thing to note here is that we are using PatternLayout to convert the logging information, and we need to tell the PatternLayout the pattern to process. In this context, we want to convert the information passed through the values bean property of CustomJDBCAppender via PatternLayout. Therefore, in the setValues() method, we create a PatternLayout with the information contained in the values bean property. At the end, we set the created PatternLayout object as the layout for CustomJDBCAppender.

The overridden execute() method does the following jobs:

1. It obtains an instance of the PreparedStatement object by calling the getPreparedStatement() method that is private to CustomJDBCAppender.

2. This method then tokenizes the formatted logging information, and each token represents the values for each column in the table.

3. The values must be supplied in the same sequence as the table columns. This condition may not be ideal, but it helps to simplify this example.

4. It then uses the setString(int, Object) method of the PreparedStatement object to set the values for each column. Again, this bit of code assumes all the columns in the table have the type VARCHAR, which is true for the table we are using for this example. But in reality, the column type can be anything, and the program needs to be able to handle that.

5. Finally, the SQL operation is performed by invoking the executeUpdate() method of PreparedStatement.

Listing 7-4, CustomJDBCAppender.java, is an example implementation of a customized JDBCAppender.

Listing 7-4. CustomJDBCAppender.java

```
package com.apress.logging.log4j.appender;

import org.apache.log4j.jdbc.JDBCAppender;
import java.sql.PreparedStatement;
import java.sql.Connection;
import java.sql.SQLException;
import org.apache.log4j.spi.LoggingEvent;
import org.apache.log4j.PatternLayout;
import java.util.StringTokenizer;

public class CustomJDBCAppender extends JDBCAppender {

    /** Holds value of property values. */
    private String values;

    /**the prepared statement object**/
    private PreparedStatement stmt = null;

    /** Holds value of property preparedSQL. */
    private String preparedSQL;

    /** Creates a new instance of CustomJDBCAppender */
    public CustomJDBCAppender() {
    }
```

```java
public void doAppend(LoggingEvent event) {
    buffer.add(event);
    if(buffer.size()>=bufferSize) {
        flushBuffer();
    }
}

/**
 * overridden method from the JDBCAppender. This method sets the
 * parameters for the prepared statement
 * before executing the statement
 **/
public void execute(String sql) throws SQLException {
    PreparedStatement stmt = getPreparedStatement();
    StringTokenizer tokenizer = new StringTokenizer(sql, ",");
    int i=1;
    while(tokenizer.hasMoreTokens()) {
        String token = tokenizer.nextToken();
        stmt.setString(i, token);
        i++;
    }
    stmt.executeUpdate();
}

/**
 * This method obtains the prepared statement object
 **/
private PreparedStatement getPreparedStatement() throws SQLException {
    //resuse the getConnection() method from the super class
    Connection conn = getConnection();
    if(stmt==null) {
        stmt = conn.prepareStatement(getPreparedSQL());
    }
    return stmt;
}

/** Getter for property values.
 * @return Value of property values.
 */
public String getValues() {
    return this.values;
}
```

```java
/** Setter for property values.
 * @param values New value of property values.
 */
public void setValues(String values) {
    PatternLayout layout = new PatternLayout(values);
    this.setLayout(layout);
    this.values = values;
}

/** Getter for property preparedSQL.
 * @return Value of property preparedSQL.
 */
public String getPreparedSQL() {
    return this.preparedSQL;
}

/** Setter for property preparedSQL.
 * @param preparedSQL New value of property preparedSQL.
 */
public void setPreparedSQL(String preparedSQL) {
    this.preparedSQL = preparedSQL;
}
}
```

Listing 7-5, "customjdbc.properties", describes the configuration file for this example. Note that it defines the custom bean properties used by CustomJDBCAppender in addition to the bean properties used by JDBCAppender.

Listing 7-5. customjdbc.properties

```
#configuring the custom logger
log4j.logger.com.apress.logging.log4j=DEBUG,DB

#log4j.appender.DB=org.apache.log4j.jdbc.JDBCAppender
log4j.appender.DB=com.apress.logging.log4j.appender.CustomJDBCAppender

#configuring the custom jdbc appender
log4j.appender.DB.URL=jdbc:odbc:dbdef
log4j.appender.DB.user=system
log4j.appender.DB.password=manager
log4j.appender.DB.preparedSQL=INSERT INTO LOGGING_DATA VALUES(?,?,?,?,?)
log4j.appender.DB.values=%x,%d{yyyy-MM-dd},%c,%p,%m
log4j.appender.DB.bufferSize=3
```

Executing this program with the "customjdbc.properties" configuration file will result in the data being inserted into in the database as usual. The only difference is that the program has now used dynamic SQL with the PreparedStatement object. Figure 7-2 presents the resulting data in the LOGGING_DATA table.

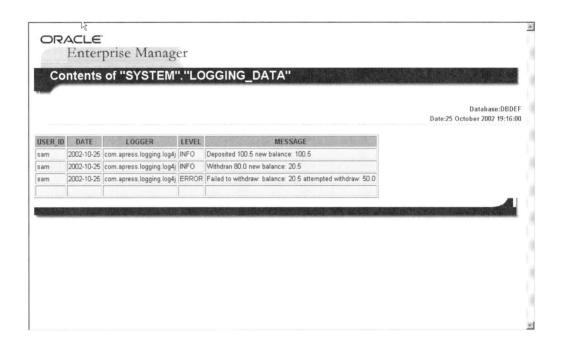

Figure 7-2. The data in the LOGGING_DATA table stored via CustomJDBCAppender

NOTE The logging information that gets stored with the default JDBCAppender and CustomJDBCAppender objects is the same. The difference between the preceding examples(Listing7-1 and Listing 7-4) lies in the way SQL statements are executed. With CustomJDBCAppender, the SQL statement is prepared, compiled once, and stored within the database for reuse. However, with the normal JDBCAppender object the SQL statement is prepared and compiled every time. The main point of using CustomJDBCAppender is the performance gain that comes with including PreparedStatement objects to execute dynamic SQL.

Finally, you can see that this example is a simplistic version of what can be done with JDBCAppender. One of the most critical issues in database-related programming is connection pooling. Most Java programmers nowadays are familiar with connection pooling and might have implemented one or two on their own. Rather than stepping through an example of connection pooling with JDBCAppender together, this is left as an exercise for you to implement on your own, to reinforce what you have learned so far about log4j.

Implementing JMS-Based Logging with JMSAppender

In the previous chapter, we discussed Appender objects that write logging information to the local machine on which an application is running. Most of these Appender objects are *synchronous*. The previous section mentioned that JDBCAppender has buffered implementation, which means the caller application gets back the control after submitting a logging event to JDBCAppender and need not wait for the actual writing to the database to finish.

But in the real world, we might want to achieve a complete *asynchronous* logging activity—that is, the logger application can send a logging message and completely forget about it. A receiver application can pick up the logging message at a later time and process that message in its own time. This is what message-oriented software is all about. Apache log4j uses this concept of messaging together with the Java Message Service to implement message-oriented logging.

With localized logging concepts such as file-based logging, logging information is scattered across the various locations in which individual application components reside. JMS-based logging becomes very useful in situations where we want to collect logging information from various distributed components and store the logging information centrally.

What Is JMS?

Because a detailed discussion about JMS is outside the scope of this book, we will only discuss how log4j fits into the JMS paradigm. JMS allows application developers to create, send, receive, and read messages. The important features of JMS or any messaging API in this sense are as follows:

- *Asynchronous:* The application module issuing messages and the application module receiving messages can operate independently of each other without knowing each other's available interfaces. The sender and receiver applications need not be up and running simultaneously.

- *Reliable:* JMS ensures that messages are sent once and only once.

Message-oriented JMS implementations can differ in the way messages are published, the way messages are consumed, and the time dependency between the sender and the receiver. In the next two sections, we will explore the two most popular messaging domains implemented by JMS.

Point-to-Point Messaging

Point-to-Point messaging is built around the concepts of messages, queues, senders, and receivers. It has the following features:

- The sender sends the messages to the queue.

- The queue retains the messages until they are consumed.

- Each message in the queue has one and only one consumer (the receiver).

- The sender and the receiver have no time dependency. The receiver can fetch the message even if it was not running at the time the message was sent.

- The receiver or the consumer acknowledges the receipt of the message.

Publish-Subscribe Messaging

Publish-Subscribe messaging is centered on the concept of messages, Topics, Publisher, and Subscriber. It has the following features:

- The sender publishes the messages to a Topic.

- Each message can have zero or multiple Subscribers.

- The system takes care of distributing messages to Subscribers.

- Publishers and Subscribers have a time dependency. A Subscriber can only subscribe to messages if it is up and running at the time the message is published to a Topic.

- Topics retain messages only as long it takes to distribute them to Subscribers subscribing to the same Topic.

JMS and log4j

Apache log4j provides the `org.apache.log4j.net.JMSAppender` object to perform JMS-based logging activity. `JMSAppender` uses the Publish-Subscribe messaging domain to send logging event–related messages to a specified Topic. Any application interested in a logging event published in a specified Topic will have to subscribe to the same Topic and listen for any messages arriving to process them.

To connect to a JMS Topic, the `JMSAppender` object will have to perform these steps:

- It has to obtain a connection to the JMS provider.

- It has to subscribe to the Topic destination.

- After it successfully obtains a connection to the provider and to the Topic, it needs to create a session to interact with the provider and the Topic.

The JMS provider manages the `Connection` and `Topic` objects itself rather than the application program controlling them. These are called `Administered` objects. As the various providers manage `Connection` and other core objects differently, it is best that the providers themselves manage the objects. The application module gains access to these objects through portable interfaces and remain unaffected by the underlying technology of a provider.

Whenever the application requires a reference to the `Administered` objects, it does so by retrieving the `JNDIContext` object. The retrieval of the `JNDIContext` object again varies from provider to provider. To illustrate this, let's look at two scenarios using the default J2EE provider and the BEA WebLogic application server.

JNDIContext with J2EE

The J2EE environment provides a default "jndi.properties" file containing all the information required to retrieve a JNDI context. If you are using the J2EE lightweight application server, you need to use the following command to obtain a JNDI context:

```
InitialContext jndiContext = new InitialContext();
```

Using a no-argument constructor will initialize a context with the default properties specified within the "jndi.properties" file local to any JMS API being used. For other JMS providers, you need to pass several other configuration parameters to obtain an initial context.

NOTE For J2SDKEE 1.3.1, the "jndi.properties" file is bundled within "j2ee.jar".

JNDIContext with WebLogic

As we discussed in the previous sections, the underlying technology for Administered objects such as Connection and Topic is different from one vendor to the next. For this reason, in order to obtain an initial JNDI context from a provider, we need to pass to it different configuration properties. For example, to obtain an initial context from WebLogic, we would use the following:

```
Properties env = new Properties( );
env.put(Context.INITIAL_CONTEXT_FACTORY,"weblogic.jndi.WLInitialContextFactory);
env.put(Context.PROVIDER_URL, "t3://localhost:7001");
InitialContext jndiContext = new InitialContext(env);
```

Other JMS providers such as JBoss will require different configuration parameters passed to them.

Configuring JMSAppender

JMSAppender collects information about all the required parameters to obtain a JMS connection through configurable bean properties, which are shown in Table 7-2.

Table 7-2. Configurable Bean Properties in JMSAppender

Bean Property	Method	Description	Default
initialContextFactoryName	setInitialContextFactoryName(String)	Sets the initial context factory name	None
locationInfo	setLocationInfo(Boolean)	If true, the caller's location information is included	false
password	setPassword(String)	Sets the password for using a JMS connection	None
providerURL	setProviderURL(String)	Specifies the URL for the provider (This varies from provider to provider.)	None
securityCredentials	setSecurityCredentials(String)	Sets the security credential attribute required by a few JMS providers	None
securityPrincipalName	setSecurityPrincipalName(String)	Sets the security principal name for the particular provider	None
topicBindingName	setTopicBindingName(String)	Sets the name of the Topic to connect to	None
topicConnectionFactoryBindingName	setTopicConnectionFactoryBindingName(String)	Sets the name of the connection factory object to use to obtain the Topic connection	None
URLPkgPrefixes	setURLPkgPrefixes(String)	Sets the package prefix property	None
userName	setUserName(String)	Sets the user name for obtaining a connection to the provider	None

Not all the configuration parameters are required for every JMS provider we might use. The JMSAppender tries to cater to a large number of the JMS providers available in the market.

An Example of Using JMSAppender

To see an example of how JMSAppender works, let's reuse the example in Listing 7-1. To direct logging information to a JMS destination, we merely need to change the configuration file passed to the log4j runtime. Listing 7-6, "jms.properties", shows the sample configuration file we will use to configure JMSAppender.

Listing 7-6. jms.properties

```
#configuring the custom logger
log4j.logger.com.apress.logging.log4j=DEBUG,JMS

#configuring the JMS appender
log4j.appender.JMS=org.apache.log4j.net.JMSAppender
log4j.appender.JMS.topicConnectionFactoryBindingName=TopicConnectionFactory
log4j.appender.JMS.topicBindingName=loggingTopic
```

In this example, we use the JMS provider implemented by the J2EE 1.3.1. To work with J2EE, the JMSAppender object will just need to create a default JNDIContext object by using the following line of code:

```
InitialContext jndiContext = new InitialContext();
```

This is the reason we do not need to pass the other configuration information to JMSAppender. The only configuration items that we pass to JMSAppender are topicConnectionFactoryBindingName and topicBindingName. Notice the Topic name we are using is loggingTopic.

With this minimum configuration, we will be able to use JMSAppender in our example application. We also need a Subscriber application that will read the messages posted in the Topic named loggingTopic. We will create a JMS sample program that listens to the Topic named loggingTopic and prints the relevant information to the console. It performs the following steps to subscribe to the named JMS Topic and then read the message sent to it:

1. The program first obtains an initial JNDI context.

2. It creates a connection Factory object with the name TopicConnectionFactory.

3. The program then uses the Topic name passed through the command line at the startup of this program and creates a Topic object.

4. It obtains a connection to the Topic and opens a session with the AUTO_ACKNOWLEDGE mode. This means that the Subscriber will automatically acknowledge the receipt of the message. As soon as this receipt is sent, the Topic will no longer retain the message.

5. The program subscribes to the Topic.

6. A custom message listener object, LogMessageListener, is attached to the Subscriber object created with the Topic session.

7. The Subscriber is now ready to listen to the Topic for any messages.

Listing 7-7, JMSLogSubscriber.java, is an example implementation of a JMS Subscriber.

Listing 7-7. JMSLogSubscriber.java

```
package com.apress.logging.log4j;

import javax.jms.*;
import javax.naming.*;

public class JMSLogSubscriber {

    /** Creates a new instance of JMSLogSubscriber */
    public JMSLogSubscriber() {
    }

    public static void main(String args[]) {
        Context ctx;
        Topic topic;
        TopicSubscriber topicSubscriber;
        TextMessage message;
        TopicConnectionFactory topicFactory;
        TopicConnection topicConnection;
        TopicSession topicSession;
```

```
        //collect the topic name from command line
        String topicName = args[0];
        try {
            //creating a default J2EE initial context
            ctx = new InitialContext();
            //obtaining the topic connection factory
            topicFactory =
(TopicConnectionFactory)ctx.lookup("TopicConnectionFactory");
            //creating the topic
            topic = (Topic)ctx.lookup(topicName);
            //opening a topic connection
            topicConnection = topicFactory.createTopicConnection();
            //creating a session to AUTO_ACKNOWLEDGE the receipt of the
            //message
            topicSession = topicConnection.createTopicSession(false,
Session.AUTO_ACKNOWLEDGE);
            //subscribe to the topic
            topicSubscriber = topicSession.createSubscriber(topic);
            //custom listener to listen to the topic for any message and
            //handle it
            LogMessageListener listener = new LogMessageListener();
            //adding the listener to this subscriber
            topicSubscriber.setMessageListener(listener);
            //start the session
            topicConnection.start();
        }catch(Exception e) {
            System.out.println(e.toString());
        }
    }
}
```

This program uses a custom listener object to listen to the Topic for any message. There is an alternative to this technique. The Subscriber can call the receive() method to obtain any message from the Topic. However, this is a *synchronous* mode of receiving and processing messages. The receive() method explicitly fetches the messages from the Topic. This method can block until a message arrives or can timeout if a message does not arrive within a specified time limit. By attaching a MessageListener object to the Subscriber, the Subscriber can *asynchronously* receive the message. As soon as a message arrives, the JMS provider will notify the MessageListener by invoking its onMessage() method.

Listing 7-8, LogMessageListener.java, is a MessageListener implementation for listening to a Topic. It provides an implementation for the onMessage() method. Within the onMessage() method, it checks for the message type. JMSAppender posts LoggingEvent objects as the ObjectMessage type to the Topic. Thus, LogMessageListener checks for the ObjectMessage, casts it back to the LoggingEvent object, and obtains all the information from the LoggingEvent object.

Listing 7-8. LogMessageListener.java

```java
package com.apress.logging.log4j;

import javax.jms.*;
import org.apache.log4j.spi.LoggingEvent;

public class LogMessageListener implements MessageListener{

    /** Creates a new instance of LogMessageListener */
    public LogMessageListener() {
    }

    /**
    * This method listens to any message coming to the subscribe topic,
    * checks if correct type
    * and prints the content.
    ***/
    public void onMessage(Message message) {
        TextMessage msg = null;
        try {
            if(message instanceof ObjectMessage){
                System.out.println("Message received: ");
                ObjectMessage obj =  (ObjectMessage)message;
                LoggingEvent event = (LoggingEvent)obj.getObject();
                System.out.println("The logger name: "+event.getLoggerName());
                System.out.println("The message: "+event.getMessage().toString());
            }else {

                System.out.println("Message of wrong type: " +
                message.getClass().getName());
            }
        } catch (JMSException e) {
            System.out.println("JMSException in onMessage(): " +
            e.toString());
```

```
        } catch (Throwable t) {
            System.out.println("Exception in onMessage():" +
            t.getMessage());
        }
    }
}
```

The `LogMessageListener` prints only the logger name and the message encapsulated within the `LoggingEvent` object. Arguably, it can extract all the information from the `LoggingEvent` object and process it in the way it wants to. This example has been kept simple to demonstrate how the JMS works with log4j.

Executing the JMS-Based Logging Example

To see the example in action, we need to go through the steps presented in the next sections.

Start the J2EE JMS Provider

First, we must make sure that the "j2ee.jar" is included in the classpath. Now, start up the J2EE application server with the following command:

```
j2ee -verbose
```

> **NOTE** Remember to set the J2EE_HOME environment to point to the j2ee location.

Creating the Topic

Next we create a new Topic named `loggingTopic` and add it to the JMS destination with the following command:

```
j2eeadmin -addJmsDestination loggingTopic topic
```

Running the Subscriber

Once the Topic is added to the JMS destination, we start `JMSLogSubscriber` with the following command:

```
java -Djms.properties=%J2EE_HOME%config/jms_client.properties
com.apress.logging.log4j.JMSLogSubscriber loggingTopic
```

Notice that we pass the Topic name `loggingTopic` as a command line parameter to the program. Also, we provide the JMS configuration parameters to the J2EE runtime via the "jms_client.properties" file, which is bundled with the J2EE.

Running the Client

Now we are ready to execute our example program. We will pass the "jms.properties" file as the log4j configuration file to the runtime. Also, we will provide the JMS configuration parameters to the J2EE runtime via the "jms_client.properties" file, which is bundled with the J2EE.

```
java -Dlog4j.configuration=jms.properties -
Djms.properties=%J2EE_HOME%config/jms_client.properties
com.apress.logging.log4j.AdvancedLogging
```

Executing this program will post all the logging information to the Topic named `loggingTopic`. In the Subscriber console, we will see the following messages arriving:

```
Message received...
Message received:
The logger name: com.apress.logging.log4j
The message: Deposited 100.5 new balance: 100.5
Message received...
Message received:
The logger name: com.apress.logging.log4j
The message: Withdrawn 80.0 new balance: 20.5
Message received...
Message received:
The logger name: com.apress.logging.log4j
The message: Failed to withdraw: balance: 20.5 attempted withdraw: 50.0
```

Note that all the logging messages are printed in the console, and the application does not terminate even after the logging message is passed to the Topic. This is because the Topic connection is closed only within the `close()` method of the `JMSAppender`. If we explicitly call the `close()` method of the `JMSAppender` or call the `LogManager.shutdown()` method as soon as we finish, the Topic connection will be closed and the console will be released.

This is all you need to know about JMSAppender. As you can see, the impressive part is it's so easy to implement without having to make any code changes in the application. With a different configuration file, we are there!

> **NOTE** JMS-based logging ensures the delivery of logging information to the receiver but does not guarantee time. The logging information passed to the receiver may not be chronological. One way to get around this problem is to use NDC information for each logging request with the timestamp from each sender. However, it is up to you to decide which is the best way to deal with this problem for your particular situation.

Working with SocketAppender

A situation in which we want to transfer logging information from one machine to another represents a distributed logging scenario. We have already seen how JMSAppender is very useful for passing logging information from distributed application components to a central location. It is also possible to pass logging information from one location to another using TCP/IP-based raw socket connections.

It may be tricky to choose between using JMS- or socket-based mechanisms to transfer logging information from one machine to another. Although the underlying implementation of any distributed architecture is TCP/IP based, the difference is in how they operate. The choice between JMS- and raw socket-based communication to transfer logging information more or less depends on the architecture of the application itself. The following few points may help you when you are faced with deciding whether to use JMS- or socket-based logging:

- JMS-based logging should be employed when the application follows a distributed architecture. Remember, an application supporting client-server technology is not necessarily distributed. True distributed architecture will have server-side components that the client(s) uses distributed across different locations. In such scenarios, JMS-based logging is more effective.

- In a true distributed application scenario, you will always have an application server running. Java-based application servers will often come with JMS support. So if your application is using any application server (for some legitimate reason), consider using JMS-based logging.

- Socket-based logging is suitable for normal client-server situations where many clients are talking to the same server component. If as a part of an application you have to write the server component, it would probably be easier for you to use socket-based logging. Remember, going for a JMS-based solution when you are not using distributed computing will require the extra cost of deploying a JMS provider.

- In any application scenario where you want to implement an asynchronous logging mechanism, a JMS-based solution would be ideal and easy to implement. If you do not need it, then a socket-based logging mechanism may win over JMS, provided other conditions discussed previously are satisfied.

org.apache.log4j.net.SocketAppender provides a means for transferring logging information to a remote server over TCP/IP. It basically sends the serialized LoggingEvent object over the TCP/IP to a remote log server. The SocketAppender object has the following features associated with it:

- The remote logging is *nonintrusive*. The timestamp, the NDC information, and the location information are preserved according to the client where the logging request was generated.

- The SocketAppender object does not use any Layout object to format its data. This is understandable as it transmits the LoggingEvent object to the server side in a serialized form.

- Logging events are automatically buffered by the native TCP implementation.

Fault Tolerance

The SocketAppender implementation is fault tolerant. It can handle or tries to resolve different network-related problems such as a link being down or link speed being slow. Typically, SocketAppender attempts to do the following things in case there is a fault:

- If the server is reachable, log events will eventually arrive at the server.

- If the remote server is down and not reachable, logging events are dropped. But as soon as the server comes back, logging activity starts transparently. This transparent connection is accomplished by a connector thread, which periodically attempts to connect to the remote server.

- If the connection to the server is slow but faster than the rate of logging event production, the client will benefit from the native TCP/IP buffered implementation, and it will not be affected by the link speed.

- If the link speed is slower than the rate of logging event production, the client will suffer because it can only go with the network speed.

- If the network link is up but the server is down, the client will not be blocked, but log events will be lost due to server unavailability.

- If the network link is down but the server is alive, the client will be blocked until it times out (normal TCP/IP timeout) or the network link comes back to life.

- `SocketAppender` does not get garbage collected automatically. It is important that the `close()` method of `SocketAppender` or the `LogManager.shutdown()` method has been explicitly called before exiting the application to make sure that `SocketAppender` is closed. However, if the JVM exits before `SocketAppender` can close gracefully, there might be untransmitted data in the pipe that might be lost.

Configuring SocketAppender

`SocketAppender` has the configurable bean properties listed in Table 7-3.

Table 7-3. Configurable Bean Properties in SocketAppender

Bean Property	Method	Description	Default
locationInfo	setLocationInfo(boolean)	Sets the location information parameter to `true` or `false`	`false`
port	setPort(int)	Sets the port number to connect to	4560
reconnectionDelay	setReconnectionDelay(int)	Number of milliseconds after which the connector thread should try to reconnect to the server, in case it is down	30,000 milliseconds
remoteHost	setRemoteHost(String)	Sets the remote host name	None

A SocketAppender Example

Writing logging event data to a remote server is easy—SocketAppender will do the job for us. We just need to pass to it the host name, the port, etc., as a part of the configurable bean properties. On the other side of the fence, we need a server program that can accept the socket connection opened by SocketAppender and process the incoming data. Listing 7-9, LoggingServer.java, is an example server-side program that accepts the data sent to it. It listens to an arbitrary port, 1000. After it receives data from the socket connection, it converts the data to the agreed LoggingEvent object and extracts all the data from it.

Listing 7-9. LoggingServer.java

```
package com.apress.logging.log4j;

import java.net.ServerSocket;
import java.net.Socket;
import java.io.ObjectInputStream;
import java.io.BufferedInputStream;

import org.apache.log4j.spi.LoggingEvent;

public class SocketServer implements Runnable{

    private String portNumber = null;
    private ServerSocket serverSocket = null;
    private Socket socket = null;
    private ObjectInputStream inStream = null;
    private LoggingEvent event = null;
    /** Creates a new instance of SocketServer */
    public SocketServer(String portNumber) {
        this.portNumber = portNumber;
        try {
            //listen to the port specified
            serverSocket = new ServerSocket(Integer.parseInt(portNumber));
            socket = serverSocket.accept();
            //creating a ObjectInputStream from the socket input stream
            inStream = new ObjectInputStream(new
BufferedInputStream(socket.getInputStream()));
            new Thread(this).start();
        }catch(Exception e) {
            System.out.println("Error: "+e.toString());
        }
    }
```

```
    public void run() {
        try {

            while(true) {

                //cast back to the LoggingEvent object
                event = (LoggingEvent)inStream.readObject();
                //print the message and logger name in this logging event
                System.out.println("THE LOGGER NAME: "+event.getLoggerName());
                System.out.println("THE MESSAGE: "+event.getMessage().toString());
            }
        }catch(Exception e) {
            System.out.println("Error: here"+e.toString());
        }
    }

    public static void main(String args[]) {
        String port = args[0];
        new SocketServer(port);
    }
}
```

Notice that SocketServer is a thread-based program, and in the run() method it is constantly listening to the port for any incoming messages. As soon as a message arrives, it is capable of printing the content of the message.

Listing 7-10, "socket.properties", shows the configuration file required to send the logging information from the example program in Listing 7-1.

Listing 7-10. socket.properties

```
#configuring the custom logger
log4j.logger.com.apress.logging.log4j=DEBUG,SOCKET

#configuring the SOCKET appender
log4j.appender.SOCKET=org.apache.log4j.net.SocketAppender
log4j.appender.SOCKET.remoteHost=oemcomputer
log4j.appender.SOCKET.port=1000
```

Running the SocketAppender Example Program

To see SocketAppender in action, we will need to first run the SocketServer program and have it listen to the same port as specified in "socket.properties" (i.e., 1000). Make sure that SocketServer and SocketAppender both talk to the same port. The host in this example is a machine named oemcomputer where the ServerSocket program is running.

Start up the server program with the following command:

```
java com.apress.logging.log4j.SocketServer 1000
```

Now try the client program by passing it "socket.properties" as the configuration file.

```
java -Dlog4j.configuration=socket.properties
com.apress.logging.log4j.AdvancvedLogging
```

We will see the following messages arriving in the server-side console:

```
THE LOGGER NAME: com.apress.logging.log4j
THE MESSAGE: Deposited 100.5 new balance: 100.5
THE LOGGER NAME: com.apress.logging.log4j
THE MESSAGE: Withdrawn 80.0 new balance: 20.5
THE LOGGER NAME: com.apress.logging.log4j
THE MESSAGE: Failed to withdraw: balance: 20.5 attempted withdraw: 50.0
```

Logging to Windows NT Event Log with NTEventLogAppender

For programs that perform system-level operations, we might need to send log information to the event log of a particular OS. In Java, we might interact with an OS by using Java Native Interface (JNI). org.apache.log4j.net.NTEventLogAppender offers us the flexibility to do this.

As log4j API is written in Java, to access the Windows NT event log, it uses JNI to talk to an "NTEventLogAppender.dll" file. This file interacts with the Windows NT event log and writes the logging information there.

The NTEventLogAppender object is very simple to use and has the configurable bean properties shown in Table 7-4.

Table 7-4. Configurable Bean Properties in NTEventLogAppender

Bean Property	Method	Description	Default
layout	SetLayout(String)	Sets the layout to be used with this appender	The default layout is TTCCLayout.
source	setSource(String)	Sets the source name for this event log	The default source name is set to "Log4j".

We will reuse the program in Listing 7-1 to see how logging information is stored in the NT event log. We will also use the configuration file in Listing 7-11, "nt.properties", to configure the logger and appenders used in this example.

Listing 7-11. nt.properties

```
#configuring the custom logger
log4j.logger.com.apress.logging.log4j=DEBUG,NT

#configuring the NT appender
log4j.appender.NT=org.apache.log4j.nt.NTEventLogAppender
log4j.appender.NT.layout=org.apache.log4j.SimpleLayout
```

This example configuration file provides a `SimpleLayout` object to `NTEventLogAppender`. Simply execute the example program with this configuration file. Once finished, if we open the Event Viewer of a Windows NT/Windows 2000/Window XP system, and we will see the events logged against the source name "Log4j" in the application log section. In each event we will find the logging information being stored.

Distributing Logging Information via SMTPAppender

The previous chapter mentioned that the greatest feature of a logging API like log4j is that it does not restrict logging activity to mere debug traces. Moreover, as we have seen from the discussions of several `Appender` objects, these objects constitute a powerful feature for distributing logging information to various components such as databases, NT event logs, sockets, etc. This useful feature can be exploited to achieve data distribution capability without having to write a separate application module to do the same.

One example of this great feature is SMTPAppender. Imagine you are writing an order processing application in which upon receiving each order the customer is subsequently updated with the details of the order received. One traditional solution to this problem is to collect the order information and pass it to a separate mailing application to e-mail it to the user. With the help of SMTPAppender, we can do this without even writing a single line of extra code.

org.apache.log4j.net.SMTPAppender is a powerful Appender object capable of sending logging information using the Simple Mail Transfer Protocol (SMTP). The SMTPAppender object has the configurable bean properties shown in Table 7-5.

Table 7-5. Configurable Bean Properties in SocketAppender

Bean Property	Method	Description	Default
bufferSize	setBufferSize(int)	Sets the size of the cyclic buffer storing the logging event	Defaults to 512 events
evaluatorClass	setEvaluatorClass(String)	Sets the name of the evaluator class to use to check for any triggering condition	Defaults to inner class DefaultEvaluator
from	setFrom(String)	Sets the e-mail address of the sender	None
layout	setLayout(String)	Sets the layout to format the logging information	None
locationInfo	setLocationInfo(boolean)	Specifies whether the location information should be included in the logging information	false
SMTPHost	setSMTPHost(String)	Sets the name of the SMTP host to be used to send e-mails	None
subject	setSubject(String)	Sets the subject of the e-mail	None
to	setTo(String)	Sets the e-mail address of the recipient	None

The last of the configuration parameters in Table 7-5 is worth discussing. SMTPAppender can have an evaluator class attached to it. This evaluator class can evaluate each logging event and decide on a triggering condition to tell the SMTPAppender to fire the e-mail activity. The triggering condition can be anything application specific, such as when a logging event has a message with a level of ERROR. The default evaluator class that SMTPAppender uses is an inner class named DefaultEvaluator. The DefaultEvaluator class only checks if the level associated with the logging event is greater or equal to the level value ERROR.

If the triggering condition is not met, the event is stored in a cyclic buffer with a default size of 512 events. As soon as a logging event arrives that satisfies the triggering condition, all the events from the buffer are retrieved and e-mailed to the recipient.

To see an example of SMTPAppender in action, we will reuse the program in Listing 7-1 with the configuration file shown in Listing 7-12, "smtp.properties". The configuration for SMTPAppender uses smtp.mail.yahoo.com as the SMTP server. You can replace this with any other SMTP server you are using. The to attribute defines the e-mail address for the recipient and from defines the e-mail address of the sender. The subject attribute defines the subject of the e-mail, and finally we assign an org.apache.log4j.SimpleLayout object to format the logging information to appear within the body of the e-mail.

Listing 7-12. smtp.properties

```
#configuring the custom logger
log4j.logger.com.apress.logging.log4j=DEBUG,SMTP

#configuring the SMTP appender
log4j.appender.SMTP=org.apache.log4j.net.SMTPAppender
log4j.appender.SMTP.SMTPHost=smtp.mail.yahoo.com
log4j.appender.SMTP.to=clientname@mailserver.com
log4j.appender.SMTP.subject=Testing the appender
log4j.appender.SMTP.from=yourname@mailserver.com
log4j.appender.SMTP.layout=org.apache.log4j.SimpleLayout
```

With this configuration file, execute the sample program. Remember, SMTPAppender relies on the Java Mail API ("mail.jar") and Java Activation API ("activation.jar"). Make sure that these two .jar files are in your classpath along with the log4j-specific .jar file.

Once executed, we will see the messages are going to the client e-mail address. In our example program, there is a message with a level of ERROR that meets the triggering condition, and thus SMTPAppender sends the e-mail with all the logging events to the specified client e-mail address.

Making Messages Available Through Telnet with TelnetAppender

On certain occasions we might want to give remote users access to the logging information we produce from an application. This is particularly important when we want to manage an application remotely. In this case, we are publishing logging data locally and want to give read-only access to the remote user. The best way of doing this is to use the existing Telnet protocol. Remote users can log in to the local machine using Telnet protocol and can read the logging information we want them to see.

The log4j API provides `org.apache.log4j.net.TelnetAppender` for us to enable this feature. `TelnetAppender` writes the data to a read-only socket. `TelnetAppender` is a multithreaded program that opens a server socket connection to a port and listens for any connection made to the same port. As soon as a connection signal arrives, it adds the connection source information to a buffer. Next, whenever a logging request arrives to the `TelnetAppender`, it writes the data to all the active connection sockets.

The `TelnetAppender` object uses the default Telnet port 23. Optionally, any other port can be specified. The maximum number of connections it can handle simultaneously is 20. `TelnetAppender` requires a specific layout to format logging data accordingly.

A good example of a situation ideal for using `TelnetAppender` is in conjunction with a servlet. A servlet handles multiple client connections at one point in time. Also, using `TelnetAppender` for server logging activity allows multiple remote managers to obtain logging information real time. This is great when remote management of an application is critical.

Instead of including an example of using `TelnetAppender` with a servlet here, this is left for to you to implement as an exercise. Remember, there is not much magic to `TelnetAppender`. You only need to configure your `Logger` object to use the `TelnetAppender`.

Conclusion

In this chapter, we have discussed some of the advanced logging concepts of log4j. We have now seen the power of the log4j API to make logging activity distributed. This is of great importance when an application is large, distributed, and interacting with several other custom or legacy applications. The remote management of the application becomes easier with log traces being managed and viewed remotely. This gives us better control over the day-to-day maintenance of our applications.

As we have also seen, most of the logging framework with log4j is configurable. In all our examples, we could change the logging behavior just by pointing the application to a different configuration file. No doubt you can appreciate the power of log4j and benefit from using it within your own applications.

In the next chapter, we will investigate how we can leverage the existing framework of log4j and extend it to write application-specific components.

CHAPTER 8

Extending log4j to Create Custom Logging Components

IN THE PREVIOUS CHAPTERS, we covered the core log4j framework. We have discussed how the Logger, Appender, Layout, and Filter objects interact with each other and publish logging information to a preferred destination. Apache log4j offers a vast range of Appender objects. These give us the power to publish logging data to a local machine and to distribute logging data over a network. Moreover, the flexible and highly configurable nature of log4j allows us to change logging behavior completely by merely changing the configuration file.

All this is great and useful. Still, there may be situations in which the default log4j capabilities do not quite fit an application's requirements. This sort of limitation is more due to the sophisticated nature of the application rather than the design of log4j. In such situations, we have to extend the log4j framework to devise our own logging components to meet our applications' requirements.

In this chapter, we will discuss how we can extend the log4j framework to create application-specific components. The topics discussed and examples provided herein will serve as a guideline for developing custom logging components specific to applications.

Creating the Custom WindowAppender

In this section, let's explore how we can create our own Appender objects. It is possible that in an application we may want Java window-based logging. It is a common application requirement to monitor log information in some sort of GUI control such as a small window. This means that the Logger objects in an application should be configured to send logging information to a Java window. To achieve this, we can create a custom appender named WindowAppender that is capable of printing all logging information to a small Java-based window.

Features of the Custom WindowAppender

As mentioned in the discussion in Chapter 5 of several Appender objects available within the log4j API, these objects all inherit from a base class called AppenderSkeleton. Any custom Appender object we want to create must adhere to this appender hierarchy. The log4j framework checks for this criterion before invoking any appender specified and ignores any that do not adhere to the appender hierarchy.

Sticking to the appender hierarchy makes it fairly easy to write custom Appender objects. In this example, we will create a WindowAppender object. Before writing the code for the WindowAppender object, let's take a look at the features we will include:

- The WindowAppender will create a small Java Frame-based window.

- The window will display logging information in a scrollable area.

- The title, width, and height properties of the window should be configurable through bean properties.

This looks simple, but we have to be aware of a few bottlenecks with this WindowAppender. We need to decide how different Logger objects within any application will access WindowAppender. The following points are important to consider before we create the WindowAppender object:

- An application may have several Logger objects, and each of them may try to use the WindowAppender object to log information.

- We need to make sure that for all the created instances of WindowAppender one and only one window is active.

- If for every Logger object using the WindowAppender object a separate logging window is created, the system will soon be full of logging windows, which is not desirable.

Architecture of the Custom WindowAppender

Considering the features we need to provide and the bottlenecks we should be aware of, we need to find a way to create a single instance of the logging window and make it available to all instances of WindowAppender. The best time to create the logging window is when the appender is initialized.

To understand this, let's go through the appender initialization process:

- If the appender configuration is specified in a configuration file, the log4j framework will read the appender configuration from that file.

- The log4j framework first creates an instance of the specified appender class by calling the default constructor of that class.

- If other bean properties are specified in the configuration file, the set() methods of the corresponding bean property are invoked to set the property values.

- Finally, the activateOptions() method of the specified appender class is invoked to initialize any optional configuration for the appender. This method is optional to any appender and therefore may or may not be present in a particular Appender object.

Now coming back to WindowAppender, what is the best place to initialize the logging window? Because we have the bean properties to set the title, height, and width attribute of the logging window, we cannot create an instance of the logging window before the initialization process sets these bean properties. Thus, the best place to create an instance of the logging window after the bean properties are set is in the activateOptions() method.

Also, we need to make sure that no more than one instance of the logging window gets created. So we should move the creation and instantiation of the logging window to a synchronized method to return a static singleton instance of the logging window.

Implementation of the Custom WindowAppender

Listing 8-1 demonstrates WindowAppender.java, the custom window-based Appender object.

Listing 8-1. WindowAppender.java

```
package com.apress.logging.log4j.appender;

import org.apache.log4j.AppenderSkeleton;
import org.apache.log4j.spi.LoggingEvent;
import javax.swing.JFrame;
import javax.swing.JTextArea;
import javax.swing.JScrollPane;
```

```java
/** This is a custom Appender object publishing the logging
 * information to a Java window. The logging Java window is a
 * singleton instance across all the instances of this Appender
 * object.
 */
public class WindowAppender extends AppenderSkeleton{

    private static JFrame frame = null;
    private static JTextArea area = null;
    private static JScrollPane pane = null;

    /** Holds value of property title. */
    private static String title;

    /** Holds value of property height. */
    private static int height;

    /** Holds value of property width. */
    private static int width;

    /** Creates a new instance of WindowAppender */
    public WindowAppender() {
    }
    /**
     *This method is called as a part of the appender initialization process
     */
    public void activateOptions() {
        getWindowInstance();
    }
    /**
     * private method to initialize the logging window
     */
    private synchronized JFrame getWindowInstance() {
        area = new JTextArea();
        pane = new JScrollPane(area);
        if(frame == null) {
            frame = new JFrame(title);
            frame.setSize(width,height);
            frame.getContentPane().add(pane);
            frame.setVisible(true);
        }
        return frame;
    }
```

Extending log4j to Create Custom Logging Components

```java
    /** This method is overridden from the super class and
     * prints the logging message to the logging window.
     * NOTE: If there is no layout specified for this Appender,
     * no message will be displayed. The logging information is
     * formatted according to the layout and the conversion pattern
     * specified.
     * @param loggingEvent encapsulates the logging information.
     */
    protected void append(LoggingEvent loggingEvent) {
        //simply extract the message and display it
        JScrollPane pane =
(JScrollPane)frame.getContentPane().getComponent(0);
        JTextArea area = (JTextArea)pane.getViewport().getView();
        if(this.layout !=null) {
            area.append(this.layout.format(loggingEvent));
        }
    }

    /** This method is overridden from the super class and disposes
     * the logging window.
     */
    public void close() {
        frame.dispose();
    }

    /** This method is overridden from the super class and always
     * returns true to indicate that a Layout is required for
     * this appender. If not specified in the conf. file, then it
     * will not print any message in the log window.
     */
    public boolean requiresLayout() {
        return true;
    }

    /** Getter for property title.
     * @return Value of property title.
     */
    public String getTitle() {
        return this.title;
    }

    /** Setter for property title.
     * @param title New value of property title.
     */
```

```java
        public void setTitle(String title) {
            this.title = title;
        }

        /** Getter for property height.
         * @return Value of property height.
         */
        public int getHeight() {
            return this.height;
        }

        /** Setter for property height.
         * @param height New value of property height.
         */
        public void setHeight(int height) {
            this.height = height;
        }

        /** Getter for property width.
         * @return Value of property width.
         */
        public int getWidth() {
            return this.width;
        }

        /** Setter for property width.
         * @param width New value of property width.
         */
        public void setWidth(int width) {
            this.width = width;
        }

}
```

As we can see in this WindowAppender, getWindowInstance() is a private synchronized method responsible for creating a JFrame instance with the specified title, width, and height bean properties. We have provided an overridden append() method that writes logging data to the JTextArea embedded within a JScrollPane attached to the JFrame. Each time a logging request arrives, the logging message is printed to the JTextArea. Notice that the requiresLayout() method in WindowAppender returns true. This means WindowAppender requires a Layout object to be associated with it, and it uses the Layout object to format the logging event before displaying the message. If no Layout object is specified, no logging message will be displayed in the window.

The activateOptions() method calls the getWindowInstance() method, which creates a new logging window JFrame instance or returns an already existing one.

If we are configuring programmatically, we have to explicitly call the activateOptions() method to get a logging window created. As the getWindowInstance() method is synchronized and returns one and only one instance of the JFrame object, it is protected against multiple programs calling the activateOptions() method of the WindowAppender. No matter how the configuration is done, we will always get one instance of the logging window per application instance.

Testing the Custom WindowAppender

To test WindowAppender, we will use the WindowAppender object as the appender for two separate Logger objects appearing in two different application class files. These files are shown in Listing 8-2 and Listing 8-3.

Listing 8-2, AnotherClass.java, creates a named logger, Logger1, and Listing 8-3, WindowAppenderDemo, creates another named logger, Logger2. Both of the classes perform some simple logging activity.

Listing 8-2. AnotherClass.java

```
package com.apress.logging.log4j.appender;

import org.apache.log4j.Logger;

public class AnotherClass {
    private static Logger logger = Logger.getLogger("Logger2");

    /** Creates a new instance of AnotherClass */
    public AnotherClass() {
    }

    public void logAnotherMessage()
    {
        logger.info("Message from Another class..");
    }
}
```

Listing 8-3. WindowAppenderDemo.java

```java
package com.apress.logging.log4j.appender;

import org.apache.log4j.Logger;

public class WindowAppenderDemo {

    private static Logger logger1 = Logger.getLogger("Logger1");
    private static Logger logger2 = Logger.getLogger("Logger2");

    /** Creates a new instance of WindowAppenderDemo */
    public WindowAppenderDemo() {
    }

    public void doLogging()
    {
        logger1.info("Message from logger1");
        logger2.info("Message from logger2");
    }

    /**
     * @param args the command line arguments
     */
    public static void main(String[] args) {
        WindowAppenderDemo demo = new WindowAppenderDemo();
        demo.doLogging();
        AnotherClass anc = new AnotherClass();
        anc.logAnotherMessage();
    }
}
```

We will write a small configuration file, "customappender.properties", to configure both the `Logger` objects used in these two classes. This file, shown in Listing 8-4, exhibits the configuration to use for this example.

Listing 8-4. customappender.properties

```
#configuring the custom logger
log4j.logger.Logger1=DEBUG,WINDOW
log4j.logger.Logger2=DEBUG,WINDOW

#configuring the WINDOW appender
log4j.appender.WINDOW=com.apress.logging.log4j.appender.WindowAppender
log4j.appender.WINDOW.layout=org.apache.log4j.SimpleLayout
log4j.appender.WINDOW.title=Custom Logging Window
log4j.appender.WINDOW.width=200
log4j.appender.WINDOW.height=200
```

In this configuration file, we pass the values for `title`, `width`, and `height` for `WindowAppender`. We also specify `SimpleLayout` as the layout to be used by `WindowAppender`.

Executing the program in Listing 8-3, we will see a small logging window appearing with logging messages displayed in it, as shown in Figure 8-1.

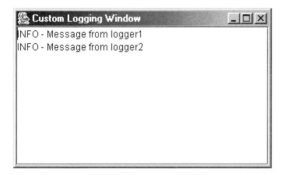

Figure 8-1. Logging information produced by WindowAppender

Configuring log4j from a Database

As we have discussed previously, one of the most important features of log4j is its highly configurable nature. We can define application-specific configuration files either in properties style or in XML style. Also, the configuration files can reside in a remote place, and we can still load configuration information provided the resource can be accessed from a URL.

The fact that logging behavior can be controlled through configuration files makes it so easy to change logging style without altering the source code, instead changing configuration information or pointing the application to a different set of configuration files.

In certain application scenarios, we might prefer to control the log4j configuration information from a central database. This can give us the power to apply a centrally controlled logging style to different application components. In this scenario, we are likely to consider that all the components in an application subscribe to a particular logging style. The `Logger`, `Appender`, `Level`, `Layout`, and `Filter` objects combined define a logging style. Another combination of these logging elements will result in a separate logging style. If we decide that all application components will collectively subscribe to a particular logging style, and when they switch over to a different logging style they do so collectively, storing the configuration information in a database in a relational way might be the solution. This means each application component does not need to maintain and load its own configuration information, and changing the configuration information centrally in a database can control the logging behavior.

It is great that we can change logging behavior so easily, but in reality how often do we need to do that? In general, we know beforehand what information we will need to log to maintain the application. It is almost always the case that we need more logging information during the development and testing phase and need only certain logging information in the deployment phase. The power of log4j lies not in the fact that we can change our application logging behavior every now and then, but in the fact that we can camouflage the capability to produce various degrees of logging information within an application, unveiling it when required. Only when we come to a stage where we need more or less information do we switch over to a different style of logging.

The Database Table Design for Storing the Logging Configuration

Recall that the structure of the configuration files and XML configuration files we used throughout the discussion of log4j is key-value based. To configure log4j from a database requires replicating the same information structure in the database. In a real-life situation, it could take a whole afternoon to decide what database structure to adopt. But for the sake of this example, we are going to use a pretty simplistic structure with two tables, LOGGER_REPOSITORY and APPENDER_DEF, that contain information about loggers and appenders, respectively.

Figure 8-2 shows the simple schema diagram for the tables we are going to use for this example.

This structure is a very simple one that excludes elements such as `Filter` objects and `Renderer` objects. We can see that the APPENDER_DEF table contains the possible properties related to different `Appender` objects, although it does not include all the `Appender` objects in order to keep this example simple. It can at present contain three appender objects: `ConsoleAppender`, `DailyRollingFileAppender`, and `JDBCAppender`.

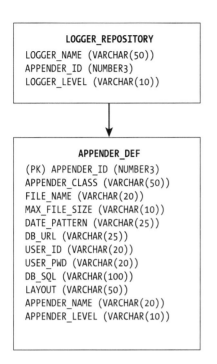

Figure 8-2. The log4j configuration schema diagram

Reading Configuration Information from the Database via the Configuration Loader

Once we have the configuration information defined in the database tables, we need some mechanism to read the information. We will now develop a small program that reads the configuration data from the database. It also creates a `java.util.Properties` object with the key and value of all the log4j configuration information and returns it to the caller. Once the data is read and loaded into the `Properties` object, the connection to the database is closed.

You might be wondering why we need to load the data in a `Properties` object. The reason will be clear once we go through this example. For the time being, you just need to know that we want to use the existing `org.apache.log4j.PropertyConfigurator` class to do the actual configuration job. The `PropertyConfigurator` class is capable of configuring the log4j framework from a `Properties` object.

Notice that the SQL to retrieve configuration data from the database is hard coded within the `DBConfigLoader` class. We also retrieve the data by referencing the column names in the tables. All this is done to keep the example simple; feel free to improve this program by changing the infrastructure wherever you like.

Listing 8-5, `DBConfigLoader.java`, is a sample implementation for reading configuration information from the database.

Listing 8-5. DBConfigLoader.java

```java
package com.apress.logging.log4j;

import java.util.Properties;
import java.sql.Connection;
import java.sql.DriverManager;
import java.sql.Statement;
import java.sql.ResultSet;
import java.sql.SQLException;

public class DBConfigLoader
{
    private Connection conn = null;
    private String dbUrl = null;
    private String dbDriver = null;
    private String dbUser = null;
    private String dbPwd = null;

    /**
     * Constructor initializing the db access params
     */
    public DBConfigLoader()
    {
        this.setDbDriver("sun.jdbc.odbc.JdbcOdbcDriver");
        this.setDbUrl("jdbc:odbc:dbdef");
        this.setDbUser("system");
        this.setDbPwd("manager");
    }

    /**
     * Sets the driver class for the db access
     */
    private void setDriver()
    {
        try
        {
            //load the driver
            Class.forName(dbDriver);
        } catch (ClassNotFoundException cnfe)
        {
            System.out.println("Could not find the driver class " + dbDriver);
        }
    }
```

Extending log4j to Create Custom Logging Components

```java
/**
 * Method to obtain a db connection
 * @return Connection object
 * @throws SQLException
 */
private Connection getConnection() throws SQLException
{
    System.out.println("CONNECTION PARAMS: ");
    System.out.println("DRIVER: " + dbDriver);
    System.out.println("URL: " + dbUrl);
    System.out.println("USER: " + dbUser);
    System.out.println("PWD: " + dbPwd);
    //load the driver
    setDriver();
    //getting the connection
    conn = DriverManager.getConnection(dbUrl, dbUser, dbPwd);

    return conn;

}

/**
 * Obtain the configuration data from the db
 * @param sql The sql to execute to get the data
 * @return ResultSet object containing the data
 * @throws SQLException
 */
private ResultSet getConfigData(String sql) throws SQLException
{
    //obtain a connection to the database
    conn = getConnection();
    //create a statement object to execute the query
    Statement stmt = conn.createStatement();
    //execute the query to get the resultset
    ResultSet rs = stmt.executeQuery(sql);
    return rs;
}

/**
 * constructs the SQL statement to execute
 * @return String the SQL statement
 */
private String getSQL()
{
    StringBuffer buffer = new StringBuffer("SELECT * FROM APPENDER_DEF
```

```
                AD, LOGGER_REPOSITORY LR WHERE ");
                    buffer.append(" LR.APPENDER_ID=AD.APPENDER_ID");
                    System.out.println("The SQL: " + buffer.toString());
                    return buffer.toString();
                }

                /**
                 * Loads all the configuration data in a Properties object
                 * and returns the Properties object back to the caller
                 */
                public Properties getConfigData()
                {
                    //properties object to store the config data
                    Properties props = new Properties();
                    String loggerName = null;
                    String loggerLevel = null;
                    String appenderName = null;
                    String appenderClass = null;
                    String appenderLevel = null;
                    String fileName = null;
                    String maxFileSize = null;
                    String jdbcURL = null;
                    String jdbcUser = null;
                    String jdbcPwd = null;
                    String jdbcSQL = null;
                    String layout = null;

                    //get the sql to obtain the config data
                    String sql = getSQL();
                    try
                    {
                        //get the result set
                        ResultSet rs = getConfigData(sql);
                        while (rs.next())
                        {

                            //getting the appender class
                            appenderClass = rs.getString("APPENDER_CLASS");
                            //getting the file name properties (can be null)
                            fileName = rs.getString("FILE_NAME");
                            //getting the max file size (can be null)
                            maxFileSize = rs.getString("MAX_FILE_SIZE");
                            //getting the jdbc url   (can be null)
                            jdbcURL = rs.getString("DB_URL");
```

```
//getting the jdbc user id (can be null)
jdbcUser = rs.getString("USER_ID");
//getting the jdbc password (can be null)
jdbcPwd = rs.getString("USER_PWD");
//getting the SQL string
jdbcSQL = rs.getString("DB_SQL");
//getting the layout information
layout = rs.getString("LAYOUT");
//getting the appender name
appenderName = rs.getString("APPENDER_NAME");
//getting the level of the appender
appenderLevel = rs.getString("APPENDER_LEVEL");

//getting the logger name
loggerName = rs.getString("LOGGER_NAME");
//getting the logger level
loggerLevel = rs.getString("LOGGER_LEVEL");

//constructing the properties with key and value
String loggerKey = "log4j.logger." + loggerName;
String appenderKey = "log4j.appender." + appenderName;

//properties for the logger  level and the appender
props.put(loggerKey, loggerLevel + "," + appenderName);
props.put(getKey(appenderKey, null), appenderClass);

if (fileName != null)
{
    props.put(getKey(appenderKey, "File"), fileName);
}
if (maxFileSize != null)
{
    props.put(getKey(appenderKey, "MaxFileSize"),
}
if (jdbcURL != null)
{
    props.put(getKey(appenderKey, "URL"), jdbcURL);
}
if (jdbcUser != null)
{
    props.put(getKey(appenderKey, "user"), jdbcUser);
}
if (jdbcPwd != null)
{
```

```java
                            props.put(getKey(appenderKey, "password"), jdbcPwd);
                        }
                        if (layout != null)
                        {
                            props.put(getKey(appenderKey, "layout"), layout);
                        }
                }
        } catch (SQLException sqle)
        {
            System.out.println("FAILED TO GET CONFIG DATA: " +
    sqle.toString());
            sqle.printStackTrace();

        } finally
        {
            closeConnection();
        }

        return props;
    }

    /**
     * constructs the key for the properties object
     * @param prefix the prefix to the key
     * @param suffix the suffix to the key
     * @return
     */
    private String getKey(String prefix, String suffix)
    {
        StringBuffer buffer = new StringBuffer(prefix);

        if (suffix != null)
        {
            buffer.append(".");
            buffer.append(suffix);
        }
        //System.out.println("returning key....."+buffer.toString());
        return buffer.toString();
    }

    private void closeConnection()
    {
        try
        {
```

```java
            if (conn != null)
            {
                conn.close();
            }
        } catch (SQLException sqle)
        {
            System.out.println("Problem closing the connection..");
        }
    }

    /**
     * Returns the db user name
     * @return   db user
     */

    public String getDbUser()
    {
        return dbUser;
    }

    /**
     * Sets the db user name
     * @param dbUser db user name
     */
    public void setDbUser(String dbUser)
    {
        this.dbUser = dbUser;
    }

    /**
     * Returns the database access password
     * @return the database password
     */
    public String getDbPwd()
    {
        return dbPwd;
    }

    /**
     * Sets the db access password
     * @param dbPwd  the db password
     */
    public void setDbPwd(String dbPwd)
    {
```

```java
            this.dbPwd = dbPwd;
        }

        /**
         * Returns the db driver
         * @return the db driver
         */
        public String getDbDriver()
        {
            return dbDriver;
        }

        /**
         * Sets the db driver
         * @param dbDriver the db driver
         */
        public void setDbDriver(String dbDriver)
        {
            this.dbDriver = dbDriver;
        }

        /**
         * Returns the db address
         * @return the db address
         */
        public String getDbUrl()
        {
            return dbUrl;
        }

        /**
         * Sets the database address
         * @param dbUrl the database address
         */
        public void setDbUrl(String dbUrl)
        {
            this.dbUrl = dbUrl;
        }
    }
```

Writing the Configuration Class

Once we have loaded log4j configuration information from the database, we need some way to access that information and configure log4j. In order to do this, we must write a custom configuration class to read the data from the database and configure the log4j framework. The log4j API already provides two classes for configuration: BasicConfigurator, which is capable of providing very basic configuration to the log4j framework, and DOMConfigurator, which is capable of loading configuration information from an XML file. We can write our own configuration class to configure the log4j framework from a database. Before we proceed to do that, let's see how the configuration takes place within the log4j framework.

Figure 8-3 shows the sequence of the log4j initialization. Each time we try to obtain a Logger by calling Logger.getLogger(loggerName), the LogManager class gets initialized. LogManager collects and inspects the system properties supplied to log4j from the command line. Remember, this is happening at class loading time of the LogManager in a static block, and this takes place once and only once. LogManager detects the configuration files specified via the command line system properties. It then calls the OptionConverter helper class to parse the information contained in the files. The OptionConverter class instantiates an appropriate Configurator class and calls the doConfigure() method to complete the configuration process.

The present state of log4j relies on the fact that configuration information should be specified in a configuration file accessible through a URL. If no configuration resource file is specified, it tries to look for its default configuration file, "log4j.properties", in the classpath of your application.

NOTE Starting with version 1.2.7, log4j looks for a "log4j.xml" or "log4j.properties" file in the classpath.

In case it cannot locate any configuration file, log4j exits, and application logging will no longer work. It is possible to override the way configuration is done by writing a custom configuration class that reads the configuration file from a location over the network. But this is restricted only to the protocols supported by the java.net.URL object.

Any custom configuration class we write must implement an interface named Configurator in log4j. The Configurator interface defines a single method, doConfigure(URL, LoggerRepository), which is the method in which the configuration takes place.

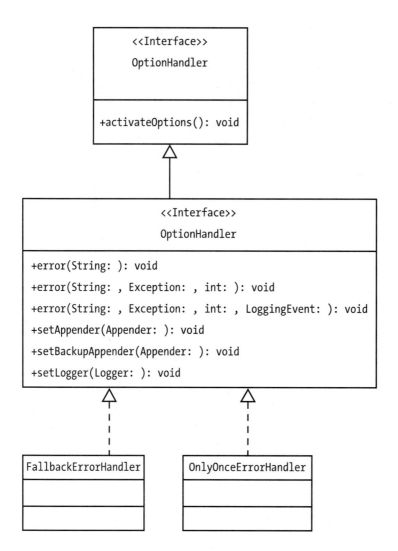

Figure 8-3. The log4j configuration process

We have already seen that the log4j framework uses URL-based configuration. In our example, we wish to configure log4j by reading the configuration information from a database. Apparently, there is a conflict of interest here. But we will be a little bit clever by exploiting the existing framework to do our job. We will use a configuration file that will contain information related to obtaining a connection to the database. DBConfigurator will parse this configuration file and use the DBConfigLoader class to read the configuration information from the database. It will then obtain the java.util.Properties object from DBConfigLoader, which contains all the configuration information. The DBConfigurator class then uses the

Extending log4j to Create Custom Logging Components

org.apache.log4j.PropertyConfigurator class to actually configure log4j by passing it the Properties object.

Listing 8-6, DBConfigurator.java, shows the custom configuration class we will use to configure the log4j framework.

Listing 8-6. DBConfigurator.java

```
package com.apress.logging.log4j;

import org.apache.log4j.spi.Configurator;
import org.apache.log4j.spi.LoggerRepository;
import org.apache.log4j.PropertyConfigurator;
import org.apache.log4j.helpers.LogLog;

import java.net.URL;
import java.util.Properties;

public class DBConfigurator implements Configurator
{
    private String dbURL = null;
    private String dbUser = null;
    private String dbPwd = null;
    private String dbDriver = null;
    private DBConfigLoader configLoader = null;
    private Properties log4jProps = null;

    public DBConfigurator()
    {
        configLoader = new DBConfigLoader();
    }

    public void doConfigure(URL url, LoggerRepository repos)
    {
        Properties props = new Properties();
        try
        {
        //collect the db access information from the config file
        props.load(url.openStream());
        dbURL = (String)props.get("DB_URL");
        dbUser = (String)props.get("DB_USER");
        dbPwd = (String)props.get("DB_PWD");
        dbDriver = (String)props.get("DB_DRIVER");
```

```
            //configure the config loader
            configLoader.setDbDriver(dbDriver);
            configLoader.setDbUrl(dbURL);
            configLoader.setDbUser(dbUser);
            configLoader.setDbPwd(dbPwd);

            //get the log4j properties
            log4jProps = configLoader.getConfigData();
            //use the PropertyConfigurator to configure
            PropertyConfigurator.configure(log4jProps);
            }catch(Exception e)
            {
                LogLog.error("could not load the configuration ", e);
            }

        }
    }
```

DBConfigurator implements the interface Configurator. Once the configuration class is specified as DBConfigurator, the LogManager class will pass the name of the configuration class to OptionConverter. OptionConverter will then create a new instance of DBConfigurator and call the doConfigure() method in it. Once the control is within the DBConfigurator class, DBConfigurator uses DBConfigLoader to obtain the configuration data and then uses PropertyConfigurator to do the actual log4j configuration.

In theory, we could configure log4j by calling PropertyConfigurator from within the DBConfigLoader class itself. But this means in the application we have to explicitly instantiate and call the configuration method of DBConfigLoader to do the configuration, which is not the ideal situation. If ever you need to use a different configuration class, you will have to change the source of your application to do so. Implementing the DBConfigurator class solves the problem and integrates the use of DBConfigLoader within the log4j framework. In turn you might argue that DBConfigLoader is hard coded within the DBConfigurator class. True, but we can easily extend DBConfigurator to read a system parameter indicating the database access class it should use, or we can specify the parameter within the configuration file.

An Example of Using Database-Based Configuration

We now have the infrastructure ready to configure log4j from a database. Let's take a look at a small demo program, LoggingDemo.java, described in Listing 8-7. The class simply has a method to write two different logging messages with levels ERROR and INFO.

Listing 8-7. LoggingDemo.java

```java
package com.apress.logging.log4j;
import org.apache.log4j.Logger;

public class LoggingDemo
{
    private static Logger logger = Logger.getLogger("APPLICATION1");
    public LoggingDemo()
    {
    }

    public void doLogging()
    {
        logger.info("INFO MESSAGE...");
        logger.error("ERROR MESSAGE...");

    }

    public static void main(String args[])
    {
        LoggingDemo demo = new LoggingDemo();
        demo.doLogging();
    }
}
```

Creating Configuration Data in the Database

In this example program, we are trying to use a Logger object named APPLICATION1. We need to create a style for this named logger in the database. The following SQL script will insert a record for the logger named APPLICATION1 and the corresponding appender record:

```
INSERT INTO LOGGER_REPOSITORY VALUES ('APPLICATION1,'1,'ERROR');
```

Now we will create some appender configuration data in the APPENDER_DEF table. The following script will insert data for the Appender object with the ID 1.

```
INSERT INTO APPENDER_DEF VALUES
(1,'org.apache.log4j.ConsoleAppender', 'org.apache.log4j. SimpleLayout',
'CONSOLE', 'DEBUG');
```

The logger named APPLICATION1 will now have a level of ERROR and will use the Appender defined with the APPENDER_ID of 1 in the APPENDER_DEF table. Referring to the data we put in the APPENDER_DEF table, the Appender with ID value 1 is a ConsoleAppender. So any logging from this application will be printed to the console. We can switch the entry in the LOGGER_REPOSITORY table any time to point the Appender to ID 2, which will then write logging data to the database using the JDBCAppender object.

The Configuration File

We also need a configuration file defining the database access parameters. Listing 8-8, "dbConfig.properties", is the configuration file for this example.

Listing 8-8. dbConfig.properties

```
DB_DRIVER=sun.jdbc.odbc.JdbcOdbcDriver
DB_URL=jdbc:odbc:dbdef
DB_USER=system
DB_PWD=manager
```

Executing the Database-Based Configuration Program

Now we need to execute the program LoggingDemo with all the required system parameters passed to it in the following manner:

```
java -Dlog4j.configuration=dbConfig.properties -
Dlog4j.configuratorClass=com.apress.logging.log4j.DBConfigurator
com.apress.logging.log4j.LoggingDemo
```

Notice that only the message with the level ERROR is printed to the console. Change the logger level in the table to INFO, and both messages will be printed.

Custom Logging Framework

Let's consider that in an application we want to trace every method entry and exit at the code optimization stage. Also, we want the level for these sorts of messages to be something below even the DEBUG level of log4j, as we do not want these messages to be published anytime at all after finishing the code optimization phase. It is a little inappropriate to use the DEBUG level for these sorts of messages, because of the likelihood that in the future the DEBUG level of messaging may need to be turned on in order to debug the application. In such cases, the messages related to method entry and exit are more likely to convolute the logging trace. Considering all these factors, we decide to introduce a new level, TRACE, to an application.

Creating a Custom Level Class

We will now examine how to write a custom level class. As mentioned in Chapter 5, each level basically corresponds to a `static final` unique integer value. We need to assign a unique integer value to the custom TRACE level we want to create. Also, log4j is capable of delegating logging messages to the UNIX Syslog via `SysLogAppender`. In this context, each logging level defined also needs to define a Syslog equivalent. The constant integer values used for Syslog are defined in the Syslog specification. For example, one sample "syslog.h" file from the UNIX implementation contains the following Syslog constants defined for different levels of logging:

```
#define LOG_EMERG 0 /* system is unusable */
#define LOG_ALERT 1 /* action must be taken immediately */
#define LOG_CRIT 2 /* critical conditions */
#define LOG_ERR 3 /* error conditions */
#define LOG_WARNING 4 /* warning conditions */
#define LOG_NOTICE 5 /* normal but signification conditions */
#define LOG_INFO 6 /* informational */
#define LOG_DEBUG 7 /* debug level messages */
```

The TRACE level should correspond to the LOG_DEBUG level of the Syslog implementation, and the `sysLogEquivalent` for this level should be 7. Finally, the `CustomLevel` class needs to provide methods to return the appropriate `Level` object and to create a TRACE level from a given `int` or `String` value.

Listing 8-9, `CustomLevel.java`, demonstrates how to implement a custom `Level` class.

Listing 8-9. CustomLevel.java

```
package com.apress.logging.log4j;

import org.apache.log4j.Level;

public class CustomLevel extends Level {

  static public final int    TRACE_INT   = Level.DEBUG_INT - 1;
  private static String TRACE_STR  = "TRACE";
```

```
    public static final CustomLevel TRACE = new CustomLevel(TRACE_INT,
TRACE_STR, 7);


  protected CustomLevel(int level, String strLevel, int syslogEquiv) {
    super(level, strLevel, syslogEquiv);
  }


  public static Level toLevel(String sArg) {
    return (Level) toLevel(sArg, CustomLevel.TRACE);
  }

  public static Level toLevel(String sArg, Level defaultValue) {

    if(sArg == null) {
      return defaultValue;
    }
    String stringVal = sArg.toUpperCase();

    if(stringVal.equals(TRACE_STR)) {
      return CustomLevel.TRACE;
    }
    return Level.toLevel(sArg, (Level) defaultValue);
  }
  public static Level toLevel(int i) {
    switch(i) {
    case TRACE_INT: return CustomLevel.TRACE;
    }
    return Level.toLevel(i);
  }
}
```

In this `CustomLevel` object, we define a new level, TRACE, with a unique integer value that is one less than the unique integer value associated with the DEBUG level to keep the priority of this level below DEBUG. This indicates that the TRACE level should be used in places where the priority is lowest. In the Syslog context, we assign it the Syslog equivalent 7 to correspond to LOG_DEBUG in the Syslog implementation.

Creating a Custom Logger

Once we have defined the CustomLevel object representing the level TRACE, we need a custom Logger object to use this level. Logger objects in essence have two responsibilities: They produce logging messages by delegating the logging request to different Appender objects with appropriate levels, and they return the instance of a named Logger object to the caller application. In the examples provided throughout the discussion of log4j, we have used the package name to name loggers. In reality, the name of a logger can be anything to identify the logger producing logging traces in a predefined destination.

In sophisticated application scenarios, we might decide to create several custom Logger classes. Depending on the name of the logger specified, we will return the appropriate Logger object to the caller application. We might in addition think about using a Factory object to decide which Logger object to return. The deciding criterion again may be the name of the logger.

Listing 8-10, CustomLogger.java, represents a custom Logger object with a method to produce TRACE-level messages. It also uses a CustomLoggerFactory object to create and return an appropriate custom Logger object.

Listing 8-10. CustomLogger.java

```java
package com.apress.logging.log4j;

import org.apache.log4j.Logger;
import com.apress.logging.log4j.CustomLevel;

public class CustomLogger extends Logger {
    private String FQCN = CustomLogger.class.getName()+".";
    private static CustomLoggerFactory factory = new CustomLoggerFactory();
    public CustomLogger(String name) {
        super(name);
    }

    public void trace(Object message) {
        //call the super log method with throwable instance as null
        super.log(FQCN, CustomLevel.TRACE, message, null);

    }
    public static Logger getLogger(String name) {
        return Logger.getLogger(name, factory);
    }
}
```

This example of CustomLogger introduces a new method to publish TRACE-level messages to the destination specified through any Appender object associated with this Logger.

Generating a Custom Logger Factory

Continuing on with our discussion of writing a custom Logger object, Listing 8-11, CustomLoggerFactory.java, is the code for generating a custom logger Factory object. If you are wondering why we need a Factory object, this will be answered towards the end of this section. The CustomLoggerFactory class implements the interface LoggerFactory and provides an implementation of the method makeNewLoggerInstance(String name). The example implementation shows a skeleton of how the Factory object can be used to return different types of logger objects.

Listing 8-11. CustomLoggerFactory.java

```
package com.apress.logging.log4j;

import org.apache.log4j.spi.LoggerFactory;
import org.apache.log4j.Logger;

public class CustomLoggerFactory implements LoggerFactory {
    public Logger makeNewLoggerInstance(String name) {
        return new CustomLogger(name);
    }
}
```

CustomLoggerFactory returns a separate CustomLogger instance based on the name of the Logger objects passed to it. This is the simplest possible scenario. The advantage of having a Factory object is that we can control how the Logger objects are made available to the caller application.

Using Custom Logging Components

We will now see a small example that demonstrates the use of the custom level, logger, and Factory object we created in the previous sections. As usual, the application that uses the logging mechanism will obtain an instance of the CustomLogger class. The application can then produce messages with the custom level TRACE by using the trace() method provided within the CustomLogger class.

Listing 8-12, CustomLoggerDemo.java, demonstrates the use of the CustomLogger class. Notice that the getLogger(String) method of the CustomLogger class actually returns an instance of the Logger class. For this reason, within the application, we need to cast the returned instance to CustomLogger.

Listing 8-12. CustomLoggerDemo.java

```
package com.apress.logging.log4j;

import org.apache.log4j.Logger;

public class CustomLoggerDemo {
    private static CustomLogger logger =
(CustomLogger)CustomLogger.getLogger(CustomLoggerDemo.class.getPackage()
.getName());

    /** Creates a new instance of CustomLoggerDemo */
    public CustomLoggerDemo()
    {
    }

    public void doLogging()
    {
        logger.trace("THIS IS A TRACE LEVEL MESSAGE...");
    }

    public static void main(String args[])
    {
        CustomLoggerDemo demo = new CustomLoggerDemo();
        demo.doLogging();
    }
}
```

The doLogging() method uses the obtained CustomLogger instance and produces a TRACE-level message by using the trace() method of the CustomLogger class.

All this is nice and simple. But we still need to address a few things regarding the configuration settings for using the custom level, logger, and Factory object. When log4j is initialized, the framework tends to use a DefaultCategoryFactory object to configure the loggers. This DefaultCategory object returns a named instance of the Logger class. In order to use the CustomLoggerFactory class, we need to specify in the configuration file the CustomLoggerFactory class as the Factory class to be used within the framework. In case the framework uses the DefaultCategoryFactory class, we will get a ClassCastException in the caller application while attempting to cast the obtained logger instance to CustomLogger.

Also, as we are using the custom level TRACE, the configuration demands that the implementation class for this level also be defined. The custom level should be defined in level#classname format. Otherwise, the framework will not be able to use any level outside the domain of normal log4j-defined levels.

Listing 8-13, "customlogger.properties", is the configuration file for the example provided in Listing 8-12.

Listing 8-13. customlogger.properties

```
#configure log4j to use the CustomLoggerFactory as the factory object
log4j.loggerFactory=com.apress.logging.log4j.CustomLoggerFactory

#set the level to TRACE and appender to ConsoleAppender
log4j.logger.com.apress.logging.log4j=TRACE#com.apress.logging.log4j
.CustomLevel,CONSOLE

#define the appender
log4j.appender.CONSOLE=org.apache.log4j.ConsoleAppender
log4j.appender.CONSOLE.layout=org.apache.log4j.SimpleLayout
```

The equivalent XML-style configuration for this example is as follows in Listing 8-14.

Listing 8-14. customlogger.xml

```
<?xml version="1.0" encoding="UTF-8"?>
<!DOCTYPE log4j:configuration SYSTEM "log4j.dtd">

<log4j:configuration xmlns:log4j="http://jakarta.apache.org/log4j/">

 <appender name="A1" class="org.apache.log4j.ConsoleAppender">

    <layout class="org.apache.log4j.PatternLayout">
      <param name="ConversionPattern" value="%t %-5p %c{2} - %m%n"/>
    </layout>

 </appender>

 <logger name="com.apress.logging.log4j">
    <level value="TRACE" class="com.apress.logging.log4j.CustomLevel"/>
    <appender-ref ref="A1"/>
 </logger>

 <categoryFactory class="com.apress.logging.log4j.CustomLoggerFactory"/>

</log4j:configuration>
```

Watch how the custom Level and custom LoggerFactory classes are configured.

CAUTION At the moment, there is a bug in log4j version 1.2.6 in that DOMConfigurator completely ignores the <categoryFactory> element. As a result, the use of custom loggers along with a custom logger Factory is not possible with XML-style configuration. Hopefully this bug will be resolved soon.

We have seen that by creating new levels and Logger classes, we are able to customize the priority of our logging messages.

CAUTION The creator group of log4j strongly discourages the use of custom logger and custom logger Factory objects.

A Simpler Approach to Use Custom Level

In the previous section, we saw how to extend the existing Logger class to create our own custom Logger class. One of the main motivations in subclassing the Logger class was to introduce a new logging method using a custom level, TRACE. To use the extended Logger class, we needed to create and supply a custom LoggerFactory class to the log4j framework. No doubt this all seems a bit complicated to achieve such a simple thing as adding a new method to the existing Logger class.

A simpler approach is to write a wrapper class around the existing Logger class. The wrapper class can provide the desired logging methods that are planned for the new logging features. For instance, Listing 8-15, LoggerWrapper.java, is a classical example of how we can still use the custom level TRACE without getting into the complexities of subclassing the Logger class.

Listing 8-15. LoggerWrapper.java

```
package com.apress.logging.log4j;

import org.apache.log4j.Logger;
import org.apache.log4j.Level;

public class LoggerWrapper
  {
    private final String name;
    private Logger log;
```

```java
    protected LoggerWrapper(String name)
    {
        this.name = name;
        log = Logger.getLogger(name);
    }

    public String getName()
    {
        return name;
    }

    public boolean isTraceEnabled()
    {
        if(!log.isEnabledFor(CustomLevel.TRACE))
            return false;
        else
            return
CustomLevel.TRACE.isGreaterOrEqual(log.getEffectiveLevel());
    }

    public void trace(Object message)
    {
        log.log(CustomLevel.TRACE, message);
    }

    public void trace(Object message, Throwable t)
    {
        log.log(CustomLevel.TRACE, message, t);
    }

    public boolean isDebugEnabled()
    {
        Level p = Level.DEBUG;
        if(!log.isEnabledFor(p))
            return false;
        else
            return p.isGreaterOrEqual(log.getEffectiveLevel());
    }

    public void debug(Object message)
    {
        log.log(Level.DEBUG, message);
    }
```

```java
public void debug(Object message, Throwable t)
{
    log.log(Level.DEBUG, message, t);
}

public boolean isInfoEnabled()
{
    Level p = Level.INFO;
    if(!log.isEnabledFor(p))
        return false;
    else
        return p.isGreaterOrEqual(log.getEffectiveLevel());
}

public void info(Object message)
{
    log.log(Level.INFO, message);
}

public void info(Object message, Throwable t)
{
    log.log(Level.INFO, message, t);
}

public void warn(Object message)
{
    log.log(Level.WARN, message);
}

public void warn(Object message, Throwable t)
{
    log.log(Level.WARN, message, t);
}

public void error(Object message)
{
    log.log(Level.ERROR, message);
}

public void error(Object message, Throwable t)
{
    log.log(Level.ERROR, message, t);
}
```

```java
        public void fatal(Object message)
        {
            log.log(Level.FATAL, message);
        }

        public void fatal(Object message, Throwable t)
        {
            log.log(Level.FATAL, message, t);
        }

        public void log(Level p, Object message)
        {
            log.log(p, message);
        }

        public void log(Level p, Object message, Throwable t)
        {
            log.log(p, message, t);
        }

        public static LoggerWrapper getLogger(String name)
        {
            LoggerWrapper logger = new LoggerWrapper(name);
            return logger;
        }

        public static LoggerWrapper getLogger(Class clazz)
        {
            LoggerWrapper logger = new LoggerWrapper(clazz.getName());
            return logger;
        }
}
```

This implementation is pretty straightforward. It just uses an internal member of the org.apache.log4j.Logger class. It also mimics all the methods from the Logger class. Internally, it delegates the method calls to the instance of the Logger class. Notably, it provides a method to use the custom TRACE level and also provides the method isTraceEnabled() to check if the level TRACE is enabled for any particular logger instance.

Listing 8-16, LoggerWrapperDemo.java, demonstrates a very simple use of the wrapper class we have just implemented.

Listing 8-16. LoggerWrapperDemo.java

```
package com.apress.logging.log4j;

public class LoggerWrapperDemo
 {
    private static LoggerWrapper logger =
LoggerWrapper.getLogger(LoggerWrapperDemo.class.getPackage().getName());
    public LoggerWrapperDemo()
    {

    }
    public void doLogging(String message)
    {
         logger.trace(message);
    }

    public static void main(String args[])
    {
        LoggerWrapperDemo demo = new LoggerWrapperDemo();
        demo.doLogging("USING LOGGER WRAPPER TO DISPLAY TRACE LEVEL
MESSAGE");

    }
}
```

To execute this example program, we need almost the same configuration file described in Listing 8-13, except that there is no logger Factory to be used for this example. The modified configuration file should read like the one listed in Listing 8-17, "loggerWrapper.properties".

Listing 8-17. loggerWrapper.properties

```
#set the level to TRACE and appender to ConsoleAppender
log4j.logger.com.apress.logging.log4j=
TRACE#com.apress.logging.log4j.CustomLevel,CONSOLE

#define the appender
log4j.appender.CONSOLE=org.apache.log4j.ConsoleAppender
log4j.appender.CONSOLE.layout=org.apache.log4j.SimpleLayout
```

Executing the example program in Listing 8-16 with this configuration file will print the following TRACE-level message to the console:

```
TRACE - USING LOGGER WRAPPER TO DISPLAY TRACE LEVEL MESSAGE
```

By writing a simple wrapper class for the logger, we have avoided the complexities of writing custom `Logger` and custom `LoggerFactory` classes. This can be quite a useful technique for adding custom features to a custom `Logger` class while retaining the normal features of the default `Logger` class.

More on Filtering

One important aspect of well-designed logging code is the control over what gets produced as the final logging information. In large application scenarios, there is always a chance that the amount of information being logged is enormous. In such situations, normal level-based filtering may become inadequate to restrict logging information to exactly the type required to analyze the system. This is when `Filter` objects become very useful. `Filter` objects are capable of filtering out logging information based on some application-specific, complex criteria that is more business logic specific. Apache log4j offers the flexibility of attaching any application-specific `Filter` object to the framework. With these `Filter` objects in place, we can control the logging information being produced in a more application- and business-specific way.

There are two ways to filter a logging request. One is to perform level-based checking, and the other is to attach a `Filter` object to the `Appender` objects. Level-based checking is limited to comparing the level of a logging request with the designated level of the corresponding `Logger` and `Appender` objects. A `Filter` object, however, can check a logging request against any application-specific criteria. We discussed `Filter` objects in Chapter 5 and also saw how to develop a custom `Filter` object. We can write any sort of `Filter` object we want and add it to a filter chain of the `Appender` object. The filters get executed sequentially in the chain, and depending on the approval or disapproval of the logging request, the log messages are processed.

The level-based filtering applied by the `Logger` and `Appender` objects is simple in principle. If a logging request falls below the level of the `Logger` and the `Appender` object, the logging request is discarded. This is useful. But what happens if we face a situation in which we want only logging messages belonging to certain level(s) to print and the rest to be discarded? For example, we might want only messages with levels between DEBUG and WARN to be printed. If we set the logger level to DEBUG, the logger will print all the messages up to the level FATAL. This is the situation where `org.apache.log4j.varia.LevelRangeFilter` comes into play.

Using LevelRangeFilter

With `LevelRangeFilter`, we can specify the lower range and the upper range of logging levels that should be approved by the logging framework. `LevelRangeFilter` has the configurable bean properties listed in Table 8-1.

Table 8-1. Bean Properties in LevelRangeFilter

Bean Property	Method	Description	Default
LevelMin	setLevelMin(Level)	Sets the minimum level to consider for logging.	None
LevelMax	setLevelMax(Level)	Sets the maximum level for which the logging request should be handled.	None
acceptOnMatch	setAcceptOnMatch(boolean)	If true, the filter returns ACCEPT, and the next filters in the chain will not be considered.	false

The Filter objects are currently configurable via an XML configuration file. Listing 8-18, "customFilter.xml", is a sample configuration file that uses LevelRangeFilter.

Listing 8-18. customFilter.xml

```xml
<?xml version="1.0" encoding="UTF-8"?>
<!DOCTYPE log4j:configuration SYSTEM "log4j.dtd">

<log4j:configuration xmlns:log4j="http://jakarta.apache.org/log4j/">

 <appender name="A1" class="org.apache.log4j.ConsoleAppender">

   <layout class="org.apache.log4j.PatternLayout">
     <param name="ConversionPattern" value="%t %-5p %c{2} - %m%n"/>
   </layout>

   <filter class="org.apache.log4j.varia.LevelRangeFilter">
     <param name="LevelMin" value="DEBUG"/>
     <param name="LevelMax" value="WARN"/>
     <param name="acceptOnMatch" value="true"/>

   </filter>
 </appender>

 <logger name="com.apress.logging.log4j">
   <level value="debug"/>
   <appender-ref ref="A1"/>
 </logger>

</log4j:configuration>
```

Notice that in this configuration file, we assign a PatternLayout to the ConsoleAppender object. ConsoleAppender also uses the LevelRangeFilter object with the minimum logging level set as DEBUG and maximum logging level set as WARN. The acceptOnMatch property is set to true. This means that if an event's level is within the specified range, the event will be logged straight away without consulting any more Filter objects in the chain. If acceptOnMatch is set to false, it means that Filter.NEUTRAL will be returned even if the event level is within the specified range. This gives the other Filter objects in the chain an opportunity to inspect the event.

Now we will write a simple program to demonstrate how LevelRangeFilter works. Listing 8-19, FilterDemo.java, is a sample program that prints logging messages with all the levels. With the help of LevelRangeFilter, we will filter out any message that is not within the range of the DEBUG and WARN levels.

Listing 8-19. FilterDemo.java

```java
package com.apress.logging.log4j;

import org.apache.log4j.Logger;
public class FilterDemo
{
    private static Logger logger =
Logger.getLogger(FilterDemo.class.getPackage().getName());

    public FilterDemo()
    {
    }
    public void doLogging()
    {
        logger.debug("DEBUG MESSAGE..");
        logger.info("INFO MESSAGE..");
        logger.error("ERROR MESSAGE..");
        logger.warn("WARN MESSAGE..");
        logger.fatal("FATAL MESSAGE...");
    }

    public static void main(String args[])
    {
        FilterDemo demo = new FilterDemo();
        demo.doLogging();
    }

}
```

Executing this program will print all the messages to the console except the messages with levels ERROR and FATAL, as they fall outside the range specified.

```
main DEBUG  logging.log4j - DEBUG MESSAGE..
main INFO   logging.log4j - INFO MESSAGE..
main WARN   logging.log4j - WARN MESSAGE..
```

NOTE Recall that the logging level sequence is ALL<DEBUG<INFO<WARN<ERROR<FATAL<OFF.

As we can see, assigning a level to the Logger objects and a threshold level to the Appender objects can always restrict the lower range of the level. LevelRangeFilter becomes useful only when we want to restrict the upper range of the level.

Using SelectedLevelFilter

We have seen how LevelRangeFilter can help us set upper and lower bounds for logging levels. In another situation, we might want to have a Filter that only allows messages with specified levels to appear in the destination. This is more precise than specifying a range of levels. For example, in one scenario, we might want only the messages with levels FATAL and INFO to be printed. One immediate solution is to write a custom Filter object to handle such situations.

We will now explore a sample Filter object designed to filter messages based on specific levels. The SelectedLevelFilter class extends the abstract class org.apache.log4j.spi.Filter and implements the abstract method decide(LoggingEvent event) to determine a certain logging event.

SelectedLevelFilter defines two configurable bean properties, acceptOnMatch and levelsToMatch. The acceptOnMatch property defines whether the filter should accept this request if a matching criterion is found. If acceptOnMatch is set to true, SelectedLevelFilter returns Filter.ACCEPT upon finding a level match, or else it returns Filter.NEUTRAL. If no match is found, it returns Filter.DENY. The levelsToMatch property accepts a comma-delimited string representation of levels we want to match. For example, if we wanted to find messages with the levels DEBUG and FATAL, we would define levelsToMatch as "DEBUG,FATAL". The sequence is immaterial here.

At initialization, the SelectedLevelFilter object stores all the specified levels in the levelsToMatch parameter in an internal java.util.ArrayList object. When a logging event arrives, it compares its level against all those specified with levelsToMatch. SelectedLevelFilter then returns an appropriate return value—Filter.ACCEPT, Filter.DENY, or Filter.NEUTRAL—depending on the result of the comparison and the value of acceptOnMatch.

Listing 8-20, SelectedLevelFilter.java, presents a sample implementation of the custom Filter object discussed in this section.

Listing 8-20. SelectedLevelFilter.java

```java
package com.apress.logging.log4j;

import org.apache.log4j.spi.Filter;
import org.apache.log4j.spi.LoggingEvent;
import org.apache.log4j.Level;
import org.apache.log4j.helpers.OptionConverter;
import java.util.ArrayList;
import java.util.Iterator;
import java.util.StringTokenizer;

public class SelectedLevelFilter extends Filter {
    private ArrayList levels = new ArrayList();
    private boolean acceptOnMatch;
    private String levelsToMatch;

    public SelectedLevelFilter() {
    }

    public int decide(LoggingEvent event)
    {
        if(levels.size() == 0)
        {
            return Filter.NEUTRAL;
        }
        Level eventLevel = event.getLevel();
        Iterator iterator = levels.iterator();
        boolean matchFound = false;

        while(iterator.hasNext())
        {
            Level level = (Level)iterator.next();
            if(level.equals(eventLevel))
            {
                matchFound = true;
                break;
            }
        }
```

```java
            if(matchFound)
            {
                if(acceptOnMatch)
                {
                    return Filter.ACCEPT;
                }else
                {
                    return Filter.NEUTRAL;
                }
            }else
            {
                return Filter.DENY;
            }
        }

        public boolean getAcceptOnMatch() {
            return this.acceptOnMatch;
        }

        public void setAcceptOnMatch(boolean acceptOnMatch) {
            this.acceptOnMatch = acceptOnMatch;
        }

        public String getLevelsToMatch() {
            return this.levelsToMatch;
        }

        public void setLevelsToMatch(String levelsToMatch) {
            this.levelsToMatch = levelsToMatch;
            if(levelsToMatch !=null)
            {
                StringTokenizer tokenizer = new StringTokenizer(levelsToMatch, ",");
                while(tokenizer.hasMoreTokens())
                {
                    String token = tokenizer.nextToken().trim();
                    Level level = OptionConverter.toLevel(token, null);
                    levels.add(level);
                }
            }

        }

}
```

Let's reuse the program `FilterDemo.java` from Listing 8-19 to demonstrate the application of `SelectedLevelFilter`. As the `Filter` objects can only be configured with an XML configuration file, we will also reuse the configuration file "customFilter.xml" shown in Listing 8-18. Make the following changes to the `<filter>` attribute in the XML file to specify `SelectedLevelFilter` as the designated filter for the defined logger:

```xml
<filter class="com.apress.logging.log4j.SelectedLevelFilter">
    <param name="LevelsToMatch" value="FATAL,INFO"/>
    <param name="acceptOnMatch" value="true"/>
</filter>
```

In the `levelsToMatch` property, we specify levels FATAL and INFO as the desired levels for the messages to be published. Now execute the `FilterDemo` program with the changed configuration file. Only the messages with level FATAL and INFO will be printed to the console.

```
main INFO  logging.log4j - INFO MESSAGE..
main FATAL logging.log4j - FATAL MESSAGE...
```

Filter Chaining

The Apache log4j API provides many `Filter` objects targeted for different purposes. As we have seen, if a particular `Filter` object returns a value of Filter.NEUTRAL, then the next filter in the chain is considered. This is called filter chaining. By chaining several `Filter` objects, we can compare a particular logging request against many filtering conditions. Sometimes, this serves as the alternative to writing a custom `Filter` object to combine the features offered by different `Filter` objects. For instance, the previous example of filtering messages only with levels INFO and FATAL can be achieved by chaining two instances of `LevelMatchFilter`. Let's see what happens when we change the XML configuration file to replace `SelectedLevelFilter` with the following entries:

```xml
<filter class="org.apache.log4j.varia.LevelMatchFilter">
   <param name="levelToMatch" value="FATAL"/>
   <param name="acceptOnMatch" value="true"/>
</filter>
<filter class="org.apache.log4j.varia.LevelMatchFilter">
   <param name="levelToMatch" value="INFO"/>
   <param name="acceptOnMatch" value="true"/>
</filter>
<filter class="org.apache.log4j.varia.DenyAllFilter"/>
```

`LevelMatchFilter` has two configuration properties, `levelToMatch` and `acceptOnMatch`. We use two instances of `LevelMatchFilter` to filter on messages with level FATAL and INFO only. The most important entry is the last filter in the chain. `DenyAllFilter` is there to deny all logging requests previously dealt with by other appenders in the chain with the return value Filter.NEUTRAL. If the `acceptOnMatch` property is set to `true`, the `LevelMatchFilter` object returns Filter.NEUTRAL if it finds no match. If a match is found, then Filter.ACCEPT is returned and the logging event is logged. All the mismatched logging events then end up in `DenyAllFilter`, and it consumes all these mismatched events without printing them.

In a similar fashion, we can use the `org.apache.log4j.varia.StringMatchFilter` object to log messages containing only "Hello" or "World". Do not forget to add `DenyAllFilter` at the end of the chain to ignore all other messages not matching the criteria.

Error Handling

However robust an application's code is, it is virtually impossible to predict and handle all potential error conditions. A good system is weighed against its resilience and how efficiently an error condition is handled. So far we have seen how to log information about the internal state of the running instance of an application. We have seen with log4j that logging information can be sent out to various destinations locally or over a network. There is every chance that these operations may generate some erroneous conditions in their process of publishing logging information.

The question is what should happen when one of the logging components encounters some problem. Here are some suggestions:

- The primary application itself should not crash just because there is some problem with the logging activity.

- In Java terms, this means that the logging component should handle errors internally without throwing the errors or exceptions back to the caller application. This saves the caller application from having to worry about the logging components.

- The logging components should allow flexibility in what the application developer might want to do in such error conditions.

Apache log4j is a resilient logging framework. It takes care of all the aspects involving erroneous logging conditions we discussed earlier. By default, the log4j `Appender` objects use the `OnlyOnceErrorHandler` object, which outputs an error message once and only once to System.err and ignores the subsequent error messages. This is graceful error handling in that it does not cause the main application to crash, and the administrator can see the error message produced and try to fix the problem in time.

Figure 8-4 presents the different error handling objects within log4j and their relationships. Note that all the error-handling objects implement a common interface, org.apache.log4j.spi.ErrorHandler. This interface defines the error handling methods that are subsequently implemented in the specific error-handling objects.

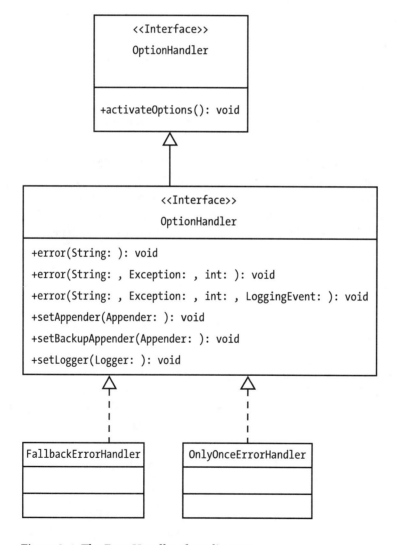

Figure 8-4. The ErrorHandler class diagram

The `ErrorHandler` interface also defines a couple of other methods in addition to the error handling methods. These methods are shown in Table 8-2.

Table 8-2. Methods in the ErrorHandler Interface

Method	Description
error(String)	Handles the error by publishing the message passed to it
error(String, Exception, int)	Handles the error by publishing the error information, including the Java exception being thrown and the integer error code describing the problem
error(String, Exception, int, LoggingEvent)	Handles the error by publishing the error message, the exception, the integer error code, and the logging event that generated the error
setLogger(Logger)	Sets the reference of the logger to which the failing appender might be attached
setAppender(Appender)	Sets the appender for which the error is handled
setBackupAppender(Appender)	Sets the backup appender to fall back to in case the primary appender fails

Apache log4j by default provides two error handling objects:

- `org.apache.log4j.helpers.OnlyOnceErrorHandler`: This is the default error handler used within log4j `Appender` objects. It prints the error message from the appender once and only once to `System.err` and ignores subsequent error messages.

- `org.apache.log4j.varia.FallbackErrorHandler`: This error handler also prints error messages to `System.err`. In addition, it can configure a secondary appender to be the backup appender for all the loggers that use this appender. This in essence means that when the first error arrives, it iterates through all the logger references associated with the primary appender defined as a part of the `FallbackErrorHandler` configuration. For each of the `Logger` objects found, it removes their primary appenders and sets the backup appender as the primary appender. This ensures for the loggers that subsequent logging requests will now be directed to the backup appender. This also ensures that no further error conditions arise due to the appender operation.

When it comes to your own applications, you won't be happy all the time with the default log4j error handling. For example, you might not be happy about producing error messages to a console, when you really want to redirect all logging events to use a different appender to send information to a secondary destination. Say you are using `JDBCAppender` to log information to a database, and the database goes down while your application is still running. What do you want to do now? You may want to log the error report and then continue logging information in a file instead. How to achieve this? You can write your own custom error handler to do the job and configure log4j to use your custom error handler.

ErrorCode Interface

To identify errors in a systematic way, log4j allocates error codes to different types of errors. These are encapsulated within the `ErrorCode` interface. The error codes are used within an `Appender` object to pass generated errors to the appropriate `ErrorHandler` class attached to the `Appender`. We can extend this interface to define our own error codes in case we need them.

Writing a Custom ErrorHandler

Let's write a custom error handler object. We want this custom error handler to achieve the following:

- The error handler must implement the `ErrorHandler` interface.

- The error handler must be given a logger reference.

- The error handler must be given an appender reference.

- The appender reference identifies the backup appender that will handle the error condition. The logger reference identifies the logger to which the specified `Appender` is attached.

- The error handler will keep a reference to all the loggers specified as having the primary `Appender` object associated with them.

- In the error condition, the error handler will remove the primary appender from the loggers specified and set the backup appender object to be the primary appender thereafter.

Listing 8-21, `CustomErrorHandler.java`, is designed to do the jobs iterated in the previous points. This is a very simple error handler. The implementation of error(message, exception, errorCode, LoggingEvent) is the method to do the bulk of the work.

Listing 8-21. CustomErrorHandler.java

```
package com.apress.logging.log4j;

import org.apache.log4j.spi.ErrorHandler;
import org.apache.log4j.spi.LoggingEvent;
import org.apache.log4j.Logger;
import org.apache.log4j.Appender;

import java.util.Vector;

public class CustomErrorHandler implements ErrorHandler
{
    private Appender primary;
    private Appender backup;
    private Vector loggers = new Vector();

    public CustomErrorHandler()
    {

    }

    public void activateOptions()
    {

    }

    public void setLogger(Logger logger)
    {
        if (logger != null)
        {
            loggers.add(logger);
        }
    }

    public void error(String message, Exception e, int errorCode)
    {
        error(message, e, errorCode, null);
    }
```

281

```java
    public void error(String message)
    {
        error(message, null, 0, null);
    }

    public void error(String message, Exception e, int errorCode,
LoggingEvent event)
    {
        for (int i = 0; i < loggers.size(); i++)
        {
            Logger l = (Logger) loggers.elementAt(i);
            l.removeAppender(primary);
            l.addAppender(backup);
            l.error(message, e);
        }

    }

    public void setAppender(Appender appender)
    {
        this.primary = appender;
    }

    public void setBackupAppender(Appender appender)
    {
        this.backup = appender;
    }
}
```

Configuring ErrorHandler

At the moment in log4j, error handlers can only be configured via an XML-style configuration file or programmatically. Here we will use the XML-style configuration, as it is more flexible compared to the hard-coded programmatic configuration. Listing 8-22, "errorHandler.xml", shows the code for the sample configuration file.

Listing 8-22. errorHandler.xml

```xml
<?xml version="1.0" encoding="UTF-8"?>
<!DOCTYPE log4j:configuration SYSTEM "log4j.dtd">

<log4j:configuration xmlns:log4j="http://jakarta.apache.org/log4j/">

 <appender name="FILE" class="org.apache.log4j.FileAppender">
    <param name="file" value="${user.home}/backup.log"/>
    <param name="append" value="true"/>

    <layout class="org.apache.log4j.SimpleLayout"/>

 </appender>

 <appender name="JDBC" class="org.apache.log4j.jdbc.JDBCAppender">

   <errorHandler class="com.apress.logging.log4j.CustomErrorHandler">
    <logger-ref ref="com.apress.logging.log4j"/>
    <appender-ref ref="FILE"/>
   </errorHandler>

   <param name="URL" value="jdbc:odbc:dbdef"/>
   <param name="user" value="system"/>
   <param name="password" value="manager"/>
   <param name="sql" value="INSERT INTO LOGGING_DATA VALUES('%x','%d{yyyy-MM-dd}','%C','%p','%m')"/>

 </appender>

 <logger name="com.apress.logging.log4j">
   <level value="debug"/>
   <appender-ref ref="JDBC"/>
 </logger>
</log4j:configuration>
```

The errorHandler element is defined as a child element of the JDBC appender element. This means that the defined error handler will be used in connection with the appender named JDBC. The JDBC appender writes the data to the database by using the configuration parameters defined.

In this example configuration, the error handler is set to the custom error handler `com.apress.logging.log4j.CustomErrorHandler`. `CustomErrorHandler` is defined as a child element to the JDBC appender. This means that the primary appender for `CustomErrorHandler` is set to be the JDBC appender.

The `logger-ref` element defines the logger that is using the appender JDBC. The `appender-ref` element defines the backup appender for the JDBC appender. In this example, the backup appender is the appender named `FILE`. The `FILE` appender in turn is configured to be `org.apache.log4j.FileAppender`.

Finally, the configuration of the `FILE` appender indicates that the logging information will be directed to the "backup.log" file in the "user.home" directory.

Running the Example

Running the example is very simple. To see `CustomErrorHandler` at work, change the database configuration parameters in the configuration file "errorHandler.xml"(Listing 8-22) to some invalid values. This will cause the `JDBCAppender` to fail. This is when `CustomErrorHandler` will take charge and do the backup job. Finally, go to the "user.home" directory to check what is written in the "backup.log" file.

Conclusion

In this chapter, we have examined how to extend the existing log4j framework to write our own application-specific logging components. The plug-and-play nature of log4j makes it easy to integrate custom components into the existing framework. The default capability of log4j is versatile and meets most of the routine requirements in logging activity. However, you might venture to extend the existing framework should you really need it. This chapter provides a guideline for implementing custom logging components to use with log4j.

In the next chapter, we will learn how to use log4j in the context of Java Server Pages (JSP). We will examine a new JSP tag library, Log (1.1), from Apache and see how we can apply it to using log4j in JSP. Also, we will explore some ideas for using log4j along with Enterprise Java Beans (EJB).

CHAPTER 9

Using the Apache Log Tag Library

ONE OF THE MANY advantages of a powerful logging framework such as Apache log4j is that it is not restricted to any particular application scenario. Apache log4j is a robust and extendible logging framework that can be tailored to any application-specific need. One feature that makes this logging framework so robust is the Log tag library, which is part of the Apache TagLibs project.

The Log tag library allows developers to embed log4j-based logging activity within a Java Server Page (JSP). In essence, it provides tags pertaining to all the logging levels declared by log4j and uses a configuration file to configure the log4j framework required to perform the logging activity.

In this chapter, we will examine the use of the Log tag library and also see how we can extend it to incorporate our own logging tags.

Installing the Log Tag Library

Installing and using Log with JSP is pretty straightforward. Follow these steps to set up and use Log in a Web application:

1. First, obtain the binary distribution of Log (1.1) from the Apache Web site (http://jakarta.apache.org/taglibs/doc/log-doc/intro.html).

2. Extract the archive file to the local machine.

3. Copy the tag library descriptor file, "taglibs-log.tld", to the application-specific "/WEB-INF" subdirectory.

4. Copy the "taglibs-log.jar" file to the "/WEB-INF/lib" subdirectory of the Web application.

5. Add a `<taglib>` ELEMENT to the "web.xml" file of the Web application to specify the location of the tag library descriptor as shown here:

```
<taglib>
   <taglib-uri>http://jakarta.apache.org/taglibs/log-1.0</taglib-uri>
   <taglib-location>/WEB-INF/log.tld</taglib-location>
</taglib>
```

This is all we need to do to use Log in a Web application. Now we will see a simple example of using Log from within a JSP.

NOTE   The installation procedure described in this section is specific to the Apache Tomcat Web server environment. For using Log (1.1) with other Web servers, you need to configure it to work specifically with the Web server you are using.

A Simple Example of Using the Log Tag Library

First, let's see a simple example of how we can use the Log tag library within a JSP to perform logging through log4j. Listing 9-1, `SimpleLog.jsp`, is a straightforward JSP that uses the Log tag library to print logging information to the console of a Web server. This example is demonstrated using Tomcat 3.2.1.

Listing 9-1. SimpleLog.jsp

```
<html>
<%@ taglib uri="http://jakarta.apache.org/taglibs/log-1.0" prefix="log" %>
<BODY>
<h1>Test Log Tag Library</h1>
<log:debug>Message embedded within open and close tags.</log:debug>
<log:debug message="Message passed as an attribute to the tag" />
<log:info category="test">Using category attribute.</log:info>
You should see output in the debug logs now.
</BODY>
</html>
```

As you can see, this JSP, although very simple, is enough to show how the Log tag libraries work. In this example, we are using the `<debug>` and `<info>` tags to print logging information. The Log tag library provides tags related to all the levels of logging defined in log4j. We will see all the tags available with Log later in this chapter. For the time being, let's explore the basics of using Log from within a JSP:

- First, we need to import the Log tag library in our JSP to make the tags available to the page context. This is achieved by the following line of code within the JSP:

    ```
    <%@ taglib uri=http://jakarta.apache.org/taglibs/log-1.0
       prefix="log" %>
    ```

    This line of code imports the tag library from the specified location and sets log as the tag name prefix for the tags in the library. In reality, this prefix can be any unique text.

- The tags from the Log tag library need to begin with the prefix that is defined while importing the tag library to the page. In this example, the tags are prefixed by log.

- The tags accept optional attributes and require open and close tags for each of them.

With this simple understanding of using the Log tag library, let's take a look at the configuration requirements for this example.

Configuration File for the Log Tag Library

The Log tag library uses log4j to print logging information to a desired location. As mentioned in Chapter 5, log4j does not make any assumptions about the application environment. In order to obtain logging information in a desired format and at a desired location, log4j needs a configuration file specifying all the information about the formatting and the destination of the logging information.

Log supplies a default configuration file named "log4j.properties". Listing 9-2 describes the default log4j configuration file that is shipped with the Log distribution.

Listing 9-2. log4j.properties, the Default Configuration File for Log

```
# Sample properties to initialize log4j
log4j.rootCategory=debug, stdout

log4j.appender.stdout=org.apache.log4j.ConsoleAppender
log4j.appender.stdout.layout=org.apache.log4j.PatternLayout
```

```
# Pattern to output the caller's file name and line number.
log4j.appender.stdout.layout.ConversionPattern=%5p [%t] (%F:%L) - %m%n

log4j.appender.R=org.apache.log4j.RollingFileAppender
log4j.appender.R.File=logtags.log

log4j.appender.R.MaxFileSize=100KB
# Keep one backup file
log4j.appender.R.MaxBackupIndex=2

log4j.appender.R.layout=org.apache.log4j.PatternLayout
log4j.appender.R.layout.ConversionPattern=%p %t %c - %m%n
```

This configuration file is quite simple. It uses `ConsoleAppender` and `RollingFileAppender` objects to output logging information to a Web server console and to a file. It also uses `PatternLayout` to format the logging information. The pattern specified for the logging information to be printed to the console includes the level, thread name, filename, location information, and message followed by a newline character.

The pattern for writing to a file is slightly different and includes the level, thread name, logger name, and message followed by a newline character. Although this configuration file looks simple, it highlights the following important points as to how `Log` works:

- `Log` uses the log4j root logger (synonymous to `Category` in the preceding example) to publish the logging information. The root logger has the threshold level DEBUG.

- `Log` by default writes logging information to the Web server console. In theory, `Log` can be configured to send logging information to any preferred destination by changing the configuration file. It provides a sample configuration for redirecting logging information to a rolling file by using the `RollingFileAppender` object.

- If we want to use a logger other than the root logger, then we need to configure the `Logger` object in the configuration file. Forgetting to do that may result in no logging information printing to any of the specified destinations.

- Changing the threshold level for the root logger or other custom loggers used with any of the tags can cause changes in the logging output.

NOTE If no separate logger (Category) is explicitly specified as an attribute of any of the Log tags, the tags rely on the root logger of log4j to publish logging information. Hence, it is always safe to keep the root logger configuration even though we may specify custom logger (Category) names within the tag attributes and configure them separately in the same configuration file.

Setting the Environment

Having followed the instructions in the "Installing the Log Tag Library" section, we are all ready to use the Log tag library from within a JSP. Before we can see the example JSP in Listing 9-1 in action, we need to configure the Web server to use the JSP and the log4j configuration file as described in next few steps:

1. First, put the JPS described in Listing 9-1 into a folder named "TestLogTags" (or any folder of your choice) under the "webapps" directory of the Tomcat installation.

2. In Tomcat, any Web application typically contains a "WEB-INF" directory and one "WEB-INF/classes" directory. Place the "log4j.properties" file in one of these locations. For example, you may decide to put it in the "WEB-INF/classes" directory.

3. Specify where Tomcat can find the configuration file shown in the preceding section for log4j.

4. Pass the "log4j.properties" file as a system variable to the execution environment of Tomcat.

5. Go to the "tomcat.bat" file in "%TOMCAT_HOME%\bin".

6. Add an entry to set the classpath variable to point to the directory containing the "log4j.properties" file. For this example, the entry may read as follows:

```
set CP=%CP%;C:\Jakarta-tomcat-3.2.1\webapps\
    TestLogTags\WEB-INF\classes
```

7. Add the following entry to the "tomcat.bat" file:

   ```
   set TOMCAT_OPTS=-Dlog4j.configuration=log4j.properties
   ```

 NOTE We can also configure log4j through an initialization servlet. Consult Chapter 5 for more on this topic.

This is all we need to do before we can run the example, which we will see how to do next.

The Log Example in Action

Now start up Tomcat and access the JSP page, as shown in Figure 9-1. Tomcat will load the "log4j.properties" file, and Log will use this configuration file to print the logging information.

Test Log (1.1) Tag Library

You should see output in the debug logs now.

Figure 9-1. The SimpleLog.jsp page

If we now look at the Tomcat console, we will see the following logging information printed:

```
DEBUG [Thread-11] (LoggerTag.java:109) - Message embedded within open and close tags.
DEBUG [Thread-11] (LoggerTag.java:97) - Message passed as an attribute to the tag
 INFO [Thread-11] (LoggerTag.java:109) - Using category attribute.
```

Using a Custom Logger with the Log Tag Library

In the JSP listed in Listing 9-1, we use the <log:info> tag with the category attribute specified as test. This is the name of the logger to be produced as part of the logging information. If we change the output pattern for the logging information to include information about the logger, we will see the category test appearing as part of the logging output. The whole point of specifying the category attribute is to be able to include a different set of configuration parameters for the category or logger.

Listing 9-3 presents a modified "log4j.properties" file that includes configuration for the category named test.

Listing 9-3. Modified log4j.properties File

```
# Sample properties to initialize log4j
log4j.rootCategory=debug, stdout
log4j.logger.test=debug, R

log4j.appender.stdout=org.apache.log4j.ConsoleAppender
log4j.appender.stdout.layout=org.apache.log4j.PatternLayout

# Pattern to output the caller's file name and line number.
log4j.appender.stdout.layout.ConversionPattern=%5p [%t] (%F:%L) - %m%n

log4j.appender.R=org.apache.log4j.RollingFileAppender
log4j.appender.R.File=logtags.log

log4j.appender.R.MaxFileSize=100KB
# Keep one backup file
log4j.appender.R.MaxBackupIndex=2

log4j.appender.R.layout=org.apache.log4j.PatternLayout
log4j.appender.R.layout.ConversionPattern=%p %t %c - %m%n
```

This configuration file defines the configuration for the logger test. The test logger has a threshold level of DEBUG and uses a RollingFileAppender object to print logging information to a file named "logtags.log". Notice that the conversionPattern to format the logging information includes the name of the logger (%c).

Using this configuration file for Log will write information to the "logtags.log" file in the "%TOMCAT_HOME%\bin" directory. If we execute the example JSP with this modified configuration file, we will see the following output in the "logtags.log" file:

```
DEBUG Thread-11 root - Message embedded within open and close <log> tags.
DEBUG Thread-11 root - Message passed as an attribute to the <log> tag
INFO Thread-11 test - Hello how are you?
```

This is how we can use different loggers with custom configuration to handle logging information. If we specify the category attribute in the JSP but do not specify a configuration for it, Log will use the root logger configuration to handle the logging request.

Description of Log Tags

The Log tag library provides tags corresponding to the levels declared in log4j. Table 9-1 summarizes all the Log tag library tags and their attributes.

Table 9-1. Summary of Log Tags

Tag Name	Tag Description	Attribute Name	Required
debug	Displays a DEBUG-level message	category	No
		message	No
info	Displays an INFO-level message	category	No
		message	No
warn	Displays a WARN-level message	category	No
		message	No
error	Displays a ERROR-level message	category	No~
		message	No
fatal	Displays a FATAL-level message	category	No
		message	No
dump	Displays all the variables in a specified scope	scope	Yes

As you can see, the use of these Log tags is very simple. All the tags except dump have two optional attributes, category and message. It is possible to specify the logging information as a value of the message attribute or by enclosing it within the tag. For example, we can use the error tag in following two ways:

```
<log:error message="This is an error message"> </log:error>
<log:error>This is an error message</log:error>
```

The dump tag mentioned in Table 9-1 is designed to print all variables within the scope specified through the scope attribute. Listing 9-4, SimpleLogDump.jsp, is a modified version of the JSP in Listing 9-1 and adds a dump tag within the page.

Listing 9-4. SimpleLogDump.jsp

```
<html>
<%@ taglib uri="http://jakarta.apache.org/taglibs/log-1.0" prefix="log" %>
<BODY>
<h1>Test Log Tag Library</h1>
<log:debug>Message embedded within open and close tags.</log:debug>
<log:debug message="Message passed as an attribute to the tag" />
<log:info category="test">Using category attribute.</log:info>
You should see output in the debug logs now.
<H4>request</H4>
<log:dump scope="request" />
<H4>page</H4>
<log:dump scope="page" />
<H4>session</H4>
<log:dump scope="session" />
<H4>application</H4>
<log:dump scope="application" />
</BODY>
</html>
```

In this JSP, we are displaying the output of the dump tag with all the possible scope attribute values. Figure 9-2 shows what is displayed on the page.

Test Log (1.1) Tag Library

You should see output in the debug logs now.

request

page

```
javax.servlet.jsp.jspOut
    org.apache.jasper.runtime.JspWriterImpl@1db5ec
javax.servlet.jsp.jspPage
    _0002fSimpleLogDump_0002ejspSimpleLogDump_jsp_9@92b1a1
javax.servlet.jsp.jspSession
    org.apache.tomcat.session.StandardSession@cbf9bd
javax.servlet.jsp.jspApplication
    org.apache.tomcat.facade.ServletContextFacade@7918f0
javax.servlet.jsp.jspPageContext
    org.apache.jasper.runtime.PageContextImpl@546dbc
javax.servlet.jsp.jspConfig
    org.apache.tomcat.facade.ServletConfigImpl@f08ed8
javax.servlet.jsp.jspResponse
    org.apache.tomcat.facade.HttpServletResponseFacade@322bce
javax.servlet.jsp.jspRequest
    org.apache.tomcat.facade.HttpServletRequestFacade@d9e282
```

session

application

```
javax.servlet.context.tempdir
    C:\jakarta-tomcat-3.2.1\work\localhost_8080%2Flog-examples
sun.servlet.workdir
    C:\jakarta-tomcat-3.2.1\work\localhost_8080%2Flog-examples
```

Figure 9-2. The SimpleLogDump.jsp page

Creating Custom Tags with the Log Tag Library to Use a Custom Level

In Chapter 8, we saw how to write a custom Level class, TRACE, and use it with log4j. If we want to use the TRACE custom level along with the Log tag library, we have to extend the Log tag library framework. Typically, we can do so by performing these tasks:

- Write a new Tag class to represent the custom level TRACE.

- Make the new Tag and Level classes available to the application.

- Modify the "taglib-descriptor" file to describe the new tag.

In the next sections, we will examine how we can achieve these tasks to use the TRACE level with the Log tag library.

Creating a New Tag

In the Log tag library world, all tag classes subclass from the abstract class LoggerTag. The LoggerTag class itself is a subclass of the BodyTagSupport class and does the entire job of handling tag-related operations. It also defines an abstract method, getPriority(), that is implemented in all other subclasses of the LoggerTag class. All other tag classes such as ErrorTag, InfoTag, etc., are subclasses of LoggerTag and provide implementations for the getPriority() method. Thus, to define a new tag, we simply need to extend the LoggerTag class and provide an implementation of the getPriority() method that returns the custom level TRACE. Listing 9-5, TraceTag.java, demonstrates how to write a custom tag using the custom level TRACE.

Listing 9-5. TraceTag.java

```
package com.apress.logging.log4j.customtag;

import org.apache.taglibs.log.LoggerTag;
import org.apache.log4j.Priority;
import com.apress.logging.log4j.CustomLevel;

public class TraceTag extends LoggerTag
{
    protected Priority getPriority()
    {
        return CustomLevel.TRACE;
    }
}
```

To develop this custom tag, we reuse the custom level TRACE developed in Chapter 8 (refer to Listing 8-9). As you can see, creating a new tag to use a new level is straightforward. Listing 9-6 shows the tag library description that needs to be added to the existing "taglibs-log.tld" file. (This file is shipped with the Log distribution.)

Chapter 9

Listing 9-6. Tag Description for the Custom Trace Tag

```
<tag>
    <name>trace</name>
    <tagclass>com.apress.logging.log4j.customtag.TraceTag</tagclass>
    <attribute>
      <name>category</name>
      <required>false</required>
      <rtexprvalue>true</rtexprvalue>
    </attribute>
    <attribute>
      <name>message</name>
      <required>false</required>
      <rtexprvalue>true</rtexprvalue>
    </attribute>
</tag>
```

NOTE The name of the tag is specified as trace. Therefore, within a JSP, we need to use the name trace to access this tag.

Custom Trace Tag in Action

Once we have the tag class for the level TRACE ready and also modify the "taglibs-log.tld" file to incorporate the definition of the new trace tag, we can start using it in a JSP. In order to set up Tomcat to use this new tag, we will need to go through the following steps:

1. Copy the required new TraceTag and CustomLevel class in the appropriate directory structure within the Web application. For example, if the Web application directory is "TestLogTags", then the appropriate package structure for the classes will need to be created under the "TestLogTags\WEB-INF\classes directory".

2. Edit the "Tomcat.bat" file to include the "taglibs-log.jar" file in the classpath.

3. Modify the "log4j.properties" file to set the threshold level to TRACE. The default threshold level set for the root logger is DEBUG, which is above the level of TRACE. So with default configuration, TRACE-level messages will not be published. Listing 9-7 presents the modified "log4j.properties" file for using the TRACE level.

Listing 9-7. Modified log4j.properties File for Using the TRACE Level

```
log4j.rootCategory=trace#com.apress.logging.log4j.CustomLevel, stdout

log4j.appender.stdout=org.apache.log4j.ConsoleAppender
log4j.appender.stdout.layout=org.apache.log4j.PatternLayout

# Pattern to output the caller's file name and line number.
log4j.appender.stdout.layout.ConversionPattern=%5p [%t] (%F:%L) - %m%n

log4j.appender.R=org.apache.log4j.RollingFileAppender
log4j.appender.R.File=logtags.log

log4j.appender.R.MaxFileSize=100KB
# Keep one backup file
log4j.appender.R.MaxBackupIndex=2

log4j.appender.R.layout=org.apache.log4j.PatternLayout
log4j.appender.R.layout.ConversionPattern=%p %t %c - %m%n
```

With these settings in place, execute the JSP presented in Listing 9-8. This JSP includes a TRACE-level message.

Listing 9-8. SimpleLogTrace.jsp

```
<html>
<%@ taglib uri="http://jakarta.apache.org/taglibs/log-1.0" prefix="log" %>
<BODY>
<h1>Test Log Tag Library</h1>
<log:trace>Trace level message.</log:trace>
You should see output in the debug logs now.
</BODY>
</html>
```

Executing this JSP will produce the following message with the TRACE level in the Web server console:

```
TRACE [Thread-11] (LoggerTag.java:109) - Trace level message.
```

Conclusion

In this chapter, we discussed a newly released tag library, Log, from Apache, for using log4j within a JSP to perform logging. This solves the age-old problem of having controlled logging from within a JSP. By changing the configuration, it is possible to redirect logging information to any preferred destination in any desired format. But careful consideration is required before you include in your Web application CPU-intensive logging operations such as writing logging data to a database, as it might affect the performance of that application.

This brings us to the end of the log4j discussion. All the topics explained in Chapters 5 through 9 should help you understand the internals of log4j and how to use it in practical applications. The smaller examples provided should enable you to grasp the concepts presented and see quick results to better understand the use of log4j. The more extensive examples should help you to correlate the use of log4j with real-life applications.

There is always one more thing to learn about any topic. But we have created a skeleton and given it a shape, and now you are in a position to build on it. But before we finish, we will definitely need to look at some of the best practices involved in using different logging APIs in the next chapter.

CHAPTER 10
Best Practices

IN THIS BOOK, we have discussed the two most popular Java-based logging APIs: the JDK 1.4 logging API and the Apache log4j API. Both logging APIs are similar in features, with the log4j API providing greater flexibility and more powerful logging capabilities. Both APIs allow us to configure and control logging behavior via configuration files. These APIs also offer a range of things we can do to log any message from within an application. For example, we can programmatically override the state of different components in the logging framework. We have seen that it is also possible to extend the existing logging framework in both logging APIs, and we can integrate our own custom logging components within the framework. This might help us to achieve specific logging behavior in our applications. Although this is very useful, there still remains a few points that need to be considered while using the existing logging framework or extending it by adding custom components.

Remember, logging is not the primary goal of most applications. It is there only to help us follow the internal status of the application. It helps us detect problems faster, publish messages to determine how the system is functioning, and maintain and debug the application with less time and cost. On the other hand, using logging incorrectly might affect the speed and functioning of an application. Hence, great care is needed in choosing the right components for the logging process and the best way to use those components. It is also very important to check that custom logging components do not affect the speed and integrity of existing components in any way.

In this chapter, we will discuss a few points that are critical to the performance of logging. These points are valid for both the JDK 1.4 logging API and the Apache log4j API unless otherwise mentioned.

Finally, this chapter will present a comparison between log4j and the JDK 1.4 logging API in terms of their internal workings and performance so that when it comes time to implement logging in your own applications, you know which API best serves your needs.

Obtaining a Logger

In both the JDK 1.4 logging API and log4j, the entry point to the logging framework is the Logger object. We obtain an instance of the Logger object and ask it to log different messages with different levels. Normally, in applications we will obtain named loggers. What naming convention should be used for these Logger objects?

There is no strict rule about what a logger's name should be. Still, we need to take great care in choosing a naming convention for the Logger objects in our applications. We configure a Logger through the configuration file. How do we know which application component is using which Logger object? How will it impact the whole application, if we change the configuration of a particular logger? Imagine that we have an application with hundreds of different components using a common logging configuration file. In this case, we would certainly need to come up with a naming strategy for logger objects so that we know the individual loggers each component is using. By having a well-designed naming convention, it is easy for us to assess the impact of any change we make to a particular logger configuration.

BEST PRACTICE   Use a package-based naming convention for Logger objects.

One great idea for a naming convention is package-based naming. Generally, application components are divided into several packages. Each package in turn contains related classes for certain aspects of the application. It is a good practice to use package name–based Logger objects, as this convention is easy to maintain.

BEST PRACTICE   In situations where components in the same package may require separate logging behavior, separate loggers on the basis of the tasks the components perform.

Immediately the question arises of whether a package contains classes that perform several distinct activities. For example, the package com.apress.logging.log4j.util can contain many utility classes. If all of them are using the same logger named com.apress.logging.log4j.util, then changing the configuration for this logger will affect all the utilities within this package. This may be undesirable. For example, one of the classes in the util package may be writing data to a file and another class may be sending data to a remote TCP/IP server. We might need detailed logging enabled for the class doing TCP/IP, but may not need the same level of detailed logging for the class doing file I/O. In such situations, it may be helpful to use two different loggers and name them according to the job they do.

The main point is to come up with an appropriate naming convention for loggers used within an application. This will increase the maintainability of the loggers. Also, it will help avoid the undesirable event of a configuration change in one logger affecting the others.

Using Logger Hierarchy

Both the JDK 1.4 logging API and log4j support logger hierarchy. The loggers are organized in a parent-child relationship. For example, a logger named com.foo is the parent logger of the child logger com.foo.bar. In the logger hierarchy, the child logger inherits the properties and the logger components from its immediate parent. In short, this means that all the logging events captured by the child logger will be processed by the child logger itself and also by its parent logger. This may also mean that logging messages will appear twice if both the child and parent logger use the same logging destinations, which may be undesirable. Of course, in both APIs, we can turn off the use of the parent logger in the hierarchy. To do so in the JDK 1.4 logging API, use the following:

setUseParentHandlers(false);

In log4j, use

setAdditivity(false);

or via the configuration file, add this line:

log4j.logger.[logger name].additivity=false

Again, there are situations when we might want this logger hierarchy enabled.

BEST PRACTICE In situations where one application component tries to log the same information to different destinations by using separate components belonging to the same package, try to use the logger hierarchy.

Imagine an order-processing application where component A receives an order. It processes the order and now needs to store the order-specific logging information to a file and also wants to send the same information back to a corporate logging database. Application component B writes the data to the local file and component C writes the logging information to the corporate database. Now the

301

important point to consider is whether the application components A, B, and C belong to a package hierarchy. For example, components B and C may belong to package com.processor and component A may belong to package com.processor.order. Another component, D, might deal with e-mail–based orders and may be in package com.processor.order.email. In such situations, we are in a position to use the parent-child logger relationship.

The main point is we need to judge if the loggers are able to justify the parent-child relationship on the basis of logging activity and not only by the package structure. If they are parent and child in terms of logging behavior, then use the relationship.

BEST PRACTICE If the logger hierarchy is turned on, the logging framework needs to determine the parent logger (recursively up the logger tree). This may reduce performance.

The benchmark result with log4j shows that walking through the logger hierarchy is three times slower than normal logging activity. So take great care in determining whether to use the logger hierarchy in your applications. The examples provided in this book aimed to keep the parent-child relationship turned off unless it was necessary to demonstrate how the parent-child relationship works.

Logging Messages Efficiently

What to log and how to log? The answers to these questions determine how effective a particular application's logging is. Choose carefully and come up with a strategy as to what information is needed for debugging and what information is needed for routine maintenance. Decide carefully about where to log information. Decide about the formatting of the log messages so that the information can be processed and analyzed in the future by other applications.

BEST PRACTICE Avoid logging unnecessary information. This will convolute the logging trace and make it harder to analyze.

Redundant and unnecessary logging information affects an application in terms of performance and usefulness. Even if we use a level that is turned off in the deployed application, the logger framework will have to do the extra work of checking the levels for each logging message. This level checking for logging requests with redundant and unnecessary information will affect the performance of the overall logging. So it is best to avoid having such logging requests within an application.

BEST PRACTICE Avoid using parameter construction within the logging request.

When developing your own applications, you might think that you have avoided making unnecessary logging requests in your application; however, you still may have a logging request that looks like the following:

```
logger.info("This is "+var1+" logging from the method"+var2);
```

The cost involved here is the parameter construction. Use simple Java techniques such as `StringBuffer` for the concatenation of `String` objects and avoid using "+" for joining two `String` objects. This is just one example. A badly coded application might have several of these sorts of statements.

BEST PRACTICE Check if logging is enabled before trying to log.

Suppose we have an application that logs all the entries of a list of customer orders (highly unlikely!). All information with a level of DEBUG is printed:

```
ArrayList list;
int length = list.size();

for(int k=0;k<size;k++)
{
   logger.debug("The customer: "+ ( (Customer)list.get(k) ).toString() );
}
```

What happens if the DEBUG level is turned off? Inside the `for` loop, the parameter construction will still take place, the logger will check if the DEBUG level is enabled, and if not, it will discard the request. To avoid this sort of situation, we could write

```
if(logger.isDebugEnabled())
{
    //do the for loop here
}
```

This will save the cost of unnecessary parameter construction. On the other hand, if the DEBUG level is turned on, there may be an extra cost for evaluating whether the DEBUG level is enabled. But this is an insignificant overhead compared to the parameter construction, as it takes about 1 percent of the time of actual logging.

Issues with Localization

The localization of logging information through the `java.util.ResourceBundle` object is a great feature for publishing logging information in different languages. However, the decision to use the localization feature within log4j can be tricky.

BEST PRACTICE Do not use `ResourceBundle` objects when you are not using the localization feature.

Constructing and using `ResourceBundle` objects is costly. If your application is presently supporting one language, refrain from using localization within your code. You can always enable this feature in the future to support different languages.

Using Location Information

The JDK 1.4 logging API and log4j both support location information for a logging request. The JDK 1.4 logging API tries to determine the class and method name for the logging request from the stack trace. The log4j API tries to detect the exact line number of the code from which the logging request was issued.

BEST PRACTICE Determining location information is a costly operation. It is best to avoid this in application logging, if possible.

Dynamic location information generation is not reliable. It might not work properly with many compilers that use optimization techniques. Moreover, it takes a great deal of extra overhead for the logging framework to go through the stack trace to determine location information.

Formatting Logging Information

The formatting of logging information is important. On one hand, the more information, the better. On the other hand, each bit of information costs CPU. We need to decide carefully about the formatting of logging information. There are choices available. XML formatting is costlier than simple text-based output, yet XML-formatted logging information is more reusable and portable.

PatternLayout objects in log4j provide extreme flexibility in terms of defining the elements of the final logging information and the formatting instructions. Using PatternLayout, we can precisely control the content of the logging information in any destination. For XML/HTML-based logging information, we need to use separate Layout objects. PatternLayout is responsible for formatting the content of the logging information and is not involved in the presentation of the logging information.

Dates are one of the main concerns when it comes to formatting, as they are complicated and costly in terms of performance. The log4j API provides several date formatting objects such as DateLayout and ISO8601DateFormat. The ISO8601DateFormat is the cheapest and fastest among all the date formats available.

Using Renderer Objects

In log4j, Renderer objects are used to construct a String representation of any Object passed to the logging framework to log.

BEST PRACTICE Renderer objects follow a class hierarchy. Any superclass Renderer is capable of rendering the subclass.

305

For example, if we have a `VehicleRenderer` object, it will be able to render the `Car` object so long as `Car` is a subclass of `Vehicle`.

BEST PRACTICE For a specialized rendering with the subclass, register a subclass-specific `Renderer`. In such cases, the superclass `Renderer` is not invoked.

For example, we could register a `CarRenderer` object to render all the `Car` objects, in which case `VehicleRenderer` will not be used to render the `Car` objects.

Using Asynchronous Logging

The log4j API offers the `AsyncAppender` object to perform asynchronous logging. This object stores logging events in a bounded buffer and releases the events when the maximum buffer size is reached. The JDK 1.4 logging API also provides similar functionality with the `MemoryHandler` object.

BEST PRACTICE `AsyncAppender` and `MemoryHandler` do not always increase performance.

If the bounded buffer gets filled up quickly, then there is an extra overhead for managing the bounded buffer, which slows down performance. But the use of `AsyncAppender` or `MemoryHandler` is quite effective in situations involving long blocking networks or I/O access or less CPU-intensive operations.

Using Filter Objects

In the examples of `Filter` objects in our log4j discussion in Chapter 5, we have seen that they are useful for filtering a logging request against some application-specific criteria other than the level of logging. We have also seen how filter chaining makes it possible to check a logging request against multiple criteria.

But filter chaining involves loading more than one Filter object and invoking the decide() method in each of them to filter the logging request. One alternative we demonstrated in Chapter 8 is to write a custom Filter object.

BEST PRACTICE   Try to do as much possible in one Filter object.

In situations where multiple custom Filter objects need to be created, try to design them in such a way that one Filter object can serve various common filtering purposes. No doubt, embedding various application logics within one Filter object makes it difficult to reuse and restricts it to a particular application scenario. Still, there may be situations in which this is worth considering.

Imagine we are trying to log information to a file. We want to perform checks against whether the logging event was generated from a certain application and also if it has the necessary security privileges to do the file I/O. In theory, we can come up with two Filter objects: one for checking the origin of the application and the other for the permission checking. This way, we have two reusable Filter objects for event origin checking and file I/O permission checking, which is good. But if we are not writing generic logging components to be used by other applications, this might not be that necessary. Try to combine both checking processes within one Filter object. This will save the time it takes to load and invoke two Filter objects.

In this author's opinion, the design of Filter objects is specific to an application and often requires some patience and time to decide how to design the Filter objects. Sometimes, you might need to come up with generic Filter objects reusable by many other application components, and sometimes you will write Filter objects specific to one application area. You need to make a trade-off before you decide to write single or multiple Filter objects.

Using Nested Diagnostic Context

The log4j API provides Nested Diagnostic Context (NDC) objects to populate the logging information with client-specific information. For example, server-based applications handling multiple clients (servlet is an example) often require that logging traces produced by different client activities be differentiated.

BEST PRACTICE Use NDC in server-side components handling multiple clients to distinguish clients.

The whole idea of NDC is to include unique client-specific information. Take care in deciding which information to put in the NDC and its degree of uniqueness.

Configuration Issues

The log4j API supports both properties-style and XML-style configuration files. There is also a programmatic way of configuring every log4j component. But programmatic configuration is impossible to change without modifying the source code. In order to benefit from the highly configurable nature of log4j, we must configure log4j via a configuration file.

This applies to the JDK 1.4 logging API. Although the JDK 1.4 logging API is not as highly configurable as log4j, we still must adhere to configuring it via a configuration file. Currently, the JDK 1.4 logging API supports only the properties-style of configuration.

Not all the components in log4j are configurable through the properties-style of configuration. So it is more often a good practice to use an XML-style configuration file.

If you ever need to change the configuration while your system is up and running, you must implement the configureAndWatch options for the log4j configuration. This way you can change the configuration file without bringing the system down. The log4j framework will look for any configuration change in a certain specified time interval (default 60 seconds) and reinitialize the framework if the configuration has changed.

The ConfigureAndWatch property can be used by calling

PropertyConfigurator.configureAndWatch(props);

or

DOMConfigurator.configureAndWatch(configFileName);

at the starting point of an application. The log4j framework will use the same configuration file to configure itself only with an extra facility that watches for any configuration change. This often proves quite useful when using log4j in server-based applications for situations where it may be difficult to bring the server down for every logging configuration change.

Comparing log4j and JDK 1.4 Logging API

Perhaps you have noticed the startling similarities between the log4j and JDK 1.4 logging implementations. They share the same basic components such as Logger, Level, Appender/Handler, Layout/Formatter. The two APIs also strongly resemble each other in their internal architecture. However, there are a few basic differences that are worth mentioning, some of which may be critical when choosing one logging API over the other. Table 10-1 summarizes the difference between these two logging APIs, and each point is discussed in more detail subsequently.

Table 10-1. Comparison Between the JDK 1.4 Logging API and Apache log4j

Features	JDK 1.4 Logging API	Apache log4j
Configuration	The JDK 1.4 logging API starts with a default configuration file supplied by JDK. In the JDK 1.4 logging API, the configuration order in a configuration file is sequential. The parent logger must be configured before the child logger. The JDK 1.4 logging API supports only properties-style configuration.	Apache log4j does not assume any default configuration. It looks for a "log4j.properties" or "log4j.xml" file in the classpath to initialize itself. In log4j, the order of configuration has no impact on the initialization. Apache log4j supports both properties- and XML-style configuration.
Formatting of logging information	The JDK 1.4 logging API only renders logging information in text format or XML format.	Apache log4j supports a wide variety of output formats such as HTML, XML, text, etc. The content of the logging information can be controlled by specifying patterns.
Output destination	The JDK 1.4 logging API only supports sockets, consoles, files, and memory buffers as output destinations.	Apache log4j supports a much wider variety of logging destinations including JMSs and databases, as well as protocols such as Telnet, SMTP, etc.
Filtering	The JDK 1.4 logging API allows attaching filters to Logger and Handler objects. Filterchaining to filter against multiple criteria is not possible with the JDK 1.4 logging API.	Apache log4j attaches filters to Appender objects only. Apache log4j supports filter chaining.

Table 10-1. Comparison Between the JDK 1.4 Logging API and Apache log4j (Continued)

Features	JDK 1.4 Logging API	Apache log4j
Location information	The JDK 1.4 logging API automatically tries to determine the location information for the logging request. There is no way to control this behavior.	In log4j, location information can be configured to be included in the logging information or not.
Error handling	The JDK 1.4 logging API throws back any runtime exceptions to the caller application. This may cause the application to crash unless these exceptions are handled.	In log4j, errors are handled internally without throwing them back to the caller application. This makes the application and the logging function independent of each other.

Comparing Configuration Options

Unlike log4j, JDK 1.4 ships with a default configuration file for the logging API. Even application developers need not define any custom configuration file; the JDK 1.4 logging API will configure itself with the default configuration file. However, log4j does not make any assumption about the logging environment. If a configuration file is not found in the classpath of the execution environment, log4j fails to initialize properly.

In terms of configuration options, log4j is much more versatile in that it supports both properties-style and XML-style configuration. The JDK 1.4 logging API only supports properties-style configuration.

Also, the JDK 1.4 configuration is sequential—that is, the order of configuration matters. For example, look at the following configuration order:

```
a.b.level=SEVERE
a.level=INFO
```

You might be surprised to discover that the logger a.b will be assigned its parent logger's level INFO. This is because the parent logger has been configured after the child logger, and the configuration for all the child loggers have been updated according to the configuration of the parent logger. Thus, in the JDK 1.4 logging API, the settings for the child loggers should appear after the settings of the parent logger. The parent logger updates the settings of its child loggers.

The log4j configuration is independent of the order. In log4j, the child loggers automatically inherit from their immediate parent logger by traversing the hierarchy upwards.

Comparing Formatter and Layout Objects

Both logging APIs provide mechanisms to format the logging information to be produced. In log4j, these objects are called `Layout` objects, and in the JDK 1.4 logging API, they are called `Formatter` objects. The JDK 1.4 logging API, however, only provides two `Formatter` objects: `SimpleFormatter` and `XMLFormatter`. The log4j API provides a vast range of `Layout` objects capable of formatting information in various formats such as HTML, XML, text, etc. The log4j API also provides `PatternLayout`, which is a powerful mechanism for including or excluding various parts of logging events in the final logging output.

Comparing Handler and Appender Objects

The JDK 1.4 logging API provides `Handler` objects to publish logging information to a preferred destination. Similarly, log4j provides `Appender` objects to publish logging information. Currently, the JDK 1.4 logging API can only publish to consoles, files, sockets, and memory buffers. However, log4j provides more choices for logging destinations. With log4j, we can publish logging information to various destinations such as consoles, files, databases, JMSs, NT event logs, UNIX Syslogs, and so on.

Of course, both APIs can be extended to provide any number of customized `Handler` and `Formatter` objects to support logging to any other application-specific destination. But by default, log4j covers almost all commonly required logging destinations.

Comparing Filter Objects

The JDK 1.4 logging API offers the facility to attach `Filter` objects to `Logger` and `Handler` objects. With the help of `Filter` objects, it is possible to obtain more fine-grained control over logging decisions. The JDK 1.4 logging API allows only one `Filter` object to be associated with a logger.

With log4j, however, `Filter` objects can only be attached to `Appender` objects. But log4j offers more capabilities with its `Filter` objects. As we discussed in Chapter 8, it is possible to chain several `Filter` objects to achieve complex logging decisions. We can also configure more than one `Filter` object for a particular `Appender` object. The JDK 1.4 logging API is lacking in terms of these `Filter` object features. A `Filter` object in the JDK 1.4 logging API can either accept or reject a logging request, but it cannot ignore a logging request and delegate it to any other `Filter` objects. Thus, `Filter` chaining is not possible with the JDK 1.4 logging API.

Comparing Location Information Options

The JDK 1.4 logging API and log4j both are capable of producing information about the location from which the logging request was generated. However, the production of location information is very costly in terms of performance.

In log4j, we can enable or disable location information according to the application's needs. By default, location information is not part of the logging output. We can enable it by specifying the location information attribute in the PatternLayout object as described in Chapter 6.

Unlike log4j, the JDK 1.4 logging API always tries to determine the location information, and this cannot be avoided. Also, the techniques used by the JDK 1.4 logging API for dynamic location information generation are not totally reliable. Normally, this is done by analyzing the stack trace of the application. But many compilers employ different optimization techniques that may cause this stack trace analysis to fail or produce incorrect information. Thus, application developers tend to avoid including location information as a part of the logging output.

Comparing Error Handling

The main drawback of the JDK 1.4 logging API is that it throws RunTimeExceptions back to the caller classes in the application. If these exceptions are not handled within the application, the application will crash. This is particularly undesirable if the application is crashing because of some problem with the logging rather than some problem with the application itself.

The log4j API, however, is more elegant in handling the errors and exceptions generated in the logging operation. All Appender objects in log4j have an associated ErrorHandler object. ErrorHandler objects such OnlyOnceErrorHandler produce a message to the console on the first occurrence of an error and ignore the following errors. This enables the application to continue functioning normally even though there is some problem with the logging. The problem with the logging function can be detected by analyzing the console messages and then corrected eventually.

Also in log4j, it is possible to define customized error handler components that can perform all sorts of operations to handle the error condition gracefully. This can be achieved simply by changing the configuration file to use any ErrorHandler object and requires no coding change at all.

Conclusion

This brings us to the end of this book. I hope the topics discussed in this book provide you with a sufficiently solid foundation for the two most common Java-based logging APIs, the JDK 1.4 logging API and the Apache log4j API. Both are well designed and easy to use. Considering the present status of both APIs, log4j, in my opinion, has a slight edge over the other. But again, you are not always going to need such a sophisticated logging mechanism. The important point is to understand that with every day spent, software applications are becoming more and more business critical. In this context, an application with better maintainability and quick-fix capability wins the market. A well-planned logging framework within an application will no doubt help it to gain some advantage in a competitive market. Hence, it is time for all of us to reconsider the importance of logging in our applications.

As numerous suggestions continue to flow through the mailing lists of Sun and Apache for their individual logging APIs, shortly we will see improvements and new features in both logging APIs. Whatever these new features may be, the basics presented in this book will remain the same, and I hope this book will prove useful to you now and in the future.

Index

Symbols
% conversion character, 196
%m and %n conversion patterns, 125
%t, %h, %g, %u and %% FileHandler expressions, 38, 39, 41
.war files, building, 134
/ FileHandler expression, 38

A
activateOptions( ) method, 237, 241
AdvancedLogging.java (listing), 200–202, 211
AgeFilter.java (listing), 53
ALL level
    JDK 1.4, 13
    log4j, 136
AlternateXML.java (listing)
    code, 66–67
    vs. XMLLogging.java, 66–67
aMethod( ) method, 23
anonymous loggers, 19–20
AnotherClass.java (listing), 241
Apache Log tag library. *See* Log tag library
Apache log4j, advanced logging, 199–233
    example application, 200–202
    JDBCAppender, 202–212
        configuration files, 205–206
        configuring, 203–204
        extending, 206–212
        tables, creating for storing logging information, 204
    JMSAppender, 212–223
        example, 217–223
        JMS and log4j, 214–217
        JMS basics, 212–213
    logging to databases. *See* JDBCAppender (*this heading*)
    NTEventLogAppender, 228–229
    SMTPAppender, 229–231
    SocketAppender, 223–228
        configuration, 225
        example, 226–228
        fault tolerance, 224–225
    TelnetAppender, 232
Apache log4j, basics, 121–175
    advantages of log4j, 121
    Appender object, 149–166
        adding Appenders to loggers, 150–151
        AsyncAppender, 163–166
        basics of, 122, 149–150, 168
        ConsoleAppender, 154
        DailyRollingFileAppender, 158–160
        file-based logging example, 161–163
        FileAppender, 154–156
        Logger to Appender collaboration, 151–152
        RollingFileAppender, 156–158
        WriterAppender, 152–153
    architecture, 122–125
    bug, version 1.2.6, 265
    configuring, 125–135
        basics of, 125–126
        default initialization, 127–131
        dynamic loading of configuration, 131
        with servlet, 132–133
        Tomcat setup, 133–135
        XML-style configuration, 127
    example of, 169–175
    Filter object, 166–168
    installing, 121–122
    introduction to, 8
    vs. JDK 1.4, 309–312
        basics of, 299, 309–310
        configuration options, 310
        error handling, 312
        Filter objects, 311
        Formatter and Layout objects, 311
        Handler and Appender objects, 311
        location information options, 312
    JDK compatibility with, 122
    Layout object, 123, 124, 168
    Level object, 124, 136
    Logger object, 136–145
        basics of, 122, 136–139, 168
        conditions of successful logging, 142
        configuration methods, 142–143
        example, 143–145
        logging information and, 139–142
    LogManager object, 145–146
    Message Diagnostic Context (MDC), 147–148
    Nested Diagnostic Context (NDC), 146–147
    ObjectRenderer, 168–169
Apache log4j, creating custom components, 235–283
    bug in version 1.2.6, 265
    configuring from databases, 243–258
        example, 256–258
        reading via configuration loader, 245–252
        table design for storing logging configuration, 244
        writing configuration class, 253–256
    custom logging framework, 259–270
        custom level classes, creating, 259–260
        custom levels simple approach, 265–270
        custom Logger, creating, 261–262
        custom Logger Factory, generating, 262
        custom logging components, using, 262–265
    error handling, 277–284
        basics of, 277–280
        custom ErrorHandler, 280–281
        ErrorCode interface, 280
        ErrorHandler, configuring, 282–284
        ErrorHandler, writing custom, 280–282
        running example, 284

Index

Filter object and, 270–277
    filter chaining, 276–277
    LevelRangeFilter, 270–273
    SelectedLevelFilter, 273–276
WindowAppender, 235–243
    architecture of, 236–237
    features of, 236
    implementation of, 237–241
    testing, 241–243
Apache log4j, formatting logging information, 177–198
    Layout hierarchy, 177–178
    Layout objects, 178–198
        DateLayout, 186–187
        HTMLLayout, 187–192
        methods in Layout, 179
        PatternLayout, 194–198
        SimpleLayout, 179–180
        TTCCLayout, 180–186
        XMLLayout, 192–194
append( ) method, 153
append property, and FileHandler parameters, 78
Append property, FileHandler, 40
Appender object
    JDK 1.4 vs. log4j, 311
    log4j, 149–166
        adding Appenders to loggers, 150–151
        AsyncAppender, 163–166
        basics of, 122, 124, 149–150, 168
        ConsoleAppender, 154
        DailyRollingFileAppender, 158–160
        file-based logging example, 161–163
        FileAppender, 154–156
        vs. JDK 1.4, 311
        Logger to Appender collaboration, 152
        RollingFileAppender, 156–158
        WriterAppender, 152–153
    TTCCLayout instances and, 186
    WindowAppender, 235–243
        architecture of, 236–237
        features of, 236
        implementation of, 237–241
        testing, 241–243
Appender property, 137
APPENDER_DEF, 244, 245
application logging
    vs. debugging, 2
    definition of, 2
    formatting logging information, 305–306
    introduction to, 1–10
        benefits of, 3–4
        description of, 1–3
        disadvantages of, 4–5
        effective logging mechanisms, 5–7
        evaluating logging packages, 7
        Java-based logging APIs, 7–9
application state, 3
architecture
    employee data management architecture, 102
    log4j, 122–125
    of logging, 6–7
    similarities of log4j and JDK 1.4, 309
    WindowAppender, 236–237
AsyncAppender, 163–166, 306

asynchronicity
    asynchronous logging, best practices, 306
    JMS and, 212, 219, 224
AsyncLogging.java (listing), 165–166
async.xml (listing), 164–165

B

BasicLogging.java (listing), 20–22, 61
Bean properties
    DateLayout, 186
    HTMLLayout, 187
    JDBCAppender, 204
    JMSAppender, 216
    LevelRangeFilter, 271
    NTEventLogAppender, 229
    PatternLayout, 194
    SocketAppender, 225, 230
    TTCCLayout, 184
best practices, 299–313
    asynchronous logging, 306
    configuration, 308
    efficient message logging, 302–304
    Filter objects, 306–307
    formatting logging information, 305–306
    localization, 304
    location information, 304–305
    log4j vs. JDK 1.4, 309–312
        basics of, 309–310
        configuration options, 310
        error handling, 312
        Filter objects, 311
        Formatter and Layout objects, 311
        Handler and Appender objects, 311
        location information options, 312
    Logger hierarchy, using, 301–302
    loggers, obtaining, 299–301
    Nested Diagnostic Context (NDC), 307–308
    Renderer objects, 305–306
bufferedIO property, FileAppender, 155
bufferedSize property, FileAppender, 155
buffers, and JDBCAppender, 202, 203

C

C, conversion character, PatternLayout, 195
c, conversion character, PatternLayout, 195
categoryPrefixing property, 184
child loggers
    ChildLogger.java (listing), 24
    JDK 1.4 vs. log4j, 310
    parent-child hierarchy and, 20, 25–26, 137–138
classes
    class-based configuration, JDK 1.4, 80–83
    configuration class, writing, 253–256
    custom level classes
        creating, 259–260
        implementing, 259–260
ClientComponent.java (listing), 112–116
clients
    client component of practical logging, 103, 111–116
    NDC to distinguish, 308
    remote logging client, 101–102
    running of
        JDK 1.4, 118–120
        JMS, 222–223

close( ) method
    JDBCAppender, 203
    JMSAppender, 222
    SocketAppender, 225
code. *See* listings
Commons logging API, 8–9
Complex log4j Configuration File (listing), 126
CONFIG level, 13
ConfigDemo.java (listing), 56
config.properties (listing), 57
configuration
    best practices, 308
    custom log4j components from databases, 243–258
        example, 256–258
        reading information via configuration loader, 245–252
        table design for storing logging configuration, 244
        writing configuration class, 253–256
    disadvantages of program-based, 55, 73
    ErrorHandler, 282–283
    evaluating logging packages and, 7
    file-based, 55–58
    JDBCAppender
        configuring, 203–204
        configuring files for, 205–206
    JDK 1.4 logging framework configuration, 73–83
        class-based, 80–83
        file-based, 74–80
    JDK 1.4, vs. log4j, 309, 310
    JMSAppender, 215–217
    Log tag library
        configuration file, 287–289
        configuring Web server for, 289–290
    log4j, 125–135
        basics of, 125–126
        default initialization, 127–131
        dynamic loading of configuration, 131
        vs. JDK 1.4, 309, 310
        program-based configuration, 130
        with servlet, 132–133
        Tomcat setup, 133–135
        XML-style configuration, 127, 308
    Logger object, log4j, 142–143
    properties-style, 308
    SocketAppender, 225
ConsoleAppender, 154
ConsoleHandler
    basics of, 37–38
    parameters, 77
constructors
    DailyRollingFileAppender, 160
    FileAppender, 155
    FileHandler to create objects, 40
    RollingFileAppender, 156
    turning off configuration code in, 185
    WriterAppender, 153
contextPrinting property, 184
control, and logging, 2–3
conversion characters
    defined, 195
    for PatternLayout, 195–196
cost effectiveness, and logging, 4
count property
    FileHandler default property, 40
    FileHandler parameters and, 78

customappender.properties (listing), 242
CustomerOrder.java (listing), 170–171
CustomErrorHandler.java (listing), 281–282
customFilter.xml (listing), 271
CustomFormatter.java (listing), 70
CustomFormatterTest.java (listing), 71–72
CustomHandlerDemo.java (listing), 92
CustomJDBCAppender.java (listing), 208–210, 211
customjdbc.properties (listing), 210
CustomLevel.java (listing), 259–260
CustomLoggerDemo.java (listing), 263
CustomLoggerFactory.java (listing), 262
CustomLogger.java (listing), 261
customlogger.properties (listing), 264
customlogger.xml (listing), 264–265

D

d, conversion character, PatternLayout, 195
DailyRollingFileAppender, log4j, 158–160
databases
    configuring custom log4j components from, 243–258
        example, 256–258
        reading configuration information via configuration loader, 245–252
        table design for storing logging configuration, 244
        writing configuration class, 253–256
    logging to with JDBCAppender, 202–212
        configuration files for JDBCAppender, 205–206
        configuring JDBCAppender, 203–204
        extending JDBCAppender, 206–212
        tables, creating for storing logging information, 204
date formats
    best practices, 305
    dateFormat property, 184
    DateLayout object, 186–187
DateLayout object
    basics of, 186–187
    Bean properties inherited from, 184
DatePattern configuration parameter, 158
DatePattern conventions, 159
DBConfigLoader.java (listing), 246–252
dbConfig.properties (listing), 258
DBConfigurator.java (listing), 255–256
DEBUG level
    custom logging framework and, 258
    described, 136
    filtering and, 272
    JDBCAppender and, 205
    logging best practices and, 303–304
debug Log tag, 292
debugging
    vs. logging, 2
    necessity of logging for, 1
    speed of, and logging, 4
decide( ) method, 307
destination for logging, 6, 7
doAppend( ) method, 152, 164, 194
doConfigure( ) method, 253, 256
dump Log tag, 292, 293

317

Index

E

employee data
  creating data files, 117
  database configuration, 117–118
  employee data management architecture, 102
  Employee object, 105–106
employee.xml (listing), 117
encoding property
  ConsoleAppender, 154
  ConsoleHandler
    default property, 38
    parameters and, 77
  FileAppender, 154
  FileHandler
    default property, 39
    parameters and, 78
  SocketHandler
    default properties, 48
    parameters and, 79
  StreamHandler initialization property, 35
  WriterAppender property, 152
error handling, log4j, 277–284
  basics of, 277–280
  ErrorCode interface, 280
  ErrorHandler
    basics of, 277–280
    configuring, 282–284
    custom ErrorHandler, 280–281
    writing custom, 280–282
  example, 284
  vs. JDK 1.4, 310, 312
ERROR level
  database-based configuration and, 256–257, 258
  described, 136
  SocketAppender and, 231
error Log tag, 292, 293
ErrorCode interface, 280
ErrorHandler
  basics of, 277–280
  configuring, 282–284
  writing custom, 280–282
errorHandler.xml (listing), 283
Example log4j Configuration File (listing), 125
examples
  JDK 1.4
    basic logging, 20–23
    Logger class methods, 29–33
    Logger relationship, 23–26
  Log tag library, 286–290
    configuration file, 287–289
    configuring Web server, 289–290
    custom trace tag, 296–298
    Tomcat, 286–290
  log4j
    Appender object file-based logging, 161–163
    complete log4j, 169–175
    configuring from databases, 256–258
    error handling, 284
    Example log4j Configuration File (listing), 125
    JMSAppender, 217–223
    log4j application, 200–202
    Logger object, 143–145
    SocketAppender, 226–228
execute( ) method, 207–208
executeUpdate( ) method, 202, 208

F

F, conversion character, PatternLayout, 195
Factory, generating custom, 262
FATAL level, 136
fatal Log tag, 292
fault tolerance, and SocketAppender, 224–225
file-based configuration
  JDK 1.4 basics, 55–58
  JDK 1.4 logging framework and, 74–80
    configuration order, 75–76
    global configuration, 74–75
    Handler-specific configuration, 74, 76–80
  log4j, file-based logging example, 161–163
fileAppend property, 155
FileAppender, log4j, 154–156
FileHandler
  basics of, 38–42
  demonstration of, 66–67
  parameters, 78–79
FileHandlerDemo.java (listing), 40–41
file_logging.properties (listing), 161–162
fileName property, 154
Filter object
  best practices, 306–307
  JDK 1.4
    basics of, 13, 14, 51–55
    vs. log4j, 311
  log4j
    basics, 123, 166–168
    vs. JDK 1.4, 311
  log4j, custom components, 270–277
    filter chaining, 276–277
    Filter objects usefulness, 270
    LevelRangeFilter, 270–273
    SelectedLevelFilter, 273–276
filter property
  Appender object, 149
  as default property
    ConsoleHandler, 37
    FileHandler, 39
    MemoryHandler, 43
    SocketHandler, 48
  Handler objects and, 76
  parameters and
    ConsoleHandler, 77
    FileHandler, 78
    MemoryHandler, 80
    SocketHandler, 79
  as StreamHandler initialization property, 35
  as WindowHandler configuration property, 90–91
FilterDemo.java (listing), 54–55, 272
filter_properties.xml (listing), 174
FINE/FINER/FINEST levels, 13
format( ) method, 62, 70, 194
format modifiers
  defined, 195
  in PatternLayout, 196–197
Formatter objects
  basics of, 13, 14, 58
  default, 59–68
    SimpleFormatter object, 61–63
    XMLFormatter object, 62–68
  defining custom, 69–72
  JDK 1.4 vs. log4j, 311
  in logging framework, 60–61

Index

formatter property
   as default property
      ConsoleHandler, 38
      FileHandler, 39
      SocketHandler, 48
   as parameters
      ConsoleHandler, 77
      FileHandler, 78
      SocketHandler, 79
   StreamHandler initialization property and, 35
   WindowHandler and, 90–91
formatting logging information
   basics of, 305–306
   JDK 1.4 vs. log4j, 309
framework, extending. *See* Apache log4j, creating custom components; JDK 1.4 logging API, extending the framework

G

getFooter( ) method, 191
getPriority( ) method, 295
getWindowInstance( ) method, 240–241
global configuration, 74–75

H

Handler object, 13, 33–51
   ConsoleHandler
      basics of, 37–38
      parameters, 77
   custom Handlers, writing, 83–94
      custom WindowHandler, 85–94
      introduction to, 83–84
   FileHandler
      basics of, 38–42
      parameters, 78–79
   global Handler object, 75
   Handler-specific configuration, 76–80
      ConsoleHandler parameters, 77
      FileHandler parameters, 78–79
      MemoryHandler parameters, 80
      SocketHandler parameters, 79
   JDK 1.4 vs. log4j, 311
   logging information and, 64
   MemoryHandler
      basics of, 42–47
      parameters, 80
   remote logging Handler, 99–100
   SocketHandler
      basics of, 47–51
      parameters, 79
   StreamHandler, 35–37
   WindowHandler, creating custom, 85–93
      CustomHandlerDemo.java (listing), 92
      LogWindow.java (listing), 85
      WindowHandler.java (listing), 86–89
handler property, and parent-child hierarchy, 20
handlers property, 75
hierarchy. *See also* parent-child hierarchy
   Renderer objects and, 305–306
histories. *See* logging histories, benefits of
host property
   SocketHandler default properties, 48
   SocketHandler parameters and, 79

HTML Source Code Produced by HTMLLayout (listing), 190–191
HTMLLayout object, 187–192
html.properties (listing), 188

I

immediateFlush property
   ConsoleAppender, 154
   described, 152
   FileAppender, 154
   when set to false, 153
INFO level
   JDK 1.4
      ChildLogger.java and, 24
      ConsoleHandler parameters and, 77
      described, 12
   log4j
      database-based configuration and, 256–257, 258
      described, 136
info Log tag, 292
info( ) method, 37, 65, 71, 93, 142
initialization
   log4j, 127–131
   StreamHandler initialization property, 35
installation
   Log tag library, 285–286
   log4j, 121–122
interfaces
   ErrorCode, 280
   ErrorHandler, 279, 280
   Logging, 97
   remote server, 107

J

J2EE
   JNDIContext with, 214–215
   starting J2EE JMS provider, 221
J2SDKEE 1.3.1, and jndi.properties, 215
Java-based logging APIs, 7–9
Java Server Pages (JSPs), embedding logging activity within. *See* Log tag library
Java Virtual machine (JVM), singleton instances, 11, 15, 90
java.util.logging.SimpleFormatter, 60
java.util.logging.XMLFormatter, 60
JDBCAppender, 202–212
   configuration files for, 205–206
   configuring, 203–204
   extending, 206–212
   tables, creating for storing logging information, 204
jdbc.properties (listing), 205
JDK 1.4 logging API basics, 11–58
   file-based configuration, 55–58
   Filter object, 51–55
   Formatter object, 58
   Fundamentals of, 8, 11–14
   Handler object, 33–51
      ConsoleHandler, 37–38
      FileHandler, 38–42
      MemoryHandler, 42–47
      SocketHandler, 47–51
      StreamHandler, 35–37

319

vs. log4j, 309–312
    basics of, 299, 309–310
    configuration options, 309, 310
    error handling, 312
    Filter objects, 311
    Formatter and Layout objects, 311
    Handler and Appender objects, 311
    location information options, 312
log4j compatibility with, 122
Logger object, 18–33
    basic logging methods, 26
    introduction to, 18–20
    level-based logging, 28–29
    Logger class methods, 29–33
    Logger object hierarchy, 19–20
    Logger relationship example, 23–26
    logging example, 20–23, 27
    logging information with, 22–24
    method-related logging, 29
    precise logging methods, 27–28
    ResourceBundle, 27–28
LogManager object, 15–17
LogRecord object, 17–18
JDK 1.4 logging API, extending the framework, 73–120
    configuring the framework, 73–83
        class-based configuration, 80–83
        file-based configuration, 74–80
    custom Handlers, writing, 83–94
        custom WindowHandler, 85–94
        introduction to, 83–84
    logging in practice, 102–120
        client component, 111–116
        client, running of, 118–120
        database configuration, 117–118
        employee data file, creating, 117
        Employee object, 105–106
        introduction to, 102–104
        remote logging server, 110
        remote server component, 107–109
        remote server interface, 107
        RMIManager, 110–111
        server startup, 118
    remote logging, 94–102
        remote logging client, 101–102
        remote logging Handler, 99–100
        remote logging server, 95–98
JDK 1.4 logging API, formatting logging information, 59–72
    custom formatters, writing, 69–72
    default formatter objects, 59–68
        SimpleFormatter object, 61–63
        XMLFormatter object, 62–68
    localization of logging messages, 68–69
JMS
    basics of, 212–213
    log4j and, 214–217
JMSAppender, 212–223
    configuring, 215–217
    example, 217–223
    JMS and log4j, 214–217
    JMS basics, 212–213
    vs. socket-based logging, 223–224

JMSLogSubscriber.java (listing), 218–219
jms.properties (listing), 217
JNDIContext
    with J2EE, 214–215
    with WebLogic, 215
jndi.properties, and J2SDKEE 1.3.1, 215
JSPs (Java Server Pages), embedding logging activity within. *See* Log tag library
JVM (Java Virtual machine), singleton instances, 11, 15, 90

L

L, conversion character, PatternLayout, 195
l, conversion character, PatternLayout, 195
Layout object
    DateLayout object, 186–187
    hierarchy of, 177–178
    HTMLLayout object, 187–192
    introduction to, 123, 124, 168
    JDK 1.4 vs. log4j, 311
    methods, 179
    PatternLayout object, 194–198
    SimpleLayout object, 179–180
    TTCCLayout object, 180–186
    XMLLayout object, 192–194
layout property, Appender object, 149
LayoutDemo.java (listing), 181–182
Level object, 123, 124, 136
level property
    Appender object, 149
    as common Handler property, 76
    as default property
        ConsoleHandler, 37
        FileHandler, 39
        MemoryHandler, 43
        SocketHandler, 47
    global Handler object and, 75
    parameters and
        ConsoleHandler, 77
        FileHandler, 78
        MemoryHandler, 80
        SocketHandler, 79
    parent-child hierarchy and, 20
    StreamHandler initialization property, 35
    WindowHandler, 90–91
Level property, and parent-child hierarchy, 137
levels of logging information. *See also specific* levels
    basics of, 12–13, 273
    creating custom tags for, 294–298
        example, 296–298
        new tags, 295–296
    custom levels, 265–270
    file-based configuration and, 76
    implementing a custom level class, 259–260
    level-based logging methods, 139–140
    Log tags and, 292, 293
    MemoryHandler and, 45–46
limit property
    FileHandler default property, 39
    FileHandler parameters and, 78

Index

listings
- Apache log4j, creating custom components
  - AnotherClass.java, 241
  - customappender.properties, 242
  - CustomErrorHandler.java, 281–282
  - customFilter.xml, 271
  - CustomLevel.java, 259–260
  - CustomLoggerDemo.java, 263
  - CustomLoggerFactory.java, 262
  - CustomLogger.java, 261
  - customlogger.properties, 264
  - customlogger.xml, 264–265
  - DBConfigLoader.java, 246–252
  - dbConfig.properties, 258
  - DBConfigurator.java, 255–256
  - errorHandler.xml, 283
  - FilterDemo.java, 272
  - LoggerWrapperDemo.java, 269
  - LoggerWrapper.java, 265–268
  - loggerWrapper.properties, 269
  - SelectedLevelFilter.java, 274–275
  - WindowAppenderDemo.java, 241–242
  - WindowAppender.java, 237–240
- Apache log4j, formatting logging information
  - The HTML Source Code Produced by HTMLLayout, 190–191
  - html.properties, 188
  - LayoutDemo.java, 181–182
  - ttcc.properties, 185
  - xml.properties, 193
- JDK 1.4 logging API basics
  - AgeFilter.java, 53
  - BasicLogging.java, 20–22
  - ChildLogger.java, 24
  - ConfigDemo.java, 56
  - config.properties, 57
  - FileHandlerDemo.java, 40–41
  - FilterDemo.java, 54–55
  - LoggingMonitor.java, 25
  - LoggingServer.java, 49–50
  - LogMethods.java, 30–32
  - MemoryHandlerDemo.java, 44–45
  - ParentLoggers.java, 23
  - Person.java, 52
  - SocketHandlerDemo.java, 48–49
  - StreamHandlerDemo.java, 36
- JDK 1.4 logging API, extending the framework
  - ClientComponent.java, 112–116
  - CustomHandlerDemo.java, 92
  - employee.xml, 117
  - LogWindow.java, 85
  - RemoteConfigReader.java, 81–82
  - RemoteHandlerDemo.java, 101
  - RemoteHandler.java, 99–100
  - RemoteLoggingServer.java, 95–97
  - RMIManager.java, 110–111
  - ServerComponent.java, 107–109
  - ServerInterface.java, 107
  - WindowHandler.java, 86–89
- JDK 1.4 logging, formatting information
  - AlternateXML.java, 66–67
  - BasicLogging.java (listing), 61
  - CustomFormatter.java, 70
  - CustomFormatterTest.java, 71
  - LocalizeLogging.java, 68–69
  - XMLLogging.java, 63–65
- Log tag library
  - log4j.properties, the Default Configuration File for Log, 287–288
  - Modified log4j.properties File, 291
  - Modified log4j.properties File for Using the TRACE Level, 297
  - SimpleLogDump.jsp, 293
  - SimpleLog.jsp, 286
  - The SimpleLog.jsp page, 290
  - Tag Description for the Custom Trace Tag, 296
  - TraceTag.java, 295
- log4j, advanced logging
  - AdvancedLogging.java, 200–202, 211
  - CustomJDBCAppender.java, 208–210, 211
  - customjdbc.properties, 210
  - jdbc.properties, 205
  - JMSLogSubscriber.java, 218–219
  - jms.properties, 217
  - LoggingServer.java, 226–227
  - LogMessageListener.java, 220–221
  - nt.properties, 229
  - smtp.properties, 231
  - socket.properties, 227
  - SQL for Creating the LOGGING_DATA Table, 204
- log4j basics
  - AsyncLogging.java, 165–166
  - async.xml, 164–165
  - Complex log4j Configuration File, 126
  - CustomerOrder.java, 170–171
  - Example log4j Configuration File, 125
  - FileBasedLoggingDemo.java, 162–163
  - file_logging.properties, 161–162
  - filter_properties.xml, 174
  - log4j.properties, 128–129
  - LoggerDemo.java, 143–144
  - LoggingServlet.java, 132
  - OrderRenderer.java, 173
  - ProductFilterDemo.java, 174–175
  - ProductFilter.java, 171–172
  - SimpleLogging.java, 129

localization
- best practices, 304
- logging and, 140–141

LocalizeLogging.java (listing), 68–69
location information
- best practices, 304–305
- JDK 1.4 vs. log4j, 310, 312

Log tag library, 285–298
- creating custom tags for custom levels, 294–298
  - example, 296–298
  - new tags, 295–296
- custom loggers and, 291–292
- example, 286–290
  - configuration file for Log tag library, 287–289
  - configuring Web server, 289–290
- installing, 285–286
- Log tags described, 292–294

log4j. *See* Apache log4j
log4j.dtd, 192
log4j.properties (listing), 128–129
log4j.properties, the Default Configuration File for Log (listing), 287–288

321

Index

log4j.xml, and writing configuration class, 253
Logger object, 18–33
   best practices
      obtaining instances of, 299–301
      for using Logger hierarchy, 301–302
   JDK 1.4
      basic logging methods, 26–27
      basics of, 13, 14, 18–20
      example, 20–23, 29–33
      hierarchy of, 19–20
      level-based logging, 28–29
      Logger object in architecture, 59
      Logger relationship example, 23–26
      logging information, 22–24
      method-related logging, 29
      precise logging methods, 27–28
      ResourceBundle, 27–28
   log4j, 136–145
      Appenders, adding, 150–151
      basics of, 122, 124, 136–139, 168
      conditions of successful logging, 142
      configuration methods, 142–143
      creating custom Logger, 261–262
      example, 143–145
      Logger to Appender collaboration, 152
      logging information and, 139–142
LoggerDemo.java (listing), 143–144
LOGGER_REPOSITORY, 244, 245, 258
loggers. *See also* Log tag library
   using different, with Log tag library, 291–292
LoggerWrapperDemo.java (listing), 269
LoggerWrapper.java (listing), 265–268
loggerWrapper.properties (listing), 269
logging. *See* application logging
logging histories, benefits of, 4
logging messages. *See* messages
logging statements, turning off, 5
LoggingMonitor.java (listing), 25
LoggingServer.java (listing), 49–50, 226–227
LoggingServlet.java (listing), 132
LogManager object
   JDK 1.4, 15–17
   log4j, 123, 145–146, 253
LogManager.shutDown( ) method, 191–192
LogMessageListener.java (listing), 220–221
LogMethods.java (listing), 30–32
LogRecord object
   Handler object and, 33–35
   JDK 1.4, 17–18
LogWindow.java (listing), 85

M

M, conversion character, PatternLayout, 196
m, conversion character, PatternLayout, 196
maxBackupIndex property, RollingFileAppender, 156
maxFileSize property, RollingFileAppender, 156
MDC (Message Diagnostic Context), 147–148
MemoryHandler
   asynchronous logging and, 306
   basics of, 42–47
   parameters, 80
MemoryHandlerDemo.java (listing), 44–45
Message Diagnostic Context (MDC), 147–148

messages
   efficient message logging, 302–304
   localization of, 68–69
methods. *See also specific* methods
   abstract methods and custom Handler, 84
   Bean properties and
      DateLayout, 184
      HTMLLayout, 187
      PatternLayout, 194
      TTCCLayout, 184
   custom WindowHandler, 91
   in ErrorHandler interface, 279
   JDBCAppender, 203, 207–208
   Layout object, 179
   level-based logging, 139–140
   Logger class, 26–33
      basic logging methods, 26–27
      differing logging methods, 26–27
      example of, 29–33
      level-based logging methods, 28–29
      logging with ResourceBundle methods, 27–28
      method-related logging, 29
      precise logging methods, 27–28
   LogManager, 15–17, 146
   MDC, 147
   MemoryHandler, 43–44
   NDC, 146–147
   RollingFileAppender, 156–157
   synchronizing, 84, 90
   WindowAppender, 237
Modified log4j.properties File for Using the TRACE Level (listing), 297
Modified log4j.properties File (listing), 291

N

n, conversion character, PatternLayout, 196
naming conventions, for Logger object, 300–301
Nested Diagnostic Context (NDC)
   best practices, 307–308
   log4j, 146–147
   NDC information and TTCCLayout object, 181
NTEventLogAppender, 228–229
nt.properties (listing), 229

O

ObjectRenderer, log4j, 123, 168–169
OFF level, log4j, 136
onMessage( ) method, 219–220
OrderRenderer.java (listing), 173
output destination, JDK 1.4 vs. log4j, 309

P

P, conversion character, PatternLayout, 196
parameters
   configuring log4j through system parameters, 134
   ConsoleHandler, 77
   DatePattern configuration parameter, 158
   FileHandler, 78–79
   MemoryHandler, 46–47, 80
   parameter construction, and logging requests, 303
   SocketHandler, 79

parent-child hierarchy, 20, 137–138, 302, 310
parent loggers
    hierarchy and, 20, 25–26, 137–138, 302
    JDK 1.4 vs. log4j, 310
    ParentLoggers.java (listing), 23
    reset( ) method and, 33
ParentLoggers.java (listing), 23
pattern property
    as FileHandler default property, 40
    FileHandler parameters and, 78
PatternLayout object
    basics of, 194–198
    formatting logging information and, 305
patterns
    configuring file for Log tag library and, 288
    conversion patterns in log4j, 125
    in FileHandler, 38–39, 42
permissions, and remote logging, 98
Person.java (listing), 52
Point-to-Point messaging, and JMS, 213
port property
    as SocketHandler default property, 48
    SocketHandler parameters and, 79
problem diagnosis, 3
ProductFilterDemo.java (listing), 174–175
ProductFilter.java (listing), 171–172
properties
    Appender, 149
    Bean
        DateLayout, 186
        HTMLLayout, 187
        JDBCAppender, 204
        JMSAppender, 216
        LevelRangeFilter, 271
        NTEventLogAppender, 229
        PatternLayout, 194
        SocketAppender, 225, 230
        TTCCLayout, 184
    child logger inherited, 20
    ConsoleAppender, 154
    ConsoleHandler default properties, 37–38
    FileAppender, 154–155
    FileHandler default properties, 39–40
    handlers property, 75
    MemoryHandler default properties, 43
    parent-child hierarchy and, 20
    ResourceBundle properties files, 69
    RollingFileAppender, 156
    SocketHandler default properties, 47–48
    StreamHandler initialization properties, 35
    WindowHandler, 90–91
    WriterAppender, 152
publish( ) method
    custom WindowHandler and, 91, 93
    logging information and, 64
    remote logging and, 100
    synchronizing, 84, 89, 90
Publish-Subscribe messaging, and JMS, 213
push property, and MemoryHandler parameters, 80
pushLevel property, MemoryHandler, 43

R

r, conversion character, PatternLayout, 196
refactoring, defined, 139
remote logging, 94–102
    client, 101–102
    Handler, 99–100
    server, 95–98
RemoteConfigReader.java (listing), 81–82
RemoteHandlerDemo.java (listing), 101
RemoteHandler.java (listing), 99–100
RemoteLoggingServer.java (listing), 95–97
Renderer objects, 305–306
reset( ) method, 17, 32, 33
ResourceBundle
    basics of, 27–28
    localization of logging and, 68–69, 140–141, 304
    parent-child hierarchy and, 20, 138
RMI component, 94–97, 102–103, 105–106
RMIManager, 110–111
RMIManager.java (listing), 110–111
RollingFileAppender, 156–158

S

Security Manager, configuring for remote machines, 98
SelectedLevelFilter.java (listing), 274–275
serializable, defined, 17
ServerComponent.java (listing), 107–109
ServerInterface.java (listing), 107
servers
    remote logging server, 95–98
    remote server component, 107–109
    remote server interface, 107
    server startup, 118
servlets, log4j
    configuring through, 134–135
    configuring with, 132–133
SEVERE level
    described, 12
    ParentLoggers.java and, 23
Simple Mail Transfer Protocol. *See* SMTPAppender;
    smtp.properties (listing)
SimpleFormatter object, 61–63
SimpleLayout object, 179–180
SimpleLogDump.jsp (listing), 293
SimpleLogging.java (listings), 129
SimpleLog.jsp (listing), 286
SimpleLog.jsp page (listing), 290
singleton instances, 11, 15, 90
size property
    MemoryHandler default property, 43
    MemoryHandler parameters and, 80
SMTPAppender, 229–231
smtp.properties (listing), 231
SocketAppender, 223–228
    configuration, 225
    example, 226–228
    fault tolerance, 224–225
    vs. JMS-based logging, 223–224

Index

SocketHandler
    basics of, 47–51
    parameters, 79
SocketHandlerDemo.java (listing), 48–49
socket.properties (listing), 227
SQL for Creating the LOGGING_DATA Table (listing), 204
StreamHandler, 35–37
StreamHandlerDemo.java (listing), 36
style of logging, 243–244
Subscriber, JMS
    Publish-Subscribe messaging, 213
    running, 221–222
system parameters, for configuring log4j, 134
system state, 3
System.out.println( ) style, 5

T

t, conversion character, PatternLayout, 196
tables
    creating for storing logging information, 204
        design for storing logging configuration, 244, 256–258
Tag Description for the Custom Trace Tag (listing), 296
tag library. *See* Log tag library
target property
    Appender object, 149
    ConsoleAppender, 154
    MemoryHandler default property, 43
    MemoryHandler parameters and, 80
    WriterAppender, 152
Telnet and message availability, 232
testing, WindowAppender, 241–243
threadPrinting property, 184
threshold property
    ConsoleAppender, 154
    FileAppender, 154
    WriterAppender, 152
timeZone property, 184
Tomcat
    example using. *See* Log tag library, example
    location of servlet.jar, 132
    setup, 133–135
TRACE level
    custom logging and, 258, 259, 262, 265, 268
    custom tags and, 294–298
        example, 296–298
        new tags, 295–296
trace( ) method, 262, 263
trace tag example, 296–298
TraceTag.java (listing), 295
TTCCLayout object, 180–186

U

UNIX, and configuring Tomcat, 133

W

WARN level, log4j
    described, 136
    filtering and, 272
warn Log tag, 292
WARNING level, JDK 1.4, 12
Web applications, using Log in. *See* Log tag library
Web servers, and Log tag library. *See* Log tag library
Web sites for information
    Apache, 285
    binary distribution of Log (1.1), 285
    latest version of log4j binary distribution, 122
    viewing HTML files, 133
WebLogic, and JNDIContext, 215
WindowAppenderDemo.java (listing), 241–242
WindowAppender.java (listing), 237–240
WindowHandler.java (listing), 86–89
windows
    custom logging window, 243
    logging information in client-side window, 119–120
    WindowAppender, creating custom, 235–243
        architecture of, 236–237
        features of, 236
        implementation of, 237–241
        testing, 241–243
    WindowHandler, creating custom, 85–93
        CustomHandlerDemo.java (listing), 92
        LogWindow.java (listing), 85
        WindowHandler.java (listing), 86–89
Windows NT event log, logging to, 228–229
wrappers, writing, 265–270
WriterAppender, log4j, 152–153

X

X, conversion character, PatternLayout, 196
x, conversion character, PatternLayout, 196
XML-style configuration, 127, 308
XMLFormatter object, 62–68
XMLLayout object, 192–194
XMLLogging.java (listing)
    vs. AlternateXML.java, 66–67
    code, 63–65
xml.properties (listing), 193